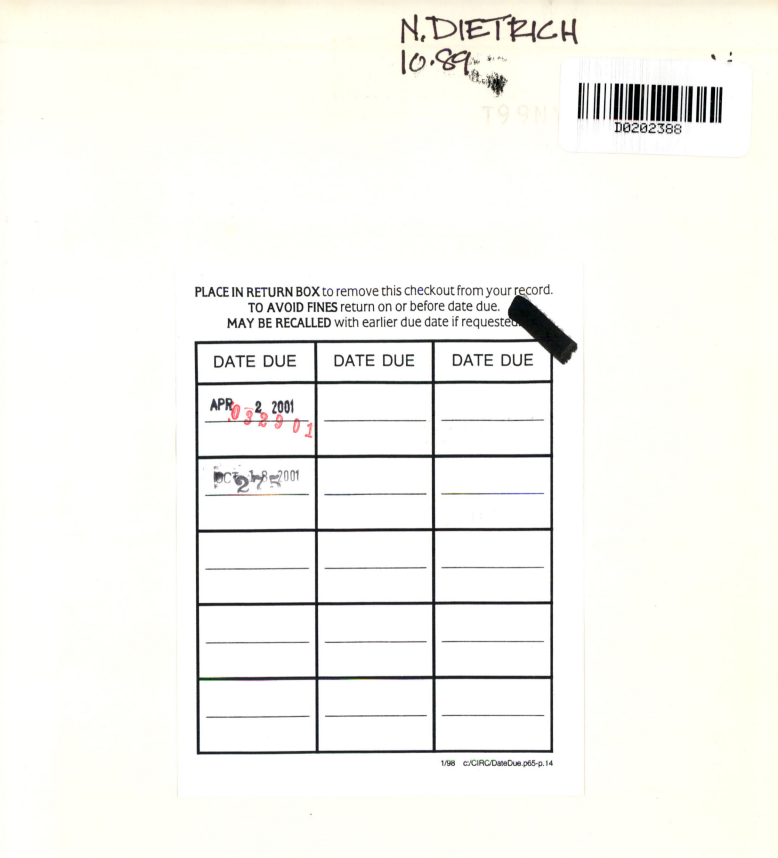

PLACE IN RETURN BOX to remove this checkout from your record.
TO AVOID FINES return on or before date due.
MAY BE RECALLED with earlier due date if requested.

DATE DUE	DATE DUE	DATE DUE
APR 0 2 2001 032901		
OCT 2 7 5 2001		

1/98 c:/CIRC/DateDue.p65-p.14

GOLF COURSE & GROUNDS

Irrigation and Drainage

Albert R. Jarrett
Associate Professor
Agricultural Engineering
The Pennsylvania State University

A RESTON BOOK
PRENTICE-HALL, INC., Englewood Cliffs, New Jersey 07632

Library of Congress Cataloging in Publication Data

Jarrett, A. R. (Albert R.)
    Golf course irrigation and drainage.

    1. Golf courses—Design and construction. 2. Drainage.
    3. Water in landscape architecture.   I. Title.
    GV975.J3 1984   712'.5   84-4895
    ISBN 0-8359-2563-3

To Ellen, Aimee, Valerie and Adam

Production supervision/interior design: Tally Morgan

© 1985 by Prentice-Hall, Inc.
A Division of Simon & Schuster
Englewood Cliffs, New Jersey 07632

10 9 8 7 6 5 4 3 2

Printed in the United States of America

CONTENTS

Preface, vii

PART ONE   IRRIGATION

Chapter 1   INTRODUCTION, 3

Atmospheric environment, 4
Soil environment, 5
Biotic environment, 6
Irrigation design, 7

Chapter 2   SPRINKLER PERFORMANCE, 9

Water distribution, 10
Sprinkler spacing, 13

Sprinkler choice, 16
Problems, 17

Chapter 3   GREENS AND TEES, 19

Irrigating putting greens, 19
Summary, 23
Irrigating tees, 24
Problem, 24

Chapter 4   FAIRWAYS, 25

Single-row sprinkler system, 26
Two-row sprinkler system, 27
Coverage near edge of fairways, 28
Coverage of approach area to
    green, 29

iii

Coverage of the area, 29
Coverage of wide fairway areas, 30
Double-row system on fairways, 30
Fairway analysis and design, 31
Golf course irrigation design
  example, 33
Problems, 39

Chapter 5   MANAGEMENT, 41

Application rate, 42
Design depth, 43
Irrigation interval, 45
Water depth, 47
Design run times, 47
Management scheme, 47
Golf course irrigation design
  example, 48
Problems, 53

Chapter 6   VALVES, 57

Gate valve, 57
Globe valve, 57
Pressure regulating valve, 58
Pressure relief valve, 58
Check valve, 58
Ball valves, 59
Specialty valves, 59
Backflow preventers, 60
Remote control valves, 62
Operating principles, 63
Selecting a control valve, 64
Golf course irrigation design
  example, 67
Problems, 67

Chapter 7   CONTROLLERS, 69

Selection factors, 70
Controller features, 71
The central-satellite system, 72
Golf course irrigation design
  example, 75
Problems, 76

Chapter 8   PIPE LAYOUT AND SIZING, 79

Pipe sizing, 81
Integrating pipe locations, pipe
  sizes, and controller systems, 85
Control and piping alternatives, 88
Golf course irrigation design
  example, 89
Problems, 93

Chapter 9   PRINCIPLES OF HYDRAULICS,
             97

Pressure, 98
Friction head, 101
Elevation, pressure and fiction, 104
Pump requirements, 106
Water hammer or surge pressure,
  107
Golf course irrigation design
  example, 110
Problems, 112

Chapter 10   PUMPS, 115

Types of water supplies, 115
Types of pumps, 119
System energy relationships, 121
Pump characteristic curves, 123
Combination of pumps, 125
Complete pumping system, 126
Pump selection, 128
Golf course irrigation design
  example, 130
Problems, 131

Chapter 11   FINAL CONSIDERATIONS, 133

Thrust blocks, 133
Drains, 135
Vents, 136
Irrigation scheduling, 136
Irrigation system design, 138
Installation details, 139
Golf course irrigation design
  example, 140
Problems, 141

PART TWO DRAINAGE

Chapter 12   INTRODUCTION, 145

Soil-water relationships, 146
Necessity for drainage, 146
Benefits of drainage, 147
Problems, 150

Chapter 13   SLOPES, GRADES, AND ELEVATIONS, 153

Grades, 154
Elevations, 154
Leveling, 155
Problems, 157

Chapter 14   SURFACE DRAINAGE, 159

Rainfall-runoff, 160
Random drains, 166
Soil modification, 169
Terraces, 170
Diversions, 171
Problems, 171

Chapter 15   SUBSURFACE DRAINAGE, 173

Introduction, 173
Types of drainage systems, 174
Subsurface drain pipe, 176
Inlets, 177
Outlets, 179
Depth of drain lines, 180
Spacing of drain lines, 181
Size of drain lines, 181
Time of installation, 190
Problems, 190

Chapter 16   SPECIAL APPLICATIONS, 193

Greens, 193
Football, soccer and field hockey fields, 194
Prescription athletic turf, 196
Baseball fields, 196
Home drainage, 196

Appendix A   SPRINKLER PERFORMANCE DATA, 201

Appendix B   PIPE PERFORMANCE DATA, 219

Index, 243

PREFACE

Water management on golf courses and other intensely managed turf areas is essential to producing durable, uniformly green turf. On these turf areas, excess natural precipitation must be removed quickly without causing displacement of turf or erosion of soil; subsurface local or regional water tables must be effectively removed or lowered; and facilities must be available for applying water to supplement natural precipitation through irrigation. *GOLF COURSE & GROUNDS: Irrigation and Drainage* provides an in-depth treatment of each of the water management techniques commonly used on turf areas. Design criteria are presented and procedures given which lead the reader through the planning, design and development of each practice.

For convenience, this book is divided into two parts. The first 11 chapters present a systematic treatment of the elements of planning and designing an irrigation system for use on golf courses and other turf areas (such as residential, commercial and recreational areas). This part begins with sprinkler performance, placement and selection. Once the sprinklers are selected and located, guidelines are developed for managing the sprinklers in light of environment, soil, turfgrass, available time and equipment constraints. Automatic control systems are discussed as a means of operating the irrigation system remotely, to minimize labor and capital costs. The development and sizing of piping systems to deliver water efficiently from a carefully designed pumping system are also discussed.

The irrigation part of the book is supported by two appendices. Appendix A presents typical sprinkler performance data for turf sprinklers manufactured by most of the major sprinkler manufacturers. Appendix B presents performance data for pipes commonly used in turf irrigation systems.

The last five chapters present an in-depth discussion of the conditions which produce surface and subsurface drainage problems. Surface drainage techniques on turf areas are often ignored in favor of removal through subsurface pipelines; limitations to this practice are discussed. Locating and sizing subsurface drainage systems are also discussed. In addition to treating drainage on golf courses and general turf areas, a special chapter is set aside to provide general guidance for draining recreation areas and athletic fields.

This book is intended as a textbook for turfgrass managers and landscape architects, and has examples and chapter problems to enhance its usefulness. Because of its layout, it can be used equally well as a reference book for practicing turf managers, landscape architects and engineers.

Part One

IRRIGATION

Chapter 1
INTRODUCTION

Turfgrasses are used for a variety of purposes. A utility turf is used primarily for soil stabilization. Utility turf, often used along roadsides and airport runways, also absorbs toxic emissions, reduces dust transport, and is an effective filter for removing suspended sediment.

Lawn turfs serve a decorative function, as well as provide areas for recreational activities and relaxation such as picnics, volleyball, and family gatherings. Lawn-quality turf is common landscaping around commercial and industrial facilities.

Sport turfs provide an arena for participants and observers. Football, baseball, soccer, and golf are a few of the many sports played on turf. These athletic areas require intensive care to overcome the stress applied by the intensive traffic that compacts the soil and wears the turfgrasses (Turgeon, 1980).

Irrigation is one of many tools that can be used by the turf manager or superintendent to manage or control the turfgrass environment. This environment has three interacting dimensions, each of which can be positively or negatively influenced by water management. These three dimensions are (a) the atmosphere above and immediately surrounding the turfgrass aerial shoots; (b) the thatch-soil environment, including roots and other below-ground plant parts; and (c) the biotic component, encompassing cultural practices, pests, and use of the turf by man (Turgeon, 1980).

ATMOSPHERIC ENVIRONMENT

Three forms of atmospheric moisture are important to turfgrass management. The first, natural precipitation, is relied upon to supply the moisture needed to grow and sustain the turf. In cases where natural precipitation is poorly distributed over the growing season or inadaquate to supply the needed moisture, supplemental irrigation must be applied. In almost all areas of the United States there are at least one or two months, usually July and August, when transpiration exceeds precipitation, making irrigation necessary.

The water vapor content, or relative humidity, of the air surrounding turfgrass shoots influences the incidence of disease through its effect on the growth and survival of pathogenic organisms. In some cases, irrigation management can be modified to influence such diseases. For example, pythium, a water mold, is favored by warm, humid weather and high soil moisture. Under these same conditions, cool-season turfgrasses may be under considerable stress and, therefore, less resistant to this fungus. Such procedures as improving air movement and soil drainage and avoiding excessive fertilization and irrigation can substantially reduce the likelihood of pythium blight (Turgeon, 1980).

The formation of dew during the early morning can result from guttation or condensation. Guttation occurs when water pressure builds up in the roots during periods of minimal transpiration and rapid water absorption. Guttation fluid contains minerals and simple organic compounds collected from the plant. The formation of these droplets cause these dissolved materials to accumulate on the leaf surfaces, which may enhance the growth of fungal pathogens as well as increase the incidence of disease. Condensation occurs when radiational cooling reduces the leaf temperature below the dew-point temperature of the air immediately adjacent to the leaf. Dew may be beneficial to turfgrass since it delays the onset of transpiration during the early morning. It may also enhance disease development, especially on greens. Traditionally, dew is removed from closely mowed turf by poling, dragging, or syringing with water during the early morning.

Turfgrass, particularly cool-season varieties used on golf greens, may suffer from high temperature on hot summer days. The practice of applying a very light irrigation to the surface of the grass has been widely used to cool the grass. This may be done once in the middle of a hot afternoon or several times on extremely hot days (Hanson and Juska, 1969).

SOIL ENVIRONMENT

Supplemental irrigation is used to maintain the soil moisture in the region between field capacity and the wilting point. Moisture contents in excess of field capacity are of little benefit since this gravitational water quickly drains from the root zone and is not available to the turf. Generally, it is desirable to keep the soil moisture content such that not more than 50% of the available moisture is removed from the soil. As the soil approaches the wilting point, the moisture is more difficult for the crop to extract, leading to slowed growth.

Soil temperature can also be influenced by soil moisture. Heat absorption occurs faster in dry soils than wet soils since the specific heat of water is five times as great as the specific heat of dry soil. Therefore, as the water content of a given soil increases, the amount of energy required to raise its temperature increases proportionately. Excessive irrigation will slow the soil warming process in the spring, tending to keep grasses in the dormant stages longer.

Irrigation is very important during seed germination and establishment. Depending on weather conditions, new seedlings may require a light irrigation daily or possibly several times a day. Soil crusting and erosion can be avoided during germination by selecting sprinkler nozzles and a pressure that will produce fine drops and a low application rate (Hanson and Juska, 1969).

Healthy turf must be fertilized regularly. Irrigation may be used to wash the fertilizer off the grass and into the soil. Application duration should be short to prevent runoff. Fertilizers may be injected into the irrigation system and applied during normal irrigation or during special daytime applications. Remember, the distribution of fertilizers dissolved in irrigation water will be no better than the uniformity of the water distribution by the irrigation system. Diluting solutions and providing a short terminal rinsing period are beneficial (Hanson and Juska, 1969).

In some parts of the United States, depending on water quality, soil salinity must be controlled. This control may require periodic applications of water in excess of that needed to replenish the water in the root zone. This additional water will move down through the soil, dissolving salts and carrying them out of the root zone. All natural waters, except rain, contain some dissolved salts, but usually at low concentrations. When these waters have moderate concentrations such as may be found in arid regions or when sewage effluent is used, precautions should be taken. Waters containing less than 650 ppm dissolved salts should not present a problem. Waters containing greater than 2,000 ppm dissolved salts should not be used for turf irrigation. Waters between these two extremes require additional management.

BIOTIC ENVIRONMENT

Irrigation can be managed to improve the overall quality of the turf. Wearability can be improved by reducing plant succulence, which is a result of reduced fertilization and irrigation. Wet soil conditions predispose the turf to serious injury from light traffic. When soil compaction becomes a problem, more frequent fertilization and irrigation are re-

quired to compensate for restricted rooting and
generally poor growth.

Irrigation is sometimes applied to soften the turf
to comply with the requests of sport participants,
particularly golfers. A light irrigation can cause a ball
to stop at or close to the spot where it lands.

IRRIGATION DESIGN

Irrigation systems are used in many ways to enhance the quality of turf. Generally, the irrigation
system is designed to meet the need that demands
the largest amount of water. In most cases this
means providing for the application of supplemental water to grow the turf. The other practices can
be applied using the same hardware, usually by adjusting the time and duration of application.

The general design procedure used to develop
a turf irrigation system has many interrelated steps
(see figure 1–1). Before an irrigation system can be

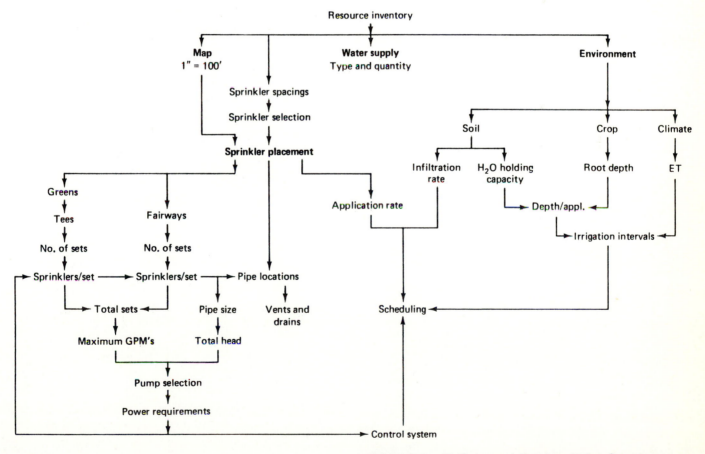

Figure 1–1   Golf course irrigation design flowchart

designed, however, it is necessary to collect the following basic information:

1. A topographic map with a horizontal scale of 1″=100′ or larger and a contour interval of not greater than 10 feet. This map must show the locations and outlines of all areas to be irrigated.

2. Knowledge of the type of water supply. An irrigation system requires a large quantity of water. This water must be available and will usually come from surface runoff, wells, or municipal water supplies. The water supply should be near the irrigated areas.

3. Information on the infiltration rate and water holding capacity of the soil, the root depth of the turfgrasses grown, and the evapotranspiration expected.

The 10 chapters that follow provide a step-by-step procedure for designing an irrigation system for turf areas, especially golf courses. Some of the chapters contain basic information needed to understand the operation and functioning of a turf irrigation system. The irrigation chapters starting with chapter 4 contain basic information, but also include a step-by-step implementation of the fundamentals in the design of a 9-hole golf course. The new material discussed in each chapter is used in the example to show how it can be applied to a real problem.

Chapter 2

SPRINKLER PERFORMANCE

The uniformity of water distribution is the weakest part of an irrigation system. Even without considering the effects from the pressure variations, wind speed, and land slopes, the depth of application from the sprinkler heads varies from a maximum near the sprinkler to zero at the outer edge of the wetted circle (see figure 2–1).

The precipitation rate, expressed in inches per hour, varies from the sprinkler outward, which means no sprinkler has a single precipitation rate. Precipitation rates may differ by as much as three to four times as one moves from one area to another between sprinkler heads. This wide variation indicates that inundating and wilting may exist within the coverage area of the same sprinkler.

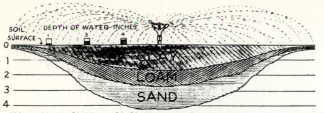

Figure 2–1 Sprinkler water distribution pattern (Redrawn with permission from Pira, 1982)

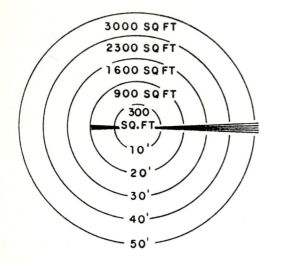

Figure 2–2 Bird's-eye-view of sprinkler head (Redrawn with permission from Toro, 1972)

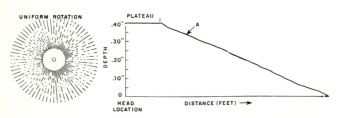

Figure 2–3 Typical sprinkler distribution (Adapted with permission from Toro, 1972)

In humid regions, this variation may exist for years without becoming noticeable because evapotranspiration is less than rainfall for most of the year. This allows the moisture levels in the soil to remain high during most of the year. In hot, arid climates, the irrigated water is the only source of moisture and uneven distribution usually results in brown or uneven turf.

WATER DISTRIBUTION

To make the best possible choice of sprinklers, it is essential to understand the principles of sprinkler water distribution patterns. In general, sprinklers have similar water distribution patterns. Usually the distribution is fairly uniform to about 30% of the radius and rapidly decreases to nothing at the outer fringes.

Taking a bird's-eye-view of the sprinkler head, it becomes apparent why the uniformity of distribution varies as one moves from the head (see figure 2–2).

Note that the first 10-foot circle covers about 300 square feet and the last segment covers 3,000 square feet. The combined effect of the sprinkler output and the difference in area covered create the sprinkler distribution illustrated in figure 2–3.

The typical distribution curve is based on a uniform rotation of the head. Should the head stop or change speed for any reason, the typical profile will be changed accordingly.

Based on the assumption that the water distribution pattern shown in figure 2–4(a) is typical of all revolving sprinklers, the depths of application shown in figure 2–4(b) can be predicted.

Figure 2–5 indicates that if a sprinkler operated long enough to apply one inch of water to the pan located a distance of approximately 30 feet from the sprinkler (30% of the sprinkler radius), the depths of water shown in table 2–1, p. 12, would be expected in the other pans. The distance from the sprinkler head to the pan, divided by the sprinkler radius, is the effective coverage (EC) in percentage.

The phrase "desired effective coverage" shall be used to mean the percentage of a sprinkler's radius that will reach a point of interest (such as the edge of a fairway). This percentage-of-radius can then be converted to a percentage of center region depth being applied to the point (see figure 2–4).

A study of figures 2–4 and 2–5 shows that choosing a sprinkler to yield an acceptable distribution of water on desired areas is a difficult task. The following examples are included to help clarify the thinking and reasoning that should be applied before making a tentative sprinkler selection based on the average fairway width.

Consider the following:

Example A 90-foot diameter sprinkler was selected and used for a 90-foot wide fairway (see figure 2–6).

Under these conditions, no water should be expected at the edge of the fairway. In addition, there is no coverage of part of the area. The effective coverage here is

$$\frac{\text{Half fairway width}}{\text{Radius of sprinkler}}(100) = \frac{45\ \text{ft}}{45\ \text{ft}}(100) = 100\%$$

Example Assume it is desired to have uniform water distribution across the entire width of the 90-foot fairway (see figure 2–7).

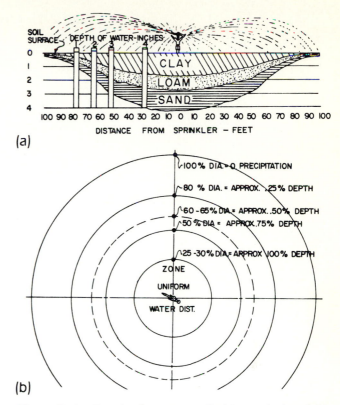

(a)

(b)

Figure 2–4   Depth of water applied by typical sprinkler (Redrawn with permission from Pira, 1982)

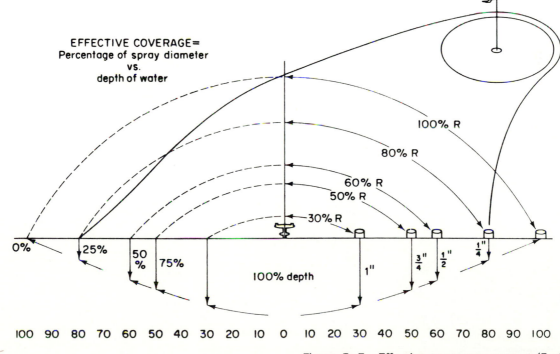

EFFECTIVE COVERAGE=
Percentage of spray diameter
vs.
depth of water

Figure 2–5   Effective coverage concept (Redrawn with permission from Pira, 1982)

Table 2–1 Effective coverage

Approximate distance of pans from sprinkler	% sprinkler radius	Approximate depth of water (in)	Depth (%)
Radius—30 ft	$\dfrac{30}{100} = 30$	1.0 (Note water distribution fairly uniform throughout)	100
Radius—50 ft	$\dfrac{50}{100} = 50$	¾	75
Radius—60 ft	$\dfrac{60}{100} = 60$	½	50
Radius—80 ft	$\dfrac{80}{100} = 80$	¼	25
Radius—100 ft	$\dfrac{100}{100} = 100$	None	0

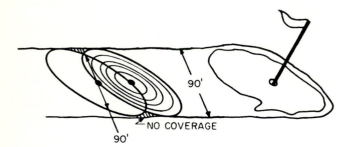

Figure 2–6 One hundred percent effective coverage (Adapted with permission from Pira, 1982)

Since the water distribution remains uniform for about 30% of the sprinkler radius, it would require a 300-foot diameter sprinkler (radius = 45/.3 = 150 ft or diameter equals 300 ft).

Another factor that must be taken into account is the distance the water overshoots the edge of the fairway to provide the desired effective coverage. An effective coverage of 70% of the sprinkler radius is recommended as first choice. Table 2–2 shows that at an EC of 60%, the depth of water may be adequate but the distance of 30 feet beyond the

Table 2–2 Selection of effective coverage

Fairway width (ft)	% sprinkler radius (EC)	Total sprinkler radius (ft)	Approx. % of depth at edge	Distance water exceeding edge (ft)
90	100	$\dfrac{45}{1.0} = 45$	None	None
90	80	$\dfrac{45}{.80} = 56$	25	11 ft
90	[a]70	$\dfrac{45}{.70} = 64$	33	19 ft
90	60	$\dfrac{45}{.60} = 75$	50	30 ft
90	50	$\dfrac{45}{.50} = 90$	75	45 ft
90	30	$\dfrac{45}{.30} = 150$	100	105 ft

[a]Recommended first choice.

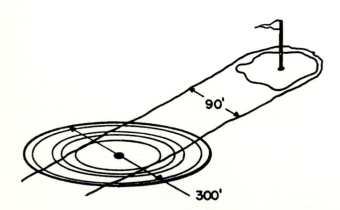

Figure 2–7 Thirty percent effective coverage (Redrawn with permission from Pira, 1982)

edge of the fairway may be unwanted or hard to justify, whereas at an EC of 80% the depth of water on the fairway becomes low for sustaining turf. Therefore, 70% is usually selected as a compromise.

The water applied by two sprinklers, A and B, to area 1 is approximately equal (see figure 2–8(b). Thus, the double application of water to area 1 brings the overall application to the area to a nearly uniform rate as desired and shown by the dotted line in figure 2–8(a).

SPRINKLER SPACING

Wind speed will also influence a sprinkler's distribution by causing the precipitation rate to increase when the sprinkler sprays against the wind and to decrease when it sprays downwind. Instead of having circles of application an egg-shaped pattern results (see figure 2–9). To compensate for the effect of wind, most sprinkler manufacturers recommend closer spacings for higher speed winds. If this is done, the precipitation rate increases during irrigation with no wind. Recommended sprinkler spacings for various wind speeds are given in figures 2–10 and 2–11. The recommended spacing between sprinklers is 50% of the spacing, that is, S = 50% of the sprinkler wetted diameter. Spacings of less than 50% (wind above 8 mph) cause considerable overwatering where triple overlapping occurs if the system is operated when the wind is not blowing.

Sprinklers can be arranged in many different geometries and still provide good distribution of

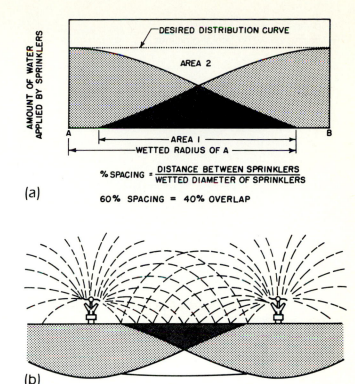

(a)

% SPACING = DISTANCE BETWEEN SPRINKLERS / WETTED DIAMETER OF SPRINKLERS

60% SPACING = 40% OVERLAP

(b)

Figure 2–8 *Creating proper coverage by overlapping sprinkler distribution areas*

S = Spacing between sprinklers
L = Spacing between lateral pipelines

Wind	%S
None	65
4 mph wind	60
8 mph wind	50

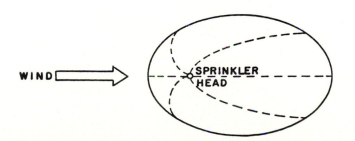

Figure 2–9 *Effect of wind (Redrawn with permission from Pira, 1982)*

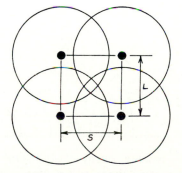

Figure 2–10 *Recommended percentage spacings for square spacings*

S = Spacing between sprinklers
L = Spacing between lateral pipelines

Wind	%S
None	75
4 mph wind	70
8 mph wind	65

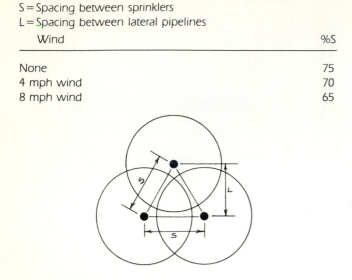

Figure 2–11 Recommended percentage spacings for triangular spacings

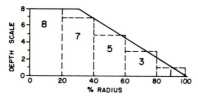

Figure 2–12 Profile of distribution curve (Adapted with permission from Toro, 1972)

water in the area being irrigated. One of the most common sprinkler patterns is the square. This spacing is used most often to supply water to greens where uniformity of coverage is very important. To illustrate the uniformity of distribution produced by various sprinkler arrangements, the depth of water distributed by one sprinkler can be represented by a series of discrete steps as the distance from the sprinkler increases. Using the model shown in figure 2–12, the zone from the sprinkler to 20% of the radius is represented by a depth of 8. The next zone, 20% to 40%, is represented by 7, and so on, until the last one, 80% to 100%, is represented by 1.

Square Spacing

When the model in figure 2–12 is used to analyze the various spacings, one can see the zones where too much or too little water will be applied. For instance, when sprinklers are arranged in a square pattern with a 60% spacing, the results shown in figure 2–13 will occur. Note the consistent coverage on the lines between the sprinklers. Note also the light coverage in the zone that normally would be the center of a green. Only half the nominal application rate of 8 occurs at this center point.

When a 50% spacing is used with a square system, the coverage improves as shown in figure 2–14. In this case, all areas receive at least a relative depth of 10 while the maximum is only 12. This is

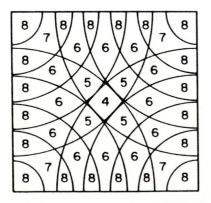

Figure 2–13 Relative depth of application using square spacing with 60% spacing (Adapted with permission from Toro, 1972)

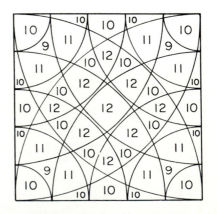

Figure 2–14 Relative depth of application using square spacing with 50% spacing

a 20% variability as compared to a 50% variability for the 60% spacing. Bringing the sprinkler closer than a 50% spacing generally does not improve the uniformity of distribution.

Triangular Spacing

A very popular spacing in the turf industry and on golf courses is the triangular spacing. Because of the interactions between the sprinklers in the pattern, sprinklers are seldom placed closer than a 60% spacing. The relative depths applied by the triangular pattern at 60% spacing are shown in figure 2–15. In this case, the minimum depth is 8 while the maximum is 9, a 13% variation. The center of the pattern is well-covered. In practice, triangular spacings vary from 60% to 75% spacing.

Single-Row Spacing

Another popular spacing, especially on fairways, is the single-row system. This pattern is analyzed in figure 2–16 for a 60% spacing and a 70% effective coverage. Note the lack of uniformity of coverage with this pattern. Within the limits of the fairway, the coverage varies from a low of 2 to a high of 8, a 75% variability. The single-row system can be improved by decreasing the distance between sprinklers as shown in figure 2–17 for a 50% spacing. This decrease in spacing improves the dis-

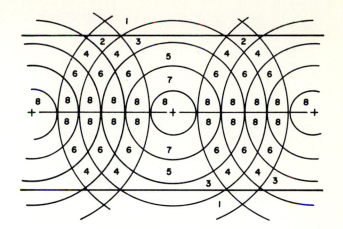

Figure 2–16 Relative depth of application using single-row spacing with 60% spacing and 70% effective coverage

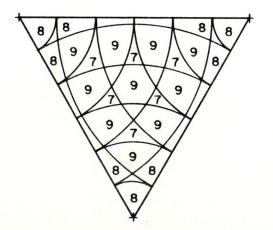

Figure 2–15 Relative depth of application using triangular spacing with 60% spacing

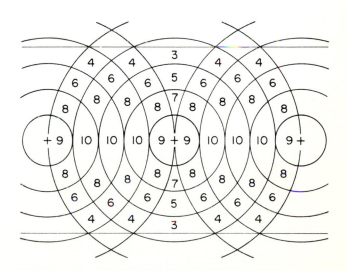

Figure 2–17 Relative depth of application using single-row spacing with 50% spacing and 70% effective coverage

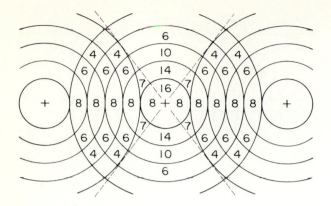

Figure 2–18   Relative depth of application using single-row, two-speed head with 60% spacing and 70% effective coverage

tribution of coverage in the central portion of the fairway but does not improve coverage near the fairway edge.

Single-Row, Two-Speed Spacing

One company has attempted to improve the overall performance of the single-row system by developing a sprinkler that operates at regular speed in the zone where the adjacent sprinklers overlap and at half speed in the zone where the sprinklers do not overlap. An analysis of this pattern is shown in figure 2–18 for a 60% spacing and 70% effective coverage. Here we see the coverage near center fairway jump to 14 and 16 as compared to 8 in the regular speed zone. The distribution is not greatly improved.

SPRINKLER CHOICE

Sprinklers are manufactured by many companies. Some companies provide features that often attract designers and operators. In general, all sprinklers are pieces of equipment that will distribute water on a certain area. Basically, all sprinklers will do about the same job. The designer dictates the overall performance of the system by choosing the percentage of spacing and percentage of effective coverage; placing the sprinklers; and designing a suitable piping, pumping, and management system. Therefore, one might choose a particular company's sprinklers not so much for the sprinkler's, water distributer pattern, but for the ease of maintenance, valving features, pressure regulation, and durability. Samples of sprinklers performance data taken from several company catalogs are given in Appendix A. Note the performance of each sprinkler. A few of the special features are also evident from the data given. To fully understand all of the features available, obtain complete sprinkler catalogs from each manufacturer. These catalogs will include information on valves, controllers, and accessories, as well as the sprinkler performance data. Do not buy products or features you do not need and probably will not use.

PROBLEMS

1. A Royal Coach Model 10110 sprinkler with $7/16$-in × $7/32$-in nozzles operating at 100 psi will apply 1.0 inches of water to a point 10 feet from the sprinkler. Sketch the expected depth of application at distances of 30%, 50%, 60%, 80%, and 100% of the radius. The sprinkler is operating by itself.

2. A Toro 694-xx-92 sprinkler operating at 70 psi will apply water, within the 30% circle, at 0.68 in/hr. If two of these sprinklers are located 100 feet apart, sketch the application rates for each sprinkler and the application rate for the two sprinklers operating simultaneously.

3. A Rain Bird Model 51A with $1/4$-in × $3/16$-in nozzles operating by itself at 65 psi applies 0.5 inches of water at the sprinkler. What depth of water is applied at 30%, 50%, 60%, 80%, and 100% of the radius?

4. A Weather-Tec/Skinner Model 30-83 sprinkler with $9/32$-in × $11/64$-in nozzles operating at 70 psi will apply water within the 30% circle at 0.26 in/hr. If two of these sprinklers are located 100 feet apart, sketch the application rate for each sprinkler and the application rate for the two sprinklers operating simultaneously. What is the percentage of spacing for these two sprinklers?

5. Select a sprinkler for each of the following. (Specify wetted diameter required, model, nozzle size(s), operating pressure, and discharge.)
   a. Spacing = 100 feet; %S = 65%
   b. Spacing = 80 feet; %S = 50%
   c. Spacing = 120 feet; %S = 70%

6. What is the minimum operating pressure recommended for each of the following:
   a. Weather-Tec/Skinner 30-83 with $13/64$-in × $11/64$-in nozzles
   b. Toro 674-xx-73
   c. Rain Bird 41 with $1/4$-in × $3/64$-in nozzles
   d. Royal Coach 10092 with $3/8$-in × $7/32$-in nozzles

7. What is the maximum operating pressure recommended for each of the following:
   a. Rain Bird 41 with $3/16$-in × $11/64$-in nozzles
   b. Toro 674-xx-73

c. Royal Coach 10090 with ⁷/₃₂-in nozzle

d. Weather-Tec/Skinner 30-84 with ⅜-in × ¹¹/₆₄-in nozzles

8. Select a V-I-H sprinkler to be placed on a 100-foot wide fairway, single-row system, with a 70% effective coverage.

9. What effect does wind have on a sprinkler's distribution? How does this effect vary with operating pressure? What can be done when placing sprinklers to compensate for the effect of wind?

Chapter 3
GREENS AND TEES

IRRIGATING PUTTING GREENS

The appearance and condition of greens is often used to judge the success or failure of a golf course superintendent. Since the superintendent's bread and butter may depend on this factor, he must develop a love for each blade of grass and give it his most tender care. Water plays a key role in growing and maintaining healthy, vigorous turf. Therefore, special emphasis should be placed on the watering system for greens.

Sprinkler Systems

The following points should be considered when planning sprinklers for putting greens:

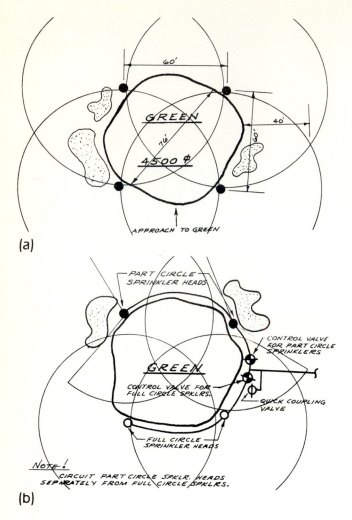

(a)

(b)

Figure 3–1 Full- and part-circle sprinklers around green (Adapted with permission from Pira, 1982)

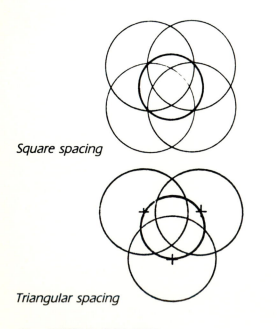

Square spacing

Triangular spacing

1. Provide a quick-coupling valve at each green for hand-watering and syringing. On automatic systems, be sure the coupling valve is installed before the remote control shut-off valve.

2. The nearest fairway sprinkler should be placed such that it does not water the green. A separation of 10 feet is usually recommended between the edge of the green and the wetted edge of the nearest fairway sprinkler.

3. Green sprinklers are usually valved in pairs as opposed to one valve for each sprinkler or one valve for all sprinklers.

4. Generally, greens require smaller sprinklers than fairways. The size and shape of the green must govern the size of the sprinklers, their location, spacing, and number. A model with approximately the same pressure requirements as the fairway sprinkler should be selected.

5. Full-circle sprinklers are usually used on greens to give good coverage of apron, collar, and approach. They make these areas easier to maintain, especially where golf carts normally travel around the greens. They also make greens look much larger.

6. Part-circle sprinklers are usually only used on special requirement areas. For example, they avoid watering on buildings, walks, or streets that lie close to a green or on sand traps that are not properly drained. Part-circle sprinklers should be put on separate control circuits from the full-circle heads so timers can be adjusted to compensate for the different application rates produced from these heads. Examples of full-circle and part-circle sprinkler layouts are shown in figure 3–1.

Spacing

Square spacing (see opposite) generally provides the best water distribution over the largest portion of the green and offers the advantage of squaring off corners. It is especially suitable for oblong-shaped greens.

Triangular spacing provides good water distribution on small, round-shaped greens.

Sprinkler types

A single permanent sprinkler requires an extra-large diameter sprinkler to uniformly cover the green. On established greens, it is necessary to trench through a portion of the green to provide for pipe installation.

A single portable sprinkler permits flexibility in adjusting to changing wind direction and in giving special attention to troublesome spots on the green. However, it is inconvenient to operate.

Procedure

Consult figure 3–2 for a typical green layout with square spacing. For any layout, each sprinkler should reach to the adjacent sprinkler (50% spacing). If a green is about 90 feet across, the sprinkler radius should be about 90 feet and the sprinklers have a 90-foot by 90-foot spacing.

The points of sprinkler-wetted diameter intersection should be a minimum of 20 feet from the green, regardless of the method used for green sprinkler selection and layouts.

Two sprinklers should be used on the approach side of the green to ensure good coverage on the approach where the transition must be made to the fairway sprinklers.

Piping Circuit Systems

Pipe lines, control valves, and sprinklers all contribute to managing water around greens. The pipelines transport the water to the sprinkler and the control valve tells the water in the pipeline when and for how long to send water to the sprinkler. Three basic types of systems or geometries are used to deliver water from the supply line to the sprinkler. The easiest to understand is the in-line system, characterized by a gang of sprinklers all on one pipeline, separated from the supply line by a control valve (see figure 3–3). Any time this one control valve is in the on position, water flows to the sprinklers. The in-line system is usually the cheapest but has limited control and flexibility since all of the sprinklers operate if any one of them is needed. In-line systems are often used around greens when more than one sprinkler is operated simultaneously

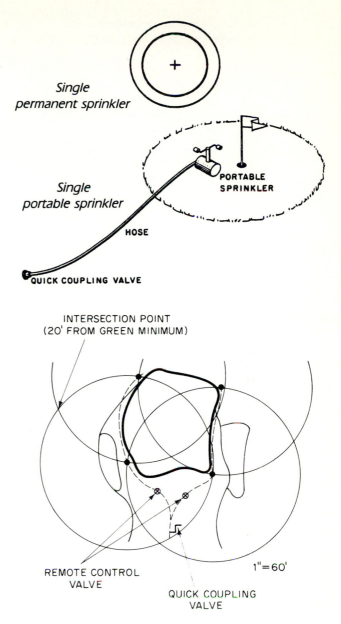

Figure 3–2   Typical green layout with square spacing

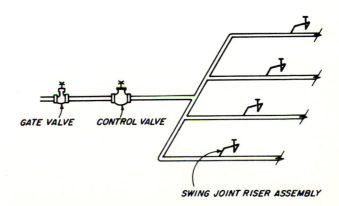

Figure 3–3   In-line valve system

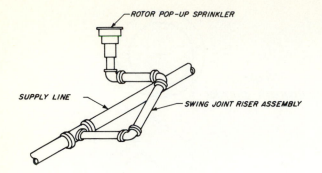

Figure 3–4   Valve-in-head system

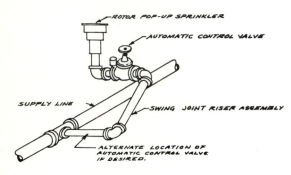

Figure 3–5   Valve-under-head system

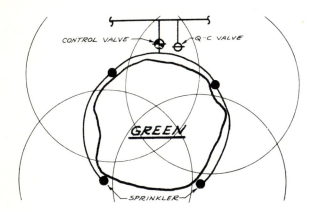

Figure 3–6   Split supply line to green sprinklers

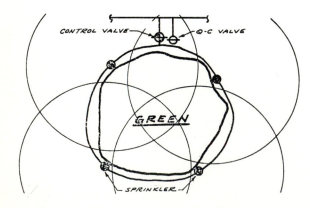

Figure 3–7   Looped circuit around green

or on fairways where large numbers of small sprinklers are used, such as with double- or triple-row systems.

When individual head control is desired, such as on single-row fairway systems or around greens or tees, it is necessary to have one control valve for every sprinkler. The two common types of systems are the valve-in-head (V-I-H) and the valve-under-head (V-U-H). The valve-in-head system (see figure 3–4) has a standard swing joint connecting the sprinkler to the supply line. In some cases, a gate valve is placed on the swing joint to serve as a manual shut-off valve. This permits sprinklers to be serviced without interrupting the supply line flow. The automatic control V-I-H is located inside the sprinkler housing and is usually accessed from the top for maintenance. The valve-under-head system is exactly like the V-I-H except the automatic control valve is located on the swing joint instead of inside the sprinkler housing (see figure 3–5). A manual gate valve can also be used with the V-U-H system for easy maintenance.

From a layout and design standpoint, the V-I-H and V-U-H systems are identical. They obviously offer the greatest flexibility of management, but are also more costly in valves, control wire, controllers, and maintenance. Many designers like the V-I-H or V-U-H systems and certain manufacturers have developed an extensive line of V-I-H sprinklers. However, many such systems have been installed and rarely used to their full potential, making the systems a poor investment.

One valve per green

Two common piping methods use one control valve for all sprinklers on a green. One method is to divide the supply line to pick up sprinkler heads to each side of the green (see figure 3–6). The other method is to circle the green with pipe, thus connecting each sprinkler (see figure 3–7).

Two circuits per green

In areas where there is a prevailing wind during the watering period or an elevation change on the green, it is desirable to control the green sprinklers with two separate circuits: one circuit on the windward or uphill side and the other on the leeward or downhill side. Each control valve is connected to a separate station of the controller to maintain maximum control over watering the green. Having two circuits also reduces the application rate on the green and is a common method of controlling green sprinklers (see figure 3–8).

Individual head control

An individual control valve for each sprinkler head at a green gives maximum watering flexibility (see figure 3–9). However, this much flexibility is questionable and is probably more than is justified or will be used effectively. The economics of a system usually will not justify this type of design and it is not generally used. Therefore, use of valve-in-head sprinklers is seldom justified on greens.

Collar sprinklers around green

On greens that are elevated and have rather high banks on the collars, there is a trend toward special consideration of the collars and area around the green. Placing a second row of sprinklers completely around the green, except for the approach area, will provide this special attention (see figure 3–10).

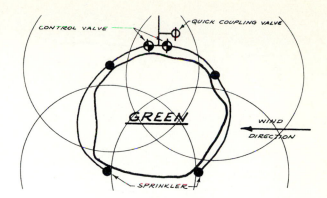

Figure 3–8   Two circuits per green

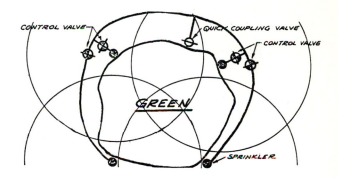

Figure 3–9   Individual sprinkler control

SUMMARY

Because every green is unique in its size, shape, and contour and in how it fits into the surrounding area, each green must be carefully studied to determine what size sprinkler is best and how many sprinklers are needed. Each green will not necessarily need the same number of sprinklers, although this may be desirable for management purposes. Large or oblong-shaped greens may need five or six sprinklers, while small, circular greens may only need three. Generally, sprinklers should be placed five to 10 feet from the edge of the green and on a square spacing, with a 50% spacing being desirable. Spacing can be increased to 60% if a triangular spacing is used.

Few specific guidelines have been given in this chapter because watering greens is an art at best. A few specific ideas will be given in the example at

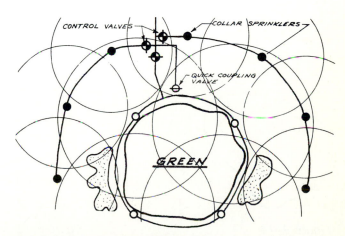

Figure 3–10   Collar sprinklers

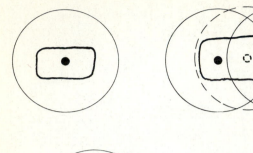

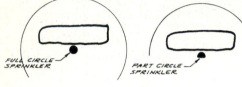

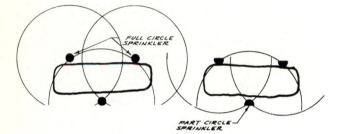

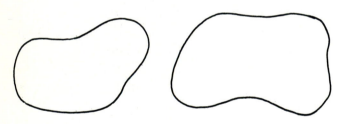

Figure 3–11   Typical tee sprinkler arrangements

the end of chapter 4, but one should not be limited by those suggestions. Remember to make sure the green is well-covered and to keep the piping circuit and control system as simple as possible without ignoring the need for management flexibility and control. Use part-circle sprinklers only where they are needed.

IRRIGATING TEES

The general practice for watering tees is to place full-circle sprinklers on or near the tees for proper coverage. Commonly, the same sprinklers used around the greens are used on tees. Although on small tees the greens sprinklers may be larger than required, they will give good coverage to the area around the tee and reduce the number of different sprinklers used in the system. This is an advantage from both maintenance and management standpoints (see figure 3–11).

PROBLEM

1.   Locate, size, and select a sprinkler to be used on the greens in figures 3–12, 3–13, 3–14, and 3–15. In each case, specify desired wetted diameter, model, nozzle size(s), operating pressure, and discharge. Draw the 100% radius circles for each sprinkler. Sketch a piping network, including one quick-coupling valve. Assume the water supply is from the bottom of the page. Assume a scale of 1″= 60′.

  a. Use V-I-H sprinklers on the green in figure 3–12.
  b. Use V-U-H sprinklers on the green in figure 3–13.
  c. Use in-line valves and lay pipe so adjacent sprinklers in figure 3–14 do not run simultaneously.
  d. Use in-line values and lay pipe so adjacent sprinklers in figure 3–15 operate simultaneously to provide irrigation in two sets.

Figure 3–12   *Figure 3–13*

Figure 3–14   *Figure 3–15*

Chapter 4
FAIRWAYS

There are many ways to irrigate fairways. However, questions must be addressed to determine which way is best for your situation. Do you want a single-row or a double-row system or do you want to irrigate the entire course (a wall-to-wall system)? How much control is necessary or cost effective? Is individual head control desired or do you want to control sprinklers in small groups with in-line valves? Do you want an automatic control system or would more manual control be better? Most of these questions do not have simple answers. In many cases the answers are based more on personal preference and experience rather than hard data or even financial considerations.

An automatic control system simply means the control valves are replaced by quick-coupling valves. With this system, the sprinklers are inserted when watering is needed instead of activating a control valve that delivers water to an existing pop-up sprinkler. All of the management evaluation and design steps are basically the same for both automatic and manual systems.

For most courses the initial question to be addressed is, Do you want or need individual head control? The single-row system is best adapted to the valve-in-head or valve-under-head concept. If you prefer running several smaller sprinklers from one valve, the two-row system may be preferred. The two-row system will usually give better uniformity-of-coverage near the center of the fairway and smaller dry areas along the fairway edge. Operating two-row value-in-head or valve-under-head systems becomes unreasonable because of the number of controller stations required. A two-row system should be used when either the practical limitations of a single-row system are being exceeded or when the advantages offered by the two-row system are preferred.

SINGLE-ROW SPRINKLER SYSTEM

Obtaining the desired effective coverage on wide fairways with a single-row sprinkler system requires very large sprinklers that usually have excessive discharge rates. To emphasize this point, select two or three possible sprinklers and record their operating characteristics for the following conditions in the chart provided:

○ Average fairway width is 175 feet.

○ Desired effective coverage is 70%.

○ Required wetted diameter is $\dfrac{175}{.70} = 250$ feet.

Name & model	Wetted diameter (ft)	Discharge (gpm)	Base pressure (psi)	Nozzle sizes(s) (in)

The following factors should be considered before installing a single-row system:

1. The availability of large-diameter sprinkler models, especially the pop-up type.

2. The operating characteristics:
   a. Sprinkler discharge rate
   b. Application rate
   c. Operating pressure

3. Reasonable number of sprinklers that can operate at one time.

4. Uniformity of water distribution.

5. Spacing of sprinklers.

6. Distance water exceeds edge of the fairway especially on smaller fairways.

TWO-ROW SPRINKLER SYSTEM

There are many advantages to a two-row sprinkler system. First, smaller sprinklers require less discharge and can result in smaller pipe sizes (see figure 4–1). Second, the system can often operate more sprinklers at one time. Third, application rates are lower,

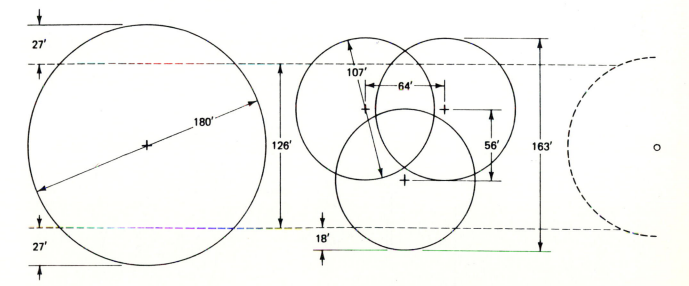

Figure 4–1 *Single-row 180-ft diameter sprinklers vs. two-row triangular system sprinklers using 60% spacing and 70% effective coverage*

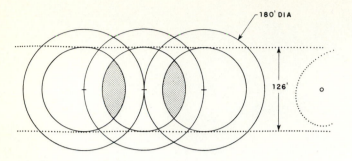

Figure 4–2 Single-row fairway system with 50% spacing and 70% effective coverage

which result in better infiltration. Fourth, lower operating pressure means smaller pump size and lower operating cost. Fifth, the system provides a wider zone of uniform coverage near center of fairway. Finally, less water is applied to rough areas. (Compare figures 4–1, 4–2, and 4–3.)

COVERAGE NEAR EDGE OF FAIRWAYS

From the discussion in chapter 2, it is evident that a single- or double-row system will not provide uniform coverage near the edge of the fairway. One major company has attempted to improve coverage in this zone by developing sprinklers that operate at two speeds. Usually, they rotate at normal speed in the zone where they overlap with an adjacent sprinkler and at one-half normal speed in the zone where there is no overlap. The effectiveness of the two-speed head is illustrated in figures 4–4 and 4–5 for a single-row system and in figures 4–6 and 4–7 for a double-row triangular spacing system. In both cases, note how the reduced speed increases the rate of application in zones where overlap does not occur. Uniformity of distribution over the entire fairway should be examined closely before deciding to use the two-speed head since areas of heavy and light coverage may still exist. Also note that the increased complexity of the drive mechanism needed

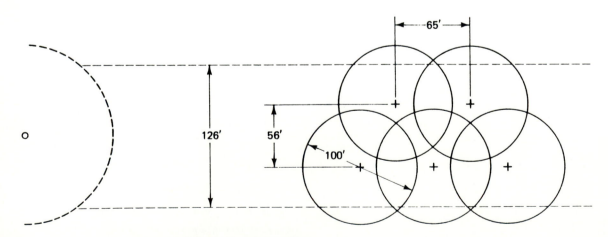

Figure 4–3 Two-row triangular fairway system with 65% spacing and 70% effective coverage

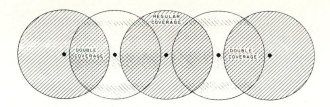

Figure 4—4 Single-row system with one-speed head (Taken with permission from Toro, 1972)

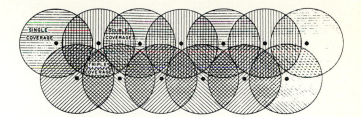

Figure 4—6 Triangular spacing with one-speed head (Taken with permission from Toro, 1972)

to create the two-speed rotation often results in increased maintenance.

In spacing sprinklers on the fairway, it is advisable to start at the green, locating the first sprinkler approximately 10 feet from the front edge of the putting surface. By placing the first sprinkler in this manner, water from the fairway sprinkler will not fall on the green which could result in overwatering of the front of the green (see figure 4—8).

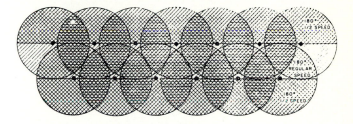

Figure 4—7 Triangular spacing with 180° two-speed heads (Taken with permission from Toro, 1972)

COVERAGE OF APPROACH AREA TO GREEN

With the growing use of golf carts and their travel around the approach areas to the greens, it is desirable to provide better coverage on the approach area. This can be effectively accomplished by placing two fairway sprinklers at the green, one to either side of the center of the green, and then continuing the fairway with a single-row or double-row system (see figure 4—9).

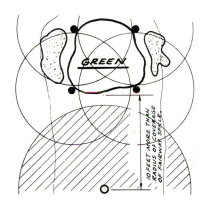

Figure 4—8 Location of first fairway sprinkler

COVERAGE OF THE AREA

On some courses, it is common to omit watering of the first 100 yards or so of the fairway, rather than

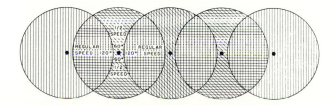

Figure 4—5 Single-row system with two-speed head (Taken with permission from Toro, 1972)

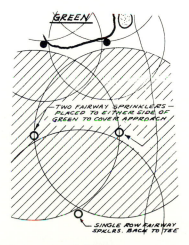

Figure 4—9 Approach sprinklers

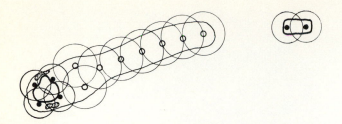

Figure 4–10   Area in front of tees not watered

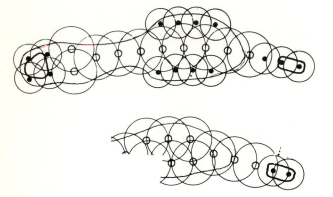

Figure 4–11   Coverage of landing areas

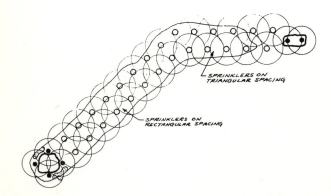

SPRINKLERS ON
TRIANGULAR SPACING

SPRINKLERS ON
RECTANGULAR SPACING

Figure 4–12   Double-row systems

water the complete fairway from green to tee. Fairway sprinklers are stopped near the end of the mowed area, in front of the tee (see figure 4–10). By stopping there, we reduce the total number of sprinkler heads and control valves (if an automatic system) and also may eliminate some piping, trenching, wiring, and controller stations.

COVERAGE OF WIDE FAIRWAY AREAS

In the design of some golf courses, the mowed fairway is increased in width at the landing areas. If it is desired to cover these wide areas, double rows of additional smaller sprinklers placed to either side of the single row may be used (see figure 4–11).

DOUBLE-ROW SYSTEM ON FAIRWAYS

To get effective coverage on the entire mowed fairway or to get some watering in the roughs, as may be required in arid climates, it may be necessary to use a double-row system. Also, in areas with high wind conditions, it may be more desirable to use a double-row system and have less damaging effect from the wind. With double-row systems, it is best to start at the green with a square spacing rather than a triangular spacing. On fairways with doglegs, the square spacing will change toward or to a triangular spacing as you go around the curve. This is an excellent method of obtaining good coverage (see figure 4–12).

Selecting sprinklers for double-row systems is more complex than selecting sprinklers for single-row systems. This is caused by the need to have the proper effective coverage at the edge of the fairways as well as to maintain the proper spacing between the two rows of sprinklers. To aid in selecting sprinklers for double-row systems, the following relationships have been developed.

Double-Row Square Spacing

The desired wetted diameter (WD) for each sprinkler in a double-row square spacing can be determined as

$$WD = \frac{W}{\% \, S + \% \, EC} \qquad \text{(Eq. 4.1)}$$

where WD = wetted diameter of sprinkler in feet
W = fairway width in feet
% S = percentage of spacing in decimal
% EC = percentage of effective coverage in decimal

Double-Row Triangular Spacing

The desired wetted diameter for each sprinkler in a double-row triangular spacing can be determined as

$$WD = \frac{W}{0.87(\% \, S) + \% \, EC} \qquad \text{(Eq. 4.2)}$$

The following example illustrates the use of these formulas.

Example Determine the required sprinkler-wetted diameter to provide a 60% effective coverage and a 70% spacing on a 130-foot wide fairway. A double-row triangular system is desired.

Solution $WD = \dfrac{W}{0.87(\% \, S) + \% \, EC} = \dfrac{130}{0.87(.7) + .6}$
$= 108 \text{ feet}$

A sprinkler with a 108-foot wetted diameter will provide proper coverage and spacing.

FAIRWAY ANALYSIS AND DESIGN

The examples that follow show how most common systems can be analyzed and/or designed. Study these in detail.

Single-Row System

Given width of fairway (W) = 130 feet
% effective coverage = 65%
% spacing = 55%

Find Desired wetted diameter (WD) and the distance between sprinklers (see figure 4–13).

Solution $WD = \dfrac{W}{\% \, EC} = \dfrac{130 \text{ ft}}{.65} = 200 \text{ feet}$

Distance between sprinklers = WD (% S) = 200 (.55) = 110 feet.

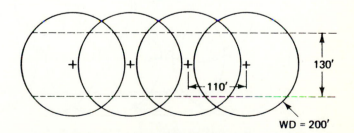

Figure 4–13   Example single-row system

Double-Row Triangular System

Given   W = 130 feet
% EC = 65%
% S = 55%

Find   WD, S, distance between laterals (L) (see figure 4–14).

Solution   From equation 4.2, WD = *115 feet;* S = % S (WD) = .55 (115) = *63 feet;* L = S (.87) = 63 (.87) = *55 feet.*

Double-Row Square System

Given   W = 130 feet
% EC = 65%
% S = 55%

Find   WD, S, L (see figure 4–15).

Solution   From equation 4.1, WD = *108 feet;* S = % S (WD) = .55 (108) = *60 feet;* L = S = *60 feet.*

Design Parameters

Given   The existing system shown in figure 4–16.

Find   % S, % EC, S.
Solution

$$S = \frac{L}{.866} = 81 \text{ ft}$$

$$\% \, S = \frac{S}{WD} = \frac{81}{180} = 45\%$$

$$\% \, EC = \frac{\text{Dist. from lateral to edge of fairway}}{\text{Dist. from lateral to edge of wetted zone}} =$$

$$\frac{140 - 70 = 70/2 = 35 \text{ ft}}{250 - 70 = 180/20 = 90 \text{ ft}} = 39\%$$

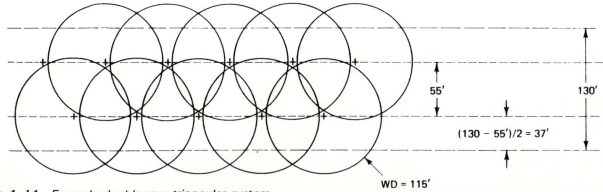

Figure 4–14   *Example double-row triangular system*

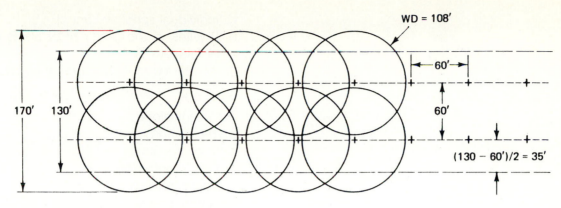

Figure 4–15   Example double-row square system

GOLF COURSE IRRIGATION DESIGN EXAMPLE

This example will take you through the steps required to completely design a 9-hole golf course irrigation system. It continues through chapter 11. The example shows some of the common methods of obtaining various parts of the design. Each golf course is different and one standard design example will not provide the best answers for all or even most courses. Another major problem with golf course design is that, before any work can be started, someone *must* make some key decisions. To say you want the best system does not mean much. A very good system could be obtained using any number of different schemes. The most important decision that must be made has to do with management. How does the golf course superintendent want to manage the watering? A typical answer is, "I want maximum flexibility; I want to be able to run any sprinkler any time!" An irrigation system designer can design such a system, but no golf course or country club could afford to buy it. In the end it all boils down to money. Therefore, you must make some decisions about

1. What kind of system you want to work with:
    a. Single-row
    b. Double-row
    c. Triple-row
    d. Valve-in-head
    e. Valve-under-head
    f. Valve for a group of heads

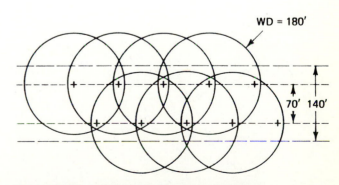

Figure 4–16   Design parameters example

g. Individual sprinkler control
h. Pipeline in the center of or along the edge of fairways
i. As needed to irrigate green, tees, fairways

2. What operating scheme is desired?
   a. Greens alone
   b. Tees with greens
   c. Fairways alone
   d. One sprinkler/fairway
   e. One sprinkler/green
   f. A whole green at once

3. What kind of water supply is available?
   a. Well
   b. Stream
   c. Ponds
   d. Combinations

This exercise is intended to help you ask the right questions and to provide a few of the answers. The sequence of operations and activities is generally about the same regardless of the decisions made about the previously mentioned questions. Before you start, have a map of the golf course. A map scale of 1″=100′ is probably best. The map should include locations, shapes, and sizes of greens, tees, fairways, sand traps, and water hazards. The water source should be included and 10-foot contours are needed.

Sprinkler Layouts

The first step in designing a golf course is to locate the sprinklers. Most companies can provide the hardware so do not be limited by one manufacturer's goods. Sprinklers are selected on the basis of their wetted diameters and the desired piping and control scheme.

Greens

The green in figure 4–17 is adequately covered by the single sprinkler placed in the green's center. The 30% circle indicates nearly uniform coverage over the green. This type of system also requires a very large sprinkler, generally wasting money and water. A better scheme for greens is to place at least three smaller sprinklers around the green (see figure 4–18). Three sprinklers work well for small greens especially if two of the three are placed on

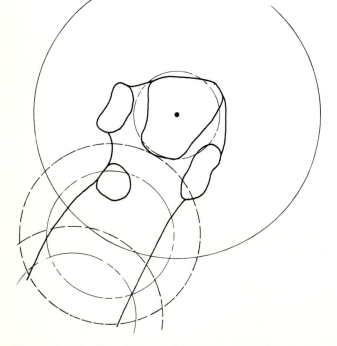

Figure 4–17   One large sprinkler on a green

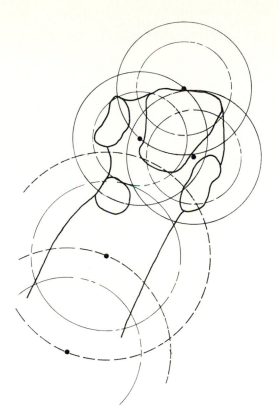

Figure 4–18   Three sprinklers on a green

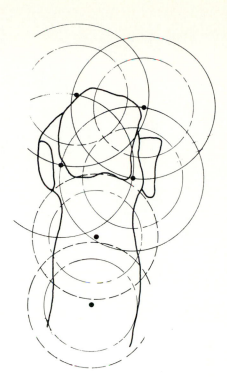

Figure 4–19   Four sprinklers on a green

a line nearly perpendicular to the line of the fairway. The distance between sprinklers should be about 50% of the sprinkler's wetted diameter.

Figure 4–19 shows four sprinklers spaced around the green. Again, a 50% spacing is best. This scheme is perhaps the best but it does take some extra resources. Some large or odd-shaped greens may need more than four sprinklers to do a good job (see figure 4–20). Remember, the greens are the key to any golf course. If you do not do a good job of watering greens, a watering system is not worth having.

Fairways

The first step with any fairway is to find the average width of the fairway. It is usually best to measure the width of the fairway at two or three locations including the maximum width. The data for the 9-hole system shown in figure 4–21 are given in table 4–1. The average fairway width is 133 feet.

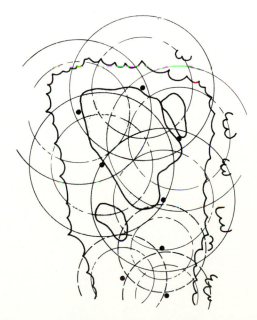

Figure 4–20   More than four sprinklers on a green

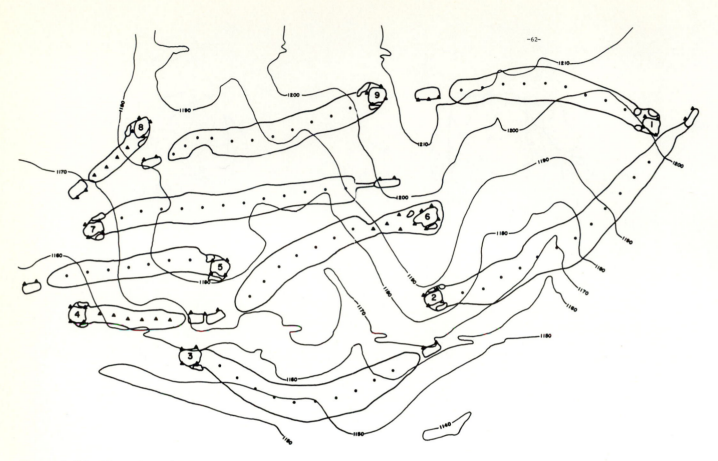

Figure 4–21 Example sprinkler layout

If the average width is used with a 70% effective coverage and a 50% spacing, the coverage would look like that shown in figure 4–22. If the average maximum width, 152 feet, is used with a

Table 4–1 Fairway width data for nine-hole course

Fairway	Width			Average width	Maximum width	Maximum width
	1	2	3			
1	172	100		136	172	172
2	170	210	130	170	210	210
3	155	185		170	185	185
4	100	90		95	100[a]	
5	95	130		112	130	130
6	150	130		140	160	160
7	150	140		145	160	160
8	70	85		78	85[a]	
9	150	150		150	170	170
		Average		133	152	170

Note: Widths expressed in feet.
[a]Exceptionally narrow fairways that may need to be considered separately.

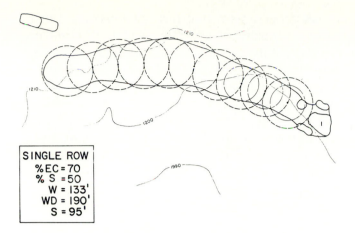

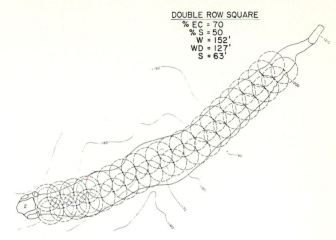

Figure 4–22 *Fairway 1 with single-row system using average fairway width*

Figure 4–24 *Fairway 2 with a square double-row system*

70% effective coverage and 50% spacing, the sprinklers cover fairway 1 as shown in figure 4–23. The coverage is better if the average maximum is used in this case. Very narrow fairways, such as fairways 4 and 8, must be considered separately, probably by using smaller sprinklers such as the green sprinkler. Another method of providing coverage on fairways is to use smaller sprinklers in a square double-row (see figure 4–24) or a triangular double-row (see figure 4–25). Either of these require smaller sprinklers than the single-row systems. These smaller sprinklers may also work well as single-row sprinklers on the narrow fairways (see figure 4–25).

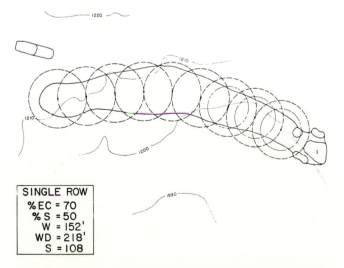

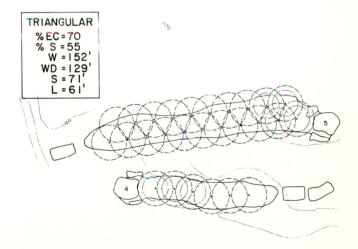

Figure 4–23 *Fairway 1 with single-row system using average maximum width*

Figure 4–25 *Fairway 5 with a triangular double-row system and fairway 4 with single-row system*

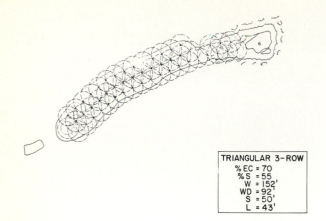

TRIANGULAR 3-ROW
%EC = 70
%S = 55
W = 152'
WD = 92'
S = 50'
L = 43'

Figure 4–26 Fairway 6 with triangular triple-row system

Another system that has not been used much but gives excellent coverage over the largest percentage of the fairway is a triangular triple-row system (see figure 4–26). Valve-in-head control is nearly impossible with this system and is seldom employed on double-row systems either.

Adequate coverage of the approach areas can be a problem if small sprinklers are used or if poor sprinkler placement occurs. The single-row and/or the triangular spacing tend to give poor coverage of the approach areas. The square double-row systems usually provide the best coverage on approaches.

Sprinkler Selection and Placement

The greens will normally be covered by four sprinklers. Since the average distance across the greens on this course is about 75 feet, the wetted diameter for green sprinklers needs to be about 150 feet, assuming a 50% spacing. A valve-in-head system was not used since individual head control was not desired. The Toro 654 with the no. 57 nozzle set operating at 80 psi and discharging 32.9 gpm was chosen. These sprinklers were also used on the tees.

A single-row system with valve-in-head sprinklers was selected for the fairways. This sprinkler was sized based on the average maximum width after deleting the widths of fairways 4 and 8. This gave an average width of 170 feet. Based on 70% effective coverage and 50% spacing, the required wetted diameter is 218 feet and the sprinklers will be spaced 108 feet apart. A Toro 694 with a no. 92 nozzle set operating at 90 psi and discharging 78.0 gpm was chosen. This sprinkler has a wetted diameter of 210 feet. The smaller green sprinklers will also be used on fairways 4, 6, and 8 as valve-in-heads. All sprinkler locations are shown on figure 4–21.

In this example, Toro sprinklers were selected. Note that other manufacturers' market sprinklers would provide equivalent performance. For those manufacturers who do not market V-I-H sprinklers, the V-U-H arrangement would provide equivalent individual head control.

PROBLEMS

1. It is desired to use a single-row system on a 130-foot-wide fairway. If the % EC = 70% and the % S = 50%, what wetted diameter is needed? Select a specific sprinkler. What is the distance between sprinklers?

2. Repeat problem 1 where the fairway is 110 feet wide, % EC = 60%, and % S = 60%.

3. Determine the required sprinkler wetted diameter, the distance between laterals, and the distance between sprinklers and select a specific sprinkler for a 100-foot-wide fairway using a 50% S and a 70% EC. Use a triangular spacing.

4. Determine the required sprinkler wetted diameter, the distance between laterals, the distance between sprinklers, and select a specific sprinkler for a 140-foot-wide fairway using a 60% S and a 50% EC. Use a triangular spacing.

5. Repeat problem 3 for a square spacing.

6. Repeat problem 4 for a square spacing.

7. Carefully draw the solution to problem 3. Note any areas that are likely to have light coverage.

8. Carefully draw the solution to problem 6. Note any areas that are likely to have light coverage.

9. Design a two-row triangular system for fairway 2 of figure 4–27. Use % S = 60% and % EC = 70%. Select specific sprinklers for the fairway, the green, and the tee. Locate each sprinkler and draw the 100% and 70% circles.

10. Repeat problem 9 using a single-row system on fairway 2. Use % S = 50% and % EC = 70%.

11. Repeat problem 9 using a two-row square system on fairway 1. Use % S = 55% and % EC = 70%.

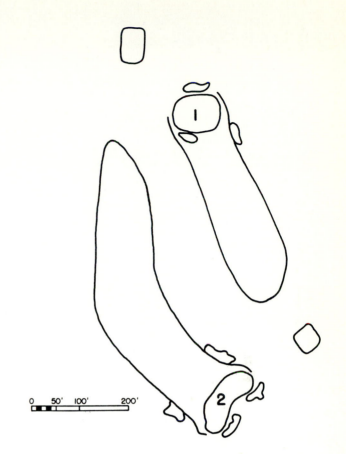

Figure 4–27   Figure for problems 9, 10 and 11

Chapter 5
MANAGEMENT

Chapters 2, 3, and 4 have provided guidance on how sprinklers perform and where the sprinklers should be located to provide uniform coverage of greens, tees, and fairways. To the superintendent, the irrigation system is a tool that can be used to meet numerous objectives as outlined in chapter 1. In most regions, the irrigation system should be designed so it can supply the water needed to grow the turfgrass on the various areas of the golf course. Supplying water to replace the soil moisture transpired through the turfgrass represents the largest water need from the standpoints of both total water volume applied and time required to apply this water. Heat suppression, turf softening, fertilizer application and/or dissolving, and other short-term water applications require less water and can usually be accomplished with the same hardware used to replace transpiration water. For these reasons, this chapter will concentrate on understanding how to manage an irrigation system to apply water required by transpiration.

APPLICATION RATE

The application rate (AR) for a sprinkler-in-pattern is a function of the individual sprinkler discharge and the area covered by that sprinkler. The effective area for a sprinkler changes depending on the type of pattern or spacing employed.

When there are two or more rows of sprinklers, the effective area covered by a given sprinkler is the distance between sprinklers (S) times the distance between rows of sprinklers (L). The distance between rows of sprinklers is the same as the spacing (S) for a square spacing. For a triangular spacing the distance between rows of sprinklers is L=0.866 (S). In the case of single-row systems, the area is approximated by 0.8 S (WD). The relationship between sprinkler discharge and area covered for common types of spacings is

$$(AR) \ (in/hr) = \frac{96.3 \ (gpm/spr)}{area}$$

where   gpm/spr = each sprinkler's discharge in gal/min

area = S^2 for square spacings

area = SL for triangular spacings

area = 0.8 S (WD) for single-row systems

This formula should be applied to all areas to be watered, yielding an application rate for all areas of the course. Average application rates for areas that may be served by only one sprinkler can be determined by the following formula:

$$AR \ (in/hr) = \frac{122 \ (gpm/spr)}{(WD)^2 \ (\% \ EC)^2} \ [0.23 + 0.77(\% \ EC)]$$

where   WD = wetted diameter of the sprinkler in feet

% EC = percentage of effective coverage, in decimal, at the edge of the area being irrigated

DESIGN DEPTH

With most sprinkler irrigation systems, the crop, in this case turfgrass, is left to extract moisture from the soil until 50% of the available moisture in the root zone has been transpired. When half the available moisture has been removed, irrigation is employed to replace the soil water, returning the soil to field capacity.

Several methods have been developed to determine how much water the turf needs to prevent moisture stress, the design depth (DD). For all methods but one, the DD is related to the amount of available moisture in the root zone of the turf. The available moisture is the amount of water in the soil between field capacity and the wilting point.

Soil Mixes

Soil Modification for Turfgrass Areas by Waddington et al. (1974) is a good source of soil data for soil mixes used for greens and tees. By assuming the effective available moisture in soil mixes occurs at 60 cm of tension, the depth of available moisture in a foot depth of root zone can be obtained from figures 5–1, 5–2, 5–3, and 5–4 for several soil mixes. If the available moisture in inches per foot of root zone is multiplied by the root zone of the turfgrasses grown, the depth of available moisture (AMC) in the root zone can be obtained as follows:

$$\text{AMC (in/ft)} \times \text{root zone (in)} \times 12\,\frac{\text{ft}}{\text{in}}$$

$$= \text{AMC (inches/root zone)}$$

The design depth (DD) can be calculated using the following relationship:

$$\text{DD (inches)} = \frac{.5\,(\text{AMC})}{\text{WAE}}$$

where   AMC = available moisture in the root zone in inches

WAE = water application efficiency in decimal

The WAE is a decimal value that reflects the portion of water taken from the water source which reaches the root zone. A WAE of .75 or 75% would

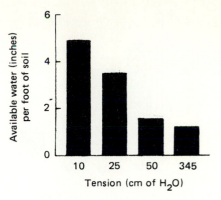

Figure 5–1   Available moisture vs. tension for an 8:1:1 (mortar sand:soil:peat) mixture (Adapted with permission from Waddington, et al., 1974)

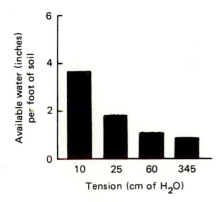

Figure 5–2   Available moisture vs. versus tension for an 8:2:2 (coarse sand:soil:peat) mixture (Adapted with permission from Waddington, et al., 1974)

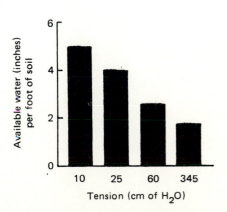

Figure 5–3   Available moisture vs. tension for a 4:5:1 (mortar sand:soil:peat) mixture (Adapted with permission from Waddington, et al., 1974)

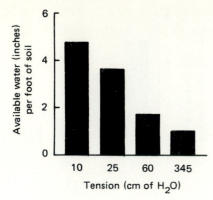

Figure 5–4   Available moisture vs. tension for an 8:2:2 (mortar sand:soil:peat) mixture (Adapted with permission from Waddington, et al., 1974)

mean that 75% of the water pumped from the source would actually get to its designated end point, the root zone of the turf. In this case, 25% of the water would be lost to pipe leakage, evaporation, runoff, and flow through the root zone. The WAE for sprinkler irrigation should be at least 70%.

Natural Soils

The available moisture capacity (AMC) of a natural soil can be determined by consulting the irrigation guides published for each state by the USDA Soil Conservation Service. The guides provide data on available moisture and maximum application rates for all soil series within the state. Sample data are summarized in table 5–1.

Table 5–1   Sample irrigation design information for natural soils

Soil characteristic	Sample series	Available moist. cap. (in/ft)	Max. app. rate (in/hr)
Deep well-drained Mod. perm. Mod. to fine texture	Allegheny Berks Elk Hublersburg Washington	2.2	0.5 C[1] 1.0 S[2] 0.5 SC[3]
Deep well-drained Mod. rapid to mod. perm. Mod. coarse to med. texture	Clymer Wooster Edgemont Fleetwood Huntington	1.7	0.5 C 1.0 S 0.5 SC
Deep well-drained Mod. rapid perm. Mod. coarse to med. texture	Chenango Howard Worth Hartleton Ottawa	1.3	0.8 C 1.3 S 0.6 SC
Mod. deep well-drained Mod. perm. Med. texture	Lordstown Penn Brooke Chambersburg Gilpin	2.0	0.8 C 1.0 S 0.5 SC
Mod. deep well-drained Mod. to med. rapid perm. Mod. coarse to med. texture	Lorain Brandywine Calvin Litz Steinsburg	1.4	0.8 C 1.0 S 0.5 SC

Table 5–1 Continued

Soil characteristic	Sample series	Available moist. cap. (in/ft)	Max. app. rate (in/hr)
Shallow well-drained Mod. perm. Mod. coarse to fine texture	Klinesville Weikert Benson	1.5	0.5 C 1.0 S 0.5 SC
Mod. deep well-drained Mod. to slow perm. Med. fine texture	Albright Bedford Troy Sweden Ernest	2.0	0.25 C 0.50 S 0.25 SC
Mod. well-drained Slowly perm. Med. fine texture	Hornell Markes Reaville	1.6	0.25 C 0.50 S 0.25 SC
Poorly drained Slowly perm. Med. texture	Fallsington Sloan	1.8	0.25 C 0.50 S 0.25 SC
Very poorly drained Very slowly perm. Med. to fine texture	Andover Robertsville	2.7	0.2 C 0.3 S 0.15 SC

[1]C = cultivated
[2]S = sod
[3]SC = sod, compacted

IRRIGATION INTERVAL

The irrigation interval (II) is the length of time required for the turf to transpire the water applied at each irrigation. It also accounts for water evaporated from the turf and soil. Together these are often referred to as evapotranspiration (ET). Maximum ET rates are given for locations in the United States and Canada in table 5–2. The irrigation interval (II) can be determined by the following relationship:

$$II \text{ (days)} = \frac{.5 \text{ (AMC)}}{ET}$$

where   AMC = available moisture in the root zone in inches

ET = evapotranspiration rate in inches per day

Table 5–2   Turf evapotranspiration data

Location	RE-ET[1] (in)	Max. ET (in/day)	Location	RF-ET (in)	Max. ET (in/day)
Mobile, Ala.	−1.61	0.25	Poplar Bluff, Mo.	−5.28	0.25
Montgomery, Ala.	−3.78	0.26	Miles City, Mont.	−5.26	0.22
Yuma, Ariz.	−10.29	0.34	Butte, Mont.	−3.72	0.16
Flagstaff, Ariz.	−4.74	0.20	Hastings, Nebr.	−5.07	0.25
El Dorado, Ark.	−4.89	0.27	Las Vegas, Nev.	−8.75	0.30
Fayetteville, Ark.	−4.02	0.27	Elko, Nev.	−5.20	0.18
Palm Springs, Cal.	−8.70	0.29	Concord, N.H.	−2.18	0.19
Squaw Valley, Cal.	−4.74	0.16	Atlantic City, N.J.	−3.02	0.22
Wray, Colo.	−4.45	0.22	Las Cruces, N.M.	−6.35	0.25
Denver, Colo.	−2.65	0.14	Santa Fe, N.M.	−3.02	0.16
New Haven, Conn.	−2.82	0.21	Buffalo, N.Y.	−3.25	0.20
Wilmington, Del.	−2.79	0.23	Charlotte, N.C.	−3.25	0.25
Key West, Fla.	−4.05	0.27	Bismark, N.Dak.	−4.36	0.21
Ft. Lauderdale, Fla.	−1.32	0.25	Grand Forks, N. Dak.	−324	0.19
Augusta, Ga.	−3.78	0.26	Toledo, Ohio	−3.49	0.22
Boise, Idaho	−6.72	0.22	Lawton, Okla.	−6.36	0.28
Hailey, Idaho	−4.39	0.16	Hugo, Okla.	−4.30	0.27
Belleville, Ill.	−4.38	0.25	Danner, Oreg.	−6.45	0.22
Rockford, Ill.	−3.31	0.23	Coos Bay, Oreg.	−3.62	0.14
Evansville, Ind.	−3.94	0.24	Pennsylvania	−3.11	0.20
Muncie, Ind.	−3.13	0.22	Rhode Island	−3.35	0.20
Knoxville, Iowa	−4.27	0.24	Greenwood, S.C.	−3.90	0.26
Waterloo, Iowa	−2.82	0.21	Rapid City, S.Dak.	−5.60	0.23
Dodge City, Kans.	−5.60	0.26	Aberdeen, S. Dak.	−4.07	0.20
Topeka, Kans.	−3.87	0.26	Memphis, Tenn.	−3.84	0.25
Louisville, Ky.	−3.09	0.23	Dallas, Tex.	−6.61	0.28
Shreveport, La.	−4.95	0.27	St. George, Utah	−7.59	0.29
New Orleans, La.	−2.16	0.26	Heber, Utah	−4.05	0.16
Augusta, Maine	−2.45	0.19	Burlington, Vt.	−1.91	0.19
Cumberland, Md.	−3.08	0.22	Norfolk, Va.	−3.06	0.24
Boston, Mass.	−3.33	0.20	Yakima, Wash.	−6.58	0.22
Midland, Mich.	−3.67	0.20	Seattle, Wash.	−3.39	0.16
St. Cloud, Minn.	−3.55	0.22	Martinsburg, W. Va.	−2.94	0.21
Greenville, Miss.	−4.89	0.27	Green Bay, Wisc.	−3.20	0.20
Cleveland, Miss.	−5.28	0.27	Cody, Wyo.	−5.09	0.19
The Pas, Man.	−3.06	0.17	Lake Yellowstone, Wyo.	−2.93	0.14
Toronto, Ont.	−2.48	0.17	Kamloops, B.C.	−4.60	0.18
Port Arthur, Ont.	−1.39	0.16	Prince Rupert, B.C.	+0.62	0.13
Montreal, P.Q.	−1.73	0.17	Calgary, Alta.	−2.33	0.16
New Brunswick	−1.30	0.14	Regina, Sask.	−2.80	0.17

Note: Adapted with permission from Toro, 1966.
[1]Rainfall minus evapotranspiration.

Because of the practicality and desire to apply water every day, every other day, or every third day, the design depth is often divided into the irrigation interval to yield the depth of water to be applied each day as:

$$\text{Depth/day} = \frac{DD}{II}$$

This value can be utilized to plan the depth required every one, two, or three days.

WATER DEPTH

Toro (1966) has developed a method of determining the depth of water to apply on a golf course. This method utilizes the data in table 5–2. If rainfall (RF) is subtracted from ET, the result is the amount of water that must be supplied by irrigation. This analysis is done using the month with the greatest deficit, usually July. It is recommended that the monthly deficit be divided by 4 to get the weekly deficit.

If the weekly deficit is less than 1.0 inches per week, 1.0 inches per week will be used. If the weekly deficit is greater than 1.0 inches per week, design for the calculated deficit.

DESIGN RUN TIMES

The design or maximum duration of run for each watering can be determined as time per day or time per set (T_s):

$$T_s = \frac{DD/ll}{AR}$$

where   DD/ll = depth per day in inches per day
            AR = application rate in inches per hour

MANAGEMENT SCHEME

The next step is to decide how to operate all the sprinklers on the course such that the needed water will be applied and the system can be conveniently operated. The management analysis can best be started by summarizing the number and type of sprinklers in the system. Deciding which sprinklers and how many sprinklers to run at each time is perhaps the most difficult part of any design. The procedure is generally by trial and error even though a procedure will be outlined in the example at the end of this chapter.

The goals of the final management scheme are as follows:

1. Be able to water the course in the time allotted each day. Usually 6 to 12 hours is selected as the maximum run time for any night's irrigation. Most superintendents desire to start watering as the last golfers leave the course each evening and to be finished before the first golfers want to start in the morning. There is often some advantage to watering critical areas such as greens just before sunrise to delay water stress during the afternoon.

2. When possible, the pump output should be constant or nearly constant during the watering cycle. This produces an efficient pumping system that reduces operating costs. When one pump rate cannot be found, it is best to keep the needed pump rates as multiples, so multiple identical pumps can be used. It is also more efficient to arrange groups of sprinklers so the runs requiring the maximum discharge are the runs requiring the longest time.

3. It is often desired to keep greens, tees, and fairways separated so separate contol systems can be used to facilitate syringing during daytime irrigation. Greens and tees are often combined on controllers to improve the efficiency in controller station usage.

GOLF COURSE IRRIGATION DESIGN EXAMPLE

The golf course irrigation design example started in chapter 4 will be continued here.

Application Rate

The application rate formula will be applied to each area of the golf course as follows:

1. For greens with a 75-ft × 75-ft spacing and a sprinkler discharge of 32.9 gpm:

$$AR = \frac{96.3 \ (32.9 \ gpm)}{75 \times 75} = 0.56 \ in/hr$$

2. For tees and narrow fairways with a 75-ft in-line spacing and a discharge of 32.9 gpm:

$$AR = \frac{96.3 \ (32.9 \ gpm)}{75 \times .8 \ (144)} = 0.37 \ in/hr$$

3. For fairways with a 108-ft in-line spacing and a discharge of 78.0 gpm:

$$AR = \frac{96.3 \ (78.0 \ gpm)}{108 \times .8 \ (210)} = 0.41 \ in/hr$$

Design Depth and Irrigation Interval

The DD and II will be calculated for the greens assuming we are using an 8:1:1 mixture of mortar sand:soil:peat. At a tension of 60 cm of water there is 1.7 inches of available water for each foot depth of mix (see figure 5–1). Assuming a 4-inch root depth, the amount of available moisture (AMC) in the root zone is 1.7 in/ft × $^{4}/_{12}$ ft = 0.57 in. The irrigation process is designed assuming that the turf has used 50% of the available moisture and therefore irrigation must supply that amount of water to the root zone. A 0.2 inch per day ET rate was also assumed. For greens:

AMC = 1.7 in/ft = 0.57 in/4-in root zone
WAE = 70%
ET (State College, Pa) = 0.20 in/day in July

$$DD = \frac{0.5 \ (AMC)}{WAE} = \frac{0.5 \ (0.57 \ in)}{.7} = 0.40 \ in$$

$$II = \frac{0.5 \ (AMC)}{ET} = \frac{0.5 \ (0.57 \ in)}{.2} = 1.42 \ day$$

The greens, therefore, need 0.40 in/1.42 day or 0.28 inches of water each day during periods when ET is greatest.

The tees are assumed to be on natural soil of the Hublersburg Series. Table 5–1 gives an AMC of 2.2 in/ft of depth for this series. Again assuming 4-inch root depth, the amount of available water in the root zone is 2.2 in/ft × $^{4}/_{12}$ ft = 0.73 in. For tees,

AMC = 2.2 in/ft = 0.73 in/4-in root zone
WAE = 70%
ET = 0.20 in/day in July

$$DD = \frac{0.5 \ (.73 \ in)}{.7} = 0.52 \ in$$

$$II = \frac{0.5 \ (.73 \ in)}{.2} = 1.83 \ day$$

The tees, therefore, need 0.52 inches of water every 1.83 days or 0.28 inches per day when ET is greatest.

The technique used here for tees is usually the most appropriate for fairways. However, to illustrate another technique that has been recommended by Toro, the fairway needs will be based on the Toro method that uses the rainfall and ET data given in table 5–2. The deficit for Pennsylvania is −3.11 inches and

$$\frac{-3.11 \text{ in}}{\text{mon}} \times \frac{\text{mon}}{4 \text{ wk}} = -0.78 \text{ in/wk}$$

In our example, the fairways will be designed for 1.0 inches per week or 0.14 inches per day. In some cases it is not necessary to water every day. Here the desire is to water fairways every other day by applying 0.28 inches at each application.

Time per Day

The time necessary to apply the required water for each type of sprinkler and turf area follows.

Greens

DD = 0.40 inches
II = 1.42 days
AR = 0.56 in/hr
$$T_s = \frac{DD/II}{AR} = \frac{0.28 \text{ in/day}}{0.56 \text{ in/hr}} = 0.50 \text{ hr} = 30 \text{ min/day}$$

Tees

DD = 0.52 inches
II = 1.83 day
AR = 0.37 in/hr
$$T_s = \frac{0.28 \text{ in/day}}{0.37 \text{ in/hr}} = 0.76 \text{ hr} = 45 \text{ min/day}$$

Fairways (large sprinklers)

DD = 0.28 inches
II = 2 days
AR = 0.41 in/hr
$$T_s = \frac{0.28 \text{ in/set}}{0.41 \text{ in/hr}} = 0.68 \text{ hr} = 41 \text{ min/set}$$

Fairways (small sprinklers)

$$DD = 0.28 \text{ inches}$$
$$II = 2 \text{ days}$$
$$AR = 0.37 \text{ in/hr}$$
$$T_s = \frac{0.28 \text{ in/set}}{0.37 \text{ in/hr}} = 0.76 \text{ hr} = 45 \text{ min/set}$$

Management Scheme

The sprinklers listed in table 5–3 are for the layout in Figure 4–21. In this example, we have already decided that tees and greens will run each night and fairways every other night. This must now be put in the context of the total time available to operate the system each night. Twelve hours was chosen as a maximum for this example.

Some possible combinations for this example are given in table 5–4. Others are possible. The combinations given in table 5–4 are obtained by trial and error and by trying combinations that make sense. The objective is to efficiently utilize the available time, which will result in smaller pipe sizes, pumps, and power units. The pump discharge should also be kept about the same. Trials 2 and 4 are fair attempts in this direction with trial 4 being better than trial 2. If all sets cannot be made to demand about the same amount of water, the runs requiring the most water should consume a majority of the time. Trial 2 is not a good attempt since the pump capacity will only be used for 1.8 hours per night. The rest of the night (8.25 hrs), the maximum pump capacity is wasted.

Table 5–3. Summary of sprinklers

Hole	Green, small	Tees, small	Fairways Large	Fairways Small
1	4	3	9	—
2	4	2	12	—
3	4	2	10	—
4	4	3	—	6
5	4	2	7	4
6	5	—	7	—
7	4	2	12	—
8	4	2	—	4
9	4	2	7	4
Totals	37	18	64	18

Table 5–4 *Summary of management possibilities*

Trials	Greens				Tees				Fairways				Total time
	Sets/night	Hrs	Spr/set	gpms	Sets/night	Hrs	Spr/set	gpms	Sets/night	Hrs	Spr/set	gpms	
1	1	0.50	37	1217	1	0.76	18	592	11	8.25	4	312	9.5
2	2	1.00	19	625	1	0.76	18	592	11	8.25	4	312	10.0
3	4	2.00	10	329	1	0.76	18	592	11	8.25	4	312	11.0
4	4	2.00	10	329	2	1.52	9	296	11	8.25	4	312	11.8
5	4	2.00	10	329	2	1.52	9	296	9	6.75	5	390	10.3
6	3	1.50	13	428	2	1.52	9	296	9	6.75	5	390	9.8
7	3	1.50	13	428	3	2.28	7	230	9	6.75	5	390	10.5
8	3	1.50	13	428	3	2.28	7	230	7	5.25	6	468	9.0
9	5	2.50	9	296	2	1.52	9	296	7	5.25	6	468	9.4

If it is not possible to have all sets require the same discharge, try to arrange to have some sets require a multiple of the larger sets, such as one-half or one-third. This leads to the need for multiple pump systems.

Trial 9 was chosen with this management scheme. First, 296 gpms are needed for 4.0 hours

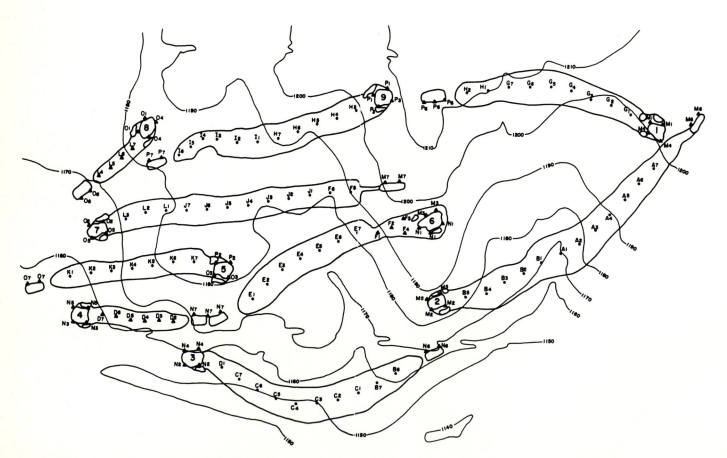

Figure 5–5 *Controller station assignments*

each night to water greens and tees. During each of the five green sets, nine sprinklers will run. Each night after the greens are completed, the tees will irrigate. Each of two tee sets will operate nine sprinklers. If eight station controllers are used on greens and tees, stations 1 to 5 will be for greens and stations 6 and 7 will be reserved for the tees (see figure 5–5).

When the greens and tees are finished each night, one-half of the fairway sprinklers will operate six at one time for a total of 42 fairway sprinklers/ night. On alternate nights, the other 42 fairway sprinklers will run.

PROBLEMS

1. A green is made up of the soil mixture shown in figure 5–2. Assuming your location is Muncie, Ind., determine the irrigation interval and design depth of water to be applied. Use a 4-inch root zone and a 70% water application efficiency (WAE). What is the depth of application required each day?

2. The mixture whose data are shown in figure 5–4 is to be used for the greens for a course near Danner, Oreg. Determine the irrigation interval and design depth of water to apply assuming a 6-inch root zone and a 50% WAE. What depth of water is required each day? Every other day? Every third day?

3. The data in figure 5–3 are for a soil to be used for the greens near Santa Fe, N.M. Determine the irrigation interval and the design depth of water to apply assuming a 4-inch root depth and a 70% WAE.

4. The soil whose data are shown in figure 5–2 text is to be used for the green and tees on a golf course near Butte, Mont. Assuming a 3-inch root depth and a 70% WAE, determine the irrigation interval and design depth.

5. Determine the irrigation interval and design depth for the soil mixture in figure 5–3 for your home area. Specify the root depth, WAE, and so on.

6. An irrigation system is planned for a course near Harrisburg, Pa. The fairways are native Calvin

soil. Determine the irrigation interval and the design depth to be applied assuming an 8-inch root zone and a 70% WAE. What depth of water is required each day? Every other day?

7. A golf course is planned for York, Pa., where Albright soil is present. If the predicted root zone on the fairways is 4 inches and a 40% WAE is expected, what is the irrigation interval an the design depth? Assuming daily applications, what depth of water actually reaches the root zone as a result of each irrigation?

8. Use the Toro method to determine the design depth of water to be applied each week for Charlotte, N.C. What depth is needed each day?

9. Use the Toro method to determine the design depth of water to be applied each week for Rockford, Ill. What depth is required each day?

10. Use the Toro method to determine the design depth of water to be applied each week for your home area.

11. A green has four Model 41 Rain Bird sprinklers with $1/4 \times 3/16$-in nozzles operating simultaneously at 80 psi. If the sprinklers have a 70-ft $\times$ 70-ft square spacing, what is the application rate on the green?

12. A Toro Model 674-xx-73 sprinkler is used at 90 psi for a single-row system with a 100-foot spacing. What is the application rate? If each sprinkler operates for 20 minutes, what depth of water will have been applied after each operation.

13. A small green is being covered by three Weather-Tec/Skinner sprinklers with $3/16$ in $\times$ $11/64$-in nozzles in a 60-foot triangular spacing operating at 80 psi. If the sprinklers operate simultaneously for 30 minutes, what depth of water will be applied?

14. Assume each green sprinkler in figure 5–6 must run 20 minutes per night, each fairway sprinkler 15 minutes per night, and each tee sprinkler 30 minutes per night. Assign each sprinkler to a controller designated by a capital letter. Station each such that green and tee sprinklers are separate from fairway sprinklers and all sprinklers will be finished in 3 hours.

15. An 18-hole golf course has 72 green sprinklers each discharging 20 gpm, 18 tee sprinklers each discharging 20 gpm, and 126 fairway sprinklers each

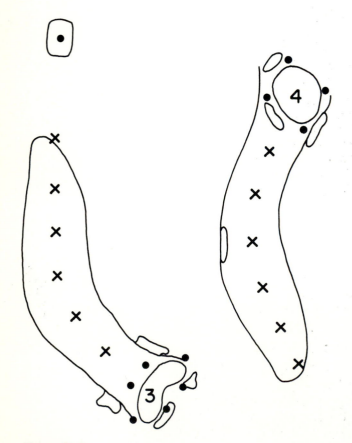

Figure 5–6

discharging 50 gpm. The green and tee sprinklers must run 30 minutes per night and the fairway sprinklers must run 40 minutes every other night. If there are 10 hours available each night for watering, how would you operate the system to minimize cost? What changes would you make in the operation to minimize pipe sizes? Pump flow rate? Labor cost?

16. Use the 9-holes laid out in figure 5–7. The fairway sprinklers each discharge 60 gpm. The green and tee sprinklers each discharge 20 gpm. The fairway sprinklers must run for 30 minutes once every 3 days and the green and tee sprinklers must run for 20 minutes each day. Assume eight station controllers will be used. Assign each sprinkler (or group of sprinklers) to a controller and station. Limit your nightly operation to 5 hours. Indicate when each sprinkler will run over a 3-day period.

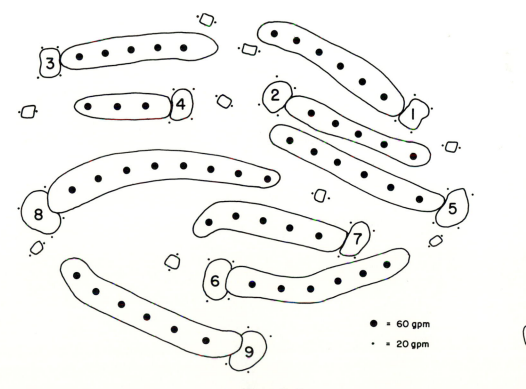

● = 60 gpm

· = 20 gpm

Figure 5–7

Chapter 6

VALVES

Many types of valves may find a practical application on a golf course irrigation system. Each of these will be described.

GATE VALVE

Gate valves (see figure 6–1) are used when the flow is to be completely unobstructed or completely closed. They are simple and when open introduce very little friction. The common application would be as section or isolation valves.

GLOBE VALVE

Almost all remote control valves used to control sprinklers are globe valves. These valves can also be

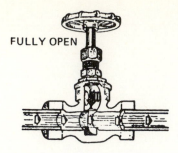

Figure 6–1   Gate valves

Figure 6–2   Globe valve

Figure 6–3   Pressure regulating valve

used to partially reduce the flow in a line and, therefore, serve as a pressure regulation valve. They are easily adapted to be opened or closed by an electric or hydraulic impulse. They impart a large amount of friction in the line (see figure 6–2).

PRESSURE REGULATING VALVE

The pressure regulator or pressure reducer valve has a fluctuating passage that can be adjusted to induce a pressure loss (see figure 6–3). The inlet pressure works against a diaphragm that is balanced by a spring force. The outlet pressure can be changed by tightening or loosening the force on the spring. Pressure regulators reduce the pressure. No pressure regulator can increase the pressure. They are used where the terrain varies greatly and they can be used on booster pumps if the pressure is too high.

PRESSURE RELIEF VALVE

Pressure relief valves are basically pressure regulators set for higher than normal pressures. If the set pressure is exceeded, the valve opens to discharge water and in turn relieve the pressure in the system. These valves are commonly used as safety devices on pumping stations.

CHECK VALVE

Check valves are used to limit water flow to one direction. The three types of check valves are swing, spring-loaded, and float (see figure 6–4). The swing type depends on its own weight to close against a backflow. The spring-loaded type is closed against a backflow by a retracting spring; with the float type a float is pushed out of the way for regular water flow but pressed into the upstream opening by backflow. Check valves can be used

1.   On the intake side of the pump suction line to prevent the pump from losing prime.

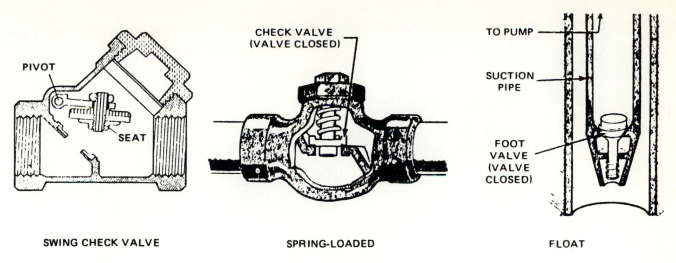

SWING CHECK VALVE

CHECK VALVE
(VALVE CLOSED)

SPRING-LOADED

TO PUMP

SUCTION
PIPE

FOOT
VALVE
(VALVE
CLOSED)

FLOAT

Figure 6–4   Check valves

2. On the discharge side of the pump where the pipe slopes upward to minimize hydraulic ram when the pump is shut off.

3. To prevent drainage from low heads in a system.

BALL VALVES

A ball valve is an on-off type valve and serves the same function as the gate valve, with different geometry (see figure 6–5).

SPECIALTY VALVES

Several specialty valves are available that a designer may use for a given installation. For example, by adding to a basic diaphragm valve, the manufacturer can add the appropriate special controls to perform many other functions. Additional special features and/or combinations of features include solenoid control, flow rate control, fast closing control, return flow control, independent operating pressure control, remote shut-off control, and motorized controls (see figure 6–6).

Figure 6–5   Ball valve

BASIC VALVE

PRESSURE REDUCING VALVE

PRESSURE REDUCING AND CHECK VALVE

PRESSURE REDUCING, PRESSURE SUSTAINING AND CHECK VALVE

Figure 6–6   Specialty valves (Adapted with permission from Rain Bird, 1977)

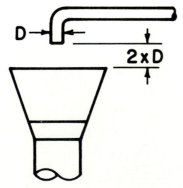

Figure 6–7   Air gap (Taken with permission from Rain Bird, 1982)

BACKFLOW PREVENTERS

Backflow preventers or cross-connections are designed to eliminate return flow to the source caused by reduced pressure at the source. Some type of backflow preventer should be used to separate an irrigation system from a potable water supply. Depending on location, local ordinances may specify certain types of backflow preventers. Some governmental units do not have codes requiring backflow preventers, but preventers should always be installed to ensure that potable water supplies are not degraded by water contaminated with fertilizer or pesticides.

There are five basic types of backflow preventers. The simplest, an air gap, is the physical separation of the potable and nonpotable water systems by an air space (see figure 6–7). The vertical distance between the supply pipe and the flood level rim should be two times the diameter of the supply pipe, but never less than 1 inch. The air gap can be used on a direct or inlet connection and for all toxic substances. However, this type protection is usually not practical for irrigation and sprinkler applications.

Atmospheric vacuum breaker backflow preventers are designed to be installed on the outlet side of a control valve or onto the hose bib to prevent backflow of polluted water into potable water supplies (see figure 6–8). These should only be used where a low degree of hazard exists (see figure 6–8).

Pressure vacuum breaker backflow preventers are to be installed on mainlines to prevent the backflow of polluted water into potable water systems where the vacuum breakers are not subject to back pressure (see figure 6–9). These units may be used under continuous supply pressure but must be installed above the usage point.

Double-check valve backflow preventers should be used as protection for all direct connections through which foreign material might enter the potable system in concentrations that would constitute a nuisance or be aesthetically objectionable (see figure 6–10). Examples of such foreign matter are air, steam, food, or other material that does not constitute a health hazard.

Reduced pressure backflow preventers should be used on all direct connections that may be subject to back pressure or back siphonage (see figure 6–11). They should also be used where there is the possibility of contamination.

As can be seen from the previous descriptions, the reduced pressure backflow preventer is the only type recommended for golf course applications. Backflow preventers are not required if water is being drawn from surface or well water.

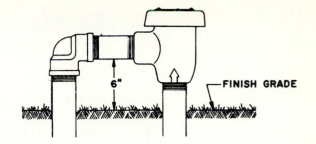

Figure 6–8 Atmospheric vacuum breaker (Taken with permission from Rain Bird, 1982)

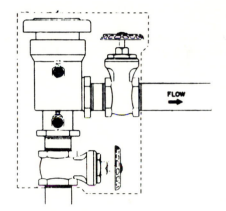

Figure 6–9 Pressure vacuum Breaker (Taken with permission from Rain Bird, 1982)

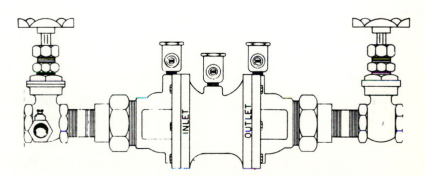

Figure 6–10 Double-check valve backflow preventer. (Taken with permission from Rain Bird, 1982)

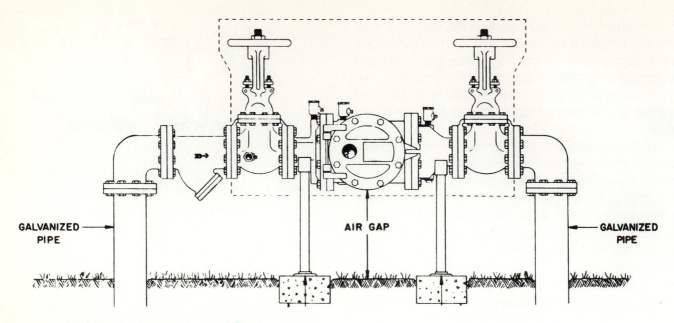

*Figure 6–11 Reduced pressure backflow preventer
(Taken with permission from Rain Bird, 1982)*

REMOTE CONTROL VALVES

The key to reduced nighttime labor and easier water management on a golf course is the remote control valve, which permits automatic controllers to activate and deactivate individual sprinklers or small groups of sprinklers on demand. All remote control valves are globe valves that operate hydraulically in that they depend on line pressure to open and close. They can be activated to open and close either hydraulically or electrically. A typical electrical remote control valve is shown in figure 6–12. Its major parts are as follows:

1. Diaphragm—A seal that divides the control chamber from the main body of the valve.

2. Control Chamber—Pressure is added or removed from this space causing the valve assembly to open or close.

3. Bonnet—The whole assembly cover and diaphragm, including the control chamber.

4. Stem—A manually operated control that can be set to limit upward lift of the diaphragm and the valve seat. It is used to control the flow and there-

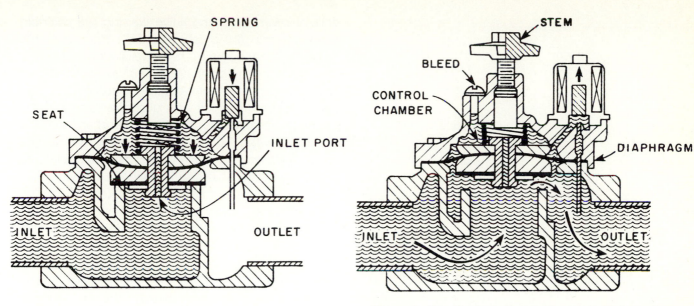

Figure 6–12 *Typical electrically controlled diaphragm valve*

fore the pressure when balancing the pressure in a system.

5. Spring—Supplies force that starts the closing of the valve.

6. Solenoid—A coil of insulated wire wrapped around an iron core. Supplying electrical energy usually at a reduced voltage (24 volts) produces an electromagnet. The electromagnet lifts a plunger that opens the outlet port, which permits flow from the control chamber. A solenoid is not used on hydraulically activated valves.

7. Bleed—A manual valve that is used for draining or bleeding air from the control chamber. It also serves as a manual control of the valve.

OPERATING PRINCIPLES

Although the geometry of globe valves may vary, in general, the operating principle remains the same. The valves are designed with an effective surface areas that is greater on the top side of the diaphragm assembly. The source of water needed to close the valve can come from either of two sources. On electrically actuated valves, water is channelled from the pipeline through a port to the control chamber of the valve. Raising the solenoid simply permits the pressure in the control chamber to be released, opening the valve. Therefore, electric valves are usually *normally closed* valves. The water in the control chamber can also be controlled by an hydraulic line from the controller. Pressure from the controller pressurizes the control chamber and closes the valve. When the pressure in the control line is released, the valve opens. Hydraulically activated valves are usually *normally open* valves.

The same operating principles outlined for diaphragm valves apply to electrically operated piston valves. The only difference is that a piston assembly is used instead of a diaphragm to open and close the valve (see figure 6–13). For hydraulically operated piston valves, a normally open valve is one that allows water to flow through the line. Pressure has to be applied to the control chamber to close it (see figure 6–14). A normally closed piston valve does not allow water to pass through; pressure must be applied to open it (see figure 6–14).

SELECTING A CONTROL VALVE

A normally open system supplies water pressure to the valve to keep it closed. If a control line is severed, the pressure is relieved, which will allow the valve, and any other valves on the same station, to open. Depending on the school of thought, this can be good or bad. The good part of such trouble

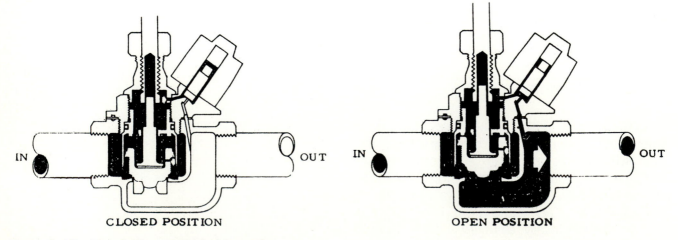

CLOSED POSITION   OPEN POSITION

Figure 6–13   Electrically operated piston valve

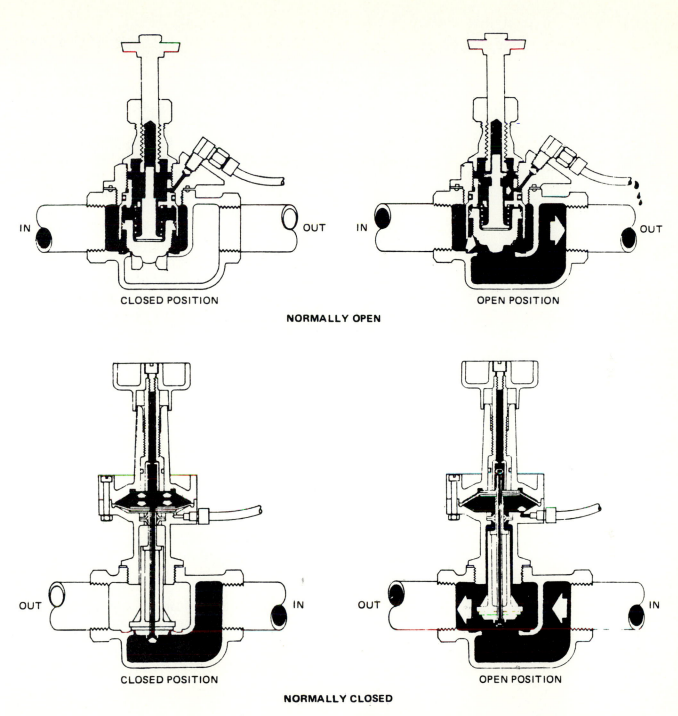

CLOSED POSITION   OPEN POSITION

NORMALLY OPEN

CLOSED POSITION   OPEN POSITION

NORMALLY CLOSED

Figure 6–14   Hydraulically operated piston valve

is that the turf manager knows immediately that a problem exists. He can then look for the cause of the problem—holes being dug for new trees or shrubs, trenching operations, deep aerofying operations, etc.—find it, and repair it with ease. The bad side of this response is that it means sprinklers will come on uncontrolled and be temporarily uncontrollable. This may be intolerable in high-use areas. The probability of control tubing being severed is much lower than the fear of it happening. The ground rodent problem is also another unjustified fear when dealing with hydraulic systems. If ground rodents are a problem, the designer should stipulate PVC tubing rather than polyethylene for control lines between the controller and the valves. The harder PVC tubing will resist the efforts of the most determined rodents.

Since an electric system employs normally closed valves, the severing of control lines will cause no immediate response. Here too, there is a good and bad side. Proponents of the normally closed, electric system point proudly to overcoming the problem of the normally open system—cut tubing causes the valves to open. With a normally closed system, valves have the fail-safe feature of not coming on if the control lines are severed. They do not, however, have a warning feature to communicate that a problem exists. Because of this, nonoperating heads are overlooked until found in maintenance inspection or when the turf manager notices the loss of turf in the area of the heads controlled by the nonoperational valve. Finding the trouble spot after the fact can be time consuming and frustrating.

The type of valve chosen may be a personal decision. Following are a few additional factors that should influence the decision:

1. Electric controllers can activate up to four electric solenoid valves on each station.

2. Electric systems are not affected by the elevation difference between the controller and valves.

3. Hydraulic controllers can activate up to 10 hydraulic control valves on each station. This may sound like an advantage but there are seldom cases where it is practical to activate more than two or three valves/station.

4. Hydraulic systems are affected by the elevation difference between the controller and the valve. Valves cannot be more than 25 feet above the controller and not more than 75 feet below the controller.

GOLF COURSE IRRIGATION DESIGN EXAMPLE

Based on the material in this chapter, an arbitrary decision was made to use an electric control system. See you at the end of chapter 7.

PROBLEMS

1. Where are gate valves typically used on golf courses?

2. What is the purpose of a backflow preventer? How does it differ from a cross-connection? Are either of these needed on golf courses? Why?

3. What is the typical use of a check valve? Where would one be found in a golf course irrigation system?

4. Sketch a typical electrically operated diaphragm globe control valve. Label all parts.

5. List the advantages and disadvantages of electric and hydraulic control systems.

Chapter 7
CONTROLLERS

Automatic control systems have been made possible by the development of two components. The remote control valves, discussed in the last chapter, can be opened or closed by an impulse delivered through a wire or a small hydraulic tube. The second component, the automatic controllers, is the heart of the control system. The controllers send signals to the remote control valves at preset times, activating or deactivating the valves. Automatic controllers have developed from simple clocks sending a signal to one valve to sophisticated units capable of controlling hundreds of valves in a sequence determined by the turf manager. The sequence causes each valve to stay open long enough for the sprinklers to apply just the depth of water needed by the turf in that area. These controllers can be programmed to sequence the valves through several programs, any one of which may be selected by the turf manager as conditions change on the course.

Because of the advent of computers and micro-processor control systems, controllers for sprinklers can be expected to advance very rapidly in the next few years. New features providing improved capability, flexibility, and reliability will certainly develop in the near future. This chapter will describe the characteristics and operating features available on today's controllers.

SELECTION FACTORS

The following factors should be reviewed when considering an automatic control system.

Versatility

Versatility should be considered in the operation sense only. The frills of lights and horns should be considered only if they aid in operational programming or use. Number of stations, timing flexibility on stations, day and hour programming, multicycle programming, and split-cycle programming are all desirable features. Pump switches, cancel switches, rain switches, master valve circuits, and moisture control circuits are frequently available either as standard or optional features.

Dependability

Because the controller is an extension of the superintendent, the irrigation system must perform dependably. A malfunction of the controller can cause dry turf, washouts, flooding, and wasted water. To be dependable, a controller cannot be overly sensitive to temperature differentials, physical jarring, and moist conditions.

Readability

Readability can be defined as the inherent ability of the controller to be understood by its human programmer. Features such as dials, settings, and switches should be clearly marked and instructions should be conveniently located and easily understood.

Serviceability

Because controllers are mechanical and electrical, the possibility of mechanical or electrical failure always exists. If a failure occurs, the controller should be engineered so the failure can be readily diagnosed and quickly repaired. Controllers should be easily removable for shop repair if a malfunction occurs that cannot be field repaired. A welcome feature when the timer fails is the ability to manually operate the controller until the timing mechanism is returned.

Cost

Except in very small turf areas, the control equipment cost is a small fraction of the total system cost. Because of this, more attention should be focused on versatility, dependability, readability, serviceability, and special features.

CONTROLLER FEATURES

The following are desirable features to have on controllers:

1. Infinite time adjustments on each station ranging from as small as 2 minutes to as much as an hour. This feature permits accurate setting of run times for syringing and growth needs.

2. The time lag between stations should be as short as possible to eliminate wasted watering time and excessive pump switching from the off-to-on and on-to-off position.

3. Minimum of two-week programming capability. This permits the turf manager to plan watering schedules in advance.

4. Maximum flexibility in programming the day and the starting time when the stations are to begin cycling.

5. Controller should have sufficient stations to control the valves in the system. Controllers with less than four stations are seldom used on golf courses. Controllers with greater than 20 stations are rarely practical since the programmer located at a controller should be able to see each sprinkler driven by the controller.

6. Multiple programming capability permits the turf manager to set more than one program on the controller then choose which one to use based on weather or other environmental conditions.

7. Manual override permits the turf manager to activate specific valves for special watering needs or testing without disturbing the watering program in the controller.

8. Weather-resistant cabinets that can be locked to prevent or reduce vandalism. It is important to keep moisture away from the controller, especially units with electrical components. If hydraulic control systems are to be used, it is necessary to prevent the controller from freezing, which could damage vital components.

9. Pump circuit control activates the pump starter circuit when the controller begins its watering cycle.

10. The off master switch permits the turf manager to cancel the preset watering program without disturbing the program. This is basically a manual override.

11. Underwriter's Laboratory (UL) listing is desirable for safety as well as qualifying the controller for use on federal, state, and municipal projects.

THE CENTRAL-SATELLITE SYSTEM

To provide control on large turf systems, the basic automatic controller, containing the features described in the previous section, has been divided into two basic parts: the central or master controller and the satellite (see figure 7–1). The central or master controller is composed of the timing mechanism (including the day and hour timers), which is used to initiate the water cycle on the area, the off mas-

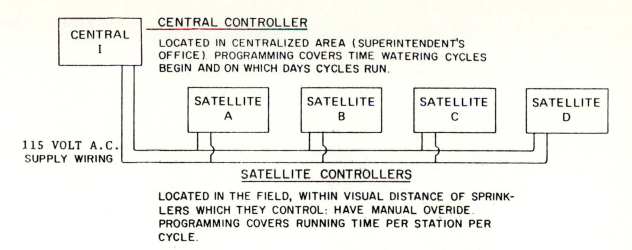

FIGURE 7–1 Central-satellite control system (Adapted with permission from Toro, 1972)

ter cancel switch, and the syringe control. These control elements have been removed from the basic controller and placed in a separate box usually located in the turf manager's office. The satellite is composed of the individual station controller features, including the timer for each station, and the manual override switch. These control elements are placed in a box located in the vicinity of the sprinklers being controlled. The satellite generally can be manually started or initiated by the central controller in the turf manager's office.

Each central controller can drive many satellite units. For example, a greens master can be connected to all of the satellites controlling green sprinklers. A second master could be used to control fairway satellites, and so on. Each manufacturer has packaged these features into varying combinations. The detailed features of each companies products should be thoroughly examined before choosing a specific system.

Communication Between Control Components

Large turf controller systems can be controlled either electrically or hydraulically. Electric systems generally used standard 120-volt power between the master and satellites and 24-volt signals between the satellite and the control valves. Most satellite control stations on electric systems are capable of driving up to four separate valves wired parallel so that one signal is received by all valves on the circuit simultaneously. Using multiple valves per station is not very common but is used for special applications.

In systems using hydraulic valves, the satellites send the control signal to the valves through a piece of small diameter tubing. The control between the master and satellite is usually electrical even if hydraulic valves are used. The closure mechanism in the valve often allows one hydraulic satellite station to drive up to eight or 10 valves. Most hydraulic control systems are filled with water that transmits the signal. The weight of the water, however, tends to limit the elevation difference between the satellite and the valve being controlled. In general, hydraulic valves may not be more than 75 feet below or 25 feet above the satellite. This limitation tends to reduce the use of hydraulic control systems in areas with much terrain. A second type of hydraulic control system uses air as the signal fluid. These hydraulic systems do not have the elevation limitation required for the water systems.

Hydraulic tubing is usually PVC or polyethylene, although copper has also been used in limited applications. PVC tubing because of its size can be coiled, unlike PVC pipe. It is generally used in large turf areas because it resists damage from burrowing rodents. Compression-type couplings and tees are used for PVC tubing because of this hardness. The compression fittings are the same as used for copper with the exception of the ferrule. The ferrule usually used for copper is sharp-edged on both ends and when compressed by tightening the compression nut cuts into the tubing. This can cause scoring of PVC tubing, which increases the chances of a break occurring. The ferrule used for PVC tubing should either be made of a plastic material or be sharp-edged only on the inner end. PVC tubing of ¼ in. and 5/16 in. ID is used.

Polyethylene (PE) tubing has the great benefit of not bursting if frozen while full of water. This ability of PE tubing to expand when necessary and return to its original shape when the water inside thaws makes its use in freezing climates highly desirable. Its softness, however, makes it vulnerable to damage by burrowing rodents. This vulnerability can be overcome by sleeving the tubing in PVC pipe, if practical.

GOLF COURSE IRRIGATION DESIGN EXAMPLE

The next task in designing a golf course is to determine exactly which sprinklers will be run together and on which nights. This assignment is tied to the specific operation of the controllers that will turn the sprinklers on and off. Since two nights are required to cover the fairways, the course has been divided into two zones, 42 sprinklers each (see figure 5–5). In larger systems, green and tee sprinklers are also zoned.

The sprinklers that operate with each controller are indicated in figure 5–5. Each night the master controller activates controllers M and N in zone I and O and P in zone II simultaneously. These four controllers cycle through their stations one at a time. This means that valves connected to stations M1, N1, O1, and P1 open and run together. When these are finished, each of these four controllers switches to station 2. Each green station on these controllers will be set to run for up to 30 minutes, depending on air temperature and soil moisture. Stations 6 and 7 of these four controllers are connected to the tee sprinklers. These two stations on each controller would be set to run for up to 45 minutes. These runs are summarized in table 7–1, along with the pump discharge required for each run.

When all four green and tee controllers have completed their cycles each night, the master or a second master will signal to controller A, B, C, D, E, and F in zone I or to controllers G, H, I, J, K, and L in zone II to start depending on the night. These 12 controllers operate the fairway sprinklers, one station for each sprinkler. These sprinklers are also summarized in table 7–1. Each station will be set to operate up to 41 minutes for the large sprinklers and up to 45 minutes for the smaller sprinklers.

Table 7–1   Management summary

Each Night
Irrigate greens and tees first
Master to M, N, O, P simultaneously at 9:00 p.m.

Zone	Controller	9:00	9:30	10:00	Start Time 10:30	11:00	11:45	12:30
				Station (no. of sprinklers/station)				
I	M	1(2)	2(2)	3(2)	4(2)	5(2)	6(2)	7(2)
	N	1(3)	2(2)	3(2)	4(2)	5(2)	6(2)	7(3)
II	O	1(2)	2(2)	3(2)	4(2)	5(2)	6(2)	7(2)
	P	1(2)	2(2)	3(2)			6(3)	7(2)
	Pump gpm =	296	263	263	197	197	296	296

Night 1—Zone I
Fairways follow greens and tees and should start no later than 1:15 a.m. and should finish by 6:30 a.m.
Master to A, B, C, D, E, F.

Controller				Station			
A	1	2	3	4	5	6	7
B	1	2	3	4	5	6	7
C	1	2	3	4	5	6	7
D	1	2^L	3^L	4^L	5^L	6^L	7^L
E	1	2	3	4	5	6	7
F	1^L	2^L	3^L	4^L	5^L	6^L	
Pump gpm =	423	378	378	378	423	423	345

Night 2—Zone II
Fairways follow greens and tees and should start no later than 1:15 a.m. and should finish by 6:30 a.m.
Master to G, H, I, J, K, L.

Controller				Station			
G	1	2	3	4	5	6	7
H	1	2	3	4	5	6	7
I	1	2	3^L	4^L	5^L	6^L	
J	1	2	3^L	4^L	5^L	6^L	7
K	1	2	3	4	5	6	7
L	1	2	3	4^L	5^L	6^L	7^L
Pump gpm =	468	468	378	333	333	333	345

PROBLEMS

1. List the desirable features that should be included on all controllers. From your experience, which of these are the most important? Least important?

2. How many valves can an electric controller operate per station?

3. How many valves can a hydraulic controller operate per station?

4. Explain how a central-satellite control system operates.

5. What features are necessary in a central controller?

6. What features are necessary in a satellite controller?

Chapter 8

PIPE LAYOUT AND SIZING

PIPE LAYOUT

In some respects the location of pipelines is almost arbitrary. One must remember, however, that all sprinklers must be connected to the system. Also, sprinkler control valves must be located to operate properly.

For single-row fairway systems, a single pipeline is usually placed in the center of each fairway. For double-row systems, it is common to place the supply lines along the edge of the fairway. From these lines, smaller pipe is run onto the fairway to connect the sprinklers or groups sprinklers to a common valve.

The general concepts of pipe layout and design will be discussed in this chapter by using a new example to show some principles. The design example that has been discussed in previous chapters will be continued at the end of the chapter.

On the section of a golf course shown in figure 8–1, plan the pipe layout for a single-row system having the pipelines placed in the center of the fairways. The water supply will be taken from the pond, which is at an elevation of 40 feet.

Locate Pipelines

First, locate all the essential pipelines. These include the connecting lines around greens, the supply lines to tees, and the supply lines to all fairway sprinklers. Because the fairway sprinklers usually require larger pipe than green or tee sprinklers, it is best to start by developing the pipelines for the fairway sprinklers (assuming fairways are to be irrigated). If fairways are not to be irrigated, the supply lines to greens and tees should be placed such that fairways can be conveniently added later. In this example, since we want a single-row system, the supply lines are located in the center of each fairway as shown in figure 8–1. The supply lines for greens and tees are usually added later since fairways provide the largest demand.

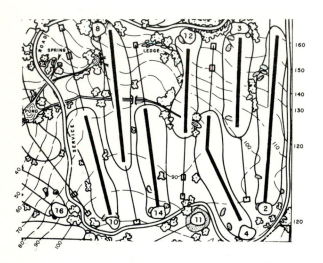

Figure 8–1   Pipe layout example (Taken with permission from Pira, 1982)

Locate Mainline

Once the supply lines for fairways are located, the next step is to locate the mainline that brings water from the pump facility to each of the supply lines.

Dead-end system

The two basic methods of pipe layout for golf courses are the dead-end system and the loop system. Figure 8–2 shows a mainline location that connects to each supply line or lateral. Note that this placement of the mainline requires that water travel up slope from the point where it leaves the mainline. Although this type of dead-end system can work properly, it is difficult to accurately calcu-

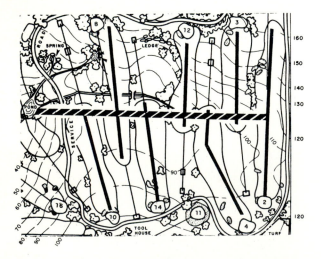

Figure 8–2   First try at a dead-end system (Adapted with permission from Pira, 1982)

late pump requirements, especially pressure requirements. This problem can be overcome by connecting the mainline to each lateral at or within 10 feet of elevation of the highest elevation on the fairway. This procedure ensures that the main delivers water to the most critical point on the golf course (elevation wise). It also simplifies computing pump requirements.

Figure 8–3 shows the main connecting to each fairway lateral at the highest point on that fairway. This system could be expected to perform very well. However, it reduces operation and maintenance flexibility since water has only one path from the pump to any given sprinkler.

Loop system

This disadvantage of the dead-end system is usually overcome by adjusting the geometry of the main so it forms a loop (see figure 8–4). The loop permits water to flow from the pump to any fairway lateral by at least two paths. If a break occurs on one side of the loop, gate valves (often called isolation valves) in the laterals and/or the main can be closed, isolating the problem until it can be repaired. Until the repair occurs, water can reach the sprinklers by one of the original two paths. The loop system also has the advantage of requiring smaller pipe than the dead-end system. This is because it can be assumed that half of the loops' demand travels each direction instead of all of the water going one direction.

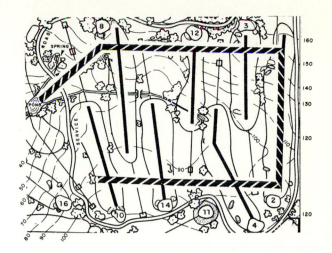

Figure 8–3 Dead-end system with laterals running downhill (Adapted with permission from Pira, 1982)

Figure 8–4 A looped piping system (Adapted with permission from Pira, 1982)

PIPE SIZING

Irrigation pipes can be sized based on one of several criteria. Some designers or engineers choose pipe sizes based on a fixed amount of friction. For agricultural irrigation systems, the limiting amount of friction will normally be 1.0 psi of friction for each 100 feet of pipe. An indepth analysis of the relative cost of an irrigation system versus the friction factor used to size the pipe shows that when a friction factor of 1.0 psi per 100 feet is used, the overall cost of the system will be minimized. The most commonly used criteria for golf course irrigation systems is to limit the velocity of water flowing in any pipe.

The logic for limiting velocity in a piping system is related to the need to stop the water, especially at valves. Electrically actuated valves usually go from the open position to the closed position in less than 0.2 seconds. This means that the water in the pipe supplying the valve must also stop in less than 0.2 seconds. This sudden stopping of the incompressible water creates very high pressures that can burst the pipes. Therefore, any pipe carrying water to an automatic control valve should be sized so that the velocity in the pipe will never exceed 5 feet per second (fps). The 5 fps criterion is usually extended to all pipes in the system. This creates a safety factor for pipes that do not terminate with a control valve. Taking this into account, some engineers extend the criteria to slightly greater than 5 fps for nonvalved pipelines, but the velocity should never exceed 6 fps.

Implementing either of these criteria requires that friction factor and velocity data be available for each pipe size and each flow rate. This data is summarized in Appendix B for most pipes used in irrigation systems.

Determine Flow Rate

Once the sprinklers have been located and sized and the pipe system has been located, the maximum discharge or flow rate for each pipe, usually in gallons per minute (gpm), must be determined. Since sprinklers are often run at different times and possibly in different combinations, determining flow rate on golf courses is often a difficult task, but an important and necessary one.

Select Pipe Size

When the maximum discharge has been determined for each pipe, the pipe size is selected by using the data in Appendix B. This procedure will be illustrated by several examples.

Example 1

Select the mainline pipe size to operate seven sprinklers at the same time on the fairway shown in figure 8–5. Use the schedule-40 steel pipe friction loss chart in table B–7 of Appendix B.

Conditions

1. Total land surface distance from pump to fairway = 1,500 ft.

2. Operate seven sprinklers at 50 gpm/sprinkler = = 350 gpm.

3. Use schedule-40 steel pipe and neglect friction losses in valves, fittings, and joints.

Solution Find the smallest pipe that can carry 350 gpm with a velocity of less than 5 fps:

1. 4-in pipe has a velocity of about 8.8 fps at 350 gpm

2. 5-in pipe has a velocity of about 5.6 fps at 350 gpm

3. 6-in pipe has a velocity of about 3.9 fps at 350 gpm

4. 8-in pipe has a velocity of about 2.2 fps at 350 gpm

The correct mainline pipe size is 6 inches.

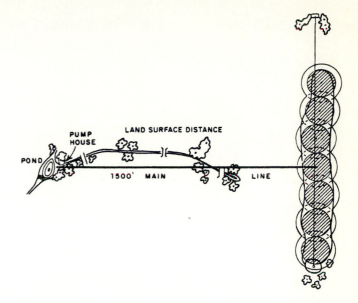

Figure 8–5 Example 1 (Adapted with permission from Pira, 1982)

Example 2

Use same pipe layout as example 1 (figure 8–2) and select the PVC 200 main pipeline size for the irrigation system designed to operate a maximum of one sprinkler in any fairway (see figure 8–6). (Ignore losses in fittings, valves, and joints.)

Conditions

1. Four 50-gpm sprinklers to be operated at the same time.

2. One sprinkler operating on each fairway.

Solution

1. Segment between fairways 2 and 3 carries 50 gpm. Therefore, use 2-in pipe. *NOTE:* Since only one sprinkler will operate at one time or any fairway, a 2-in PVC pipe can be used in all fairways.

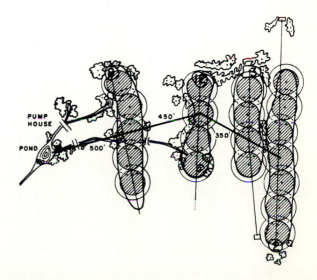

Figure 8–6 Example 2 (Adapted with permission from Pira, 1982)

2. Segment between fairways 3 and 12 must carry the water for two sprinklers or 100 gpm. Therefore, use a 3-in PVC pipe.

3. Segment between fairways 12 and 8 must carry the water for three sprinklers or 150 gpm. Therefore, use a 3.5-in PVC pipe.

4. Segment between the pump house and fairway 8 must carry the water for four sprinklers or 200 gpm. Therefore, use a 4-in PVC pipe.

Example 3

Conditions

1. Assume that the entire discharge is to be carried by the main line from the pond to fairway 10. Use a dead-end system. Each fairway has only one 50-gpm sprinkler operating (see figure 8–7). Use PVC 200 pipe.

2. Assume that all conditions are the same as in number 1, except the loop has been completed as shown by the dashed line.

Solution

1. Dead-end system.
   a. Segment 10 to 14: Q = 50 gpm, 2-in PVC pipe required.
   b. Segment 14 to 4: Q = 100 gpm, 3-in PVC pipe required.
   c. Segment 4 to 2: Q = 150 gpm, 3.5-in PVC pipe required.
   d. Segment 2 to 3: Q = 200 gpm, 4-in PVC pipe required.
   e. Segment 3 to 12: Q = 250 gpm, 5-in PVC pipe required.
   f. Segment 12 to 8: Q = 300 gpm, 5-in PVC pipe required.
   g. Segment 8 to pump: Q = 350 gpm, 6-in PVC pipe required.

2. Loop system. If the loop is completed, half of the total flow of 350 gpm will go each direction. Therefore, the pipe can be sized as follows:
   a. Pond to segment 8 and pond to segment 10: Q = 175 gpm, 4-in PVC pipe required.
   b. Segments 8 to 12 and 10 to 14: Q = 125 gpm, 3.5-in PVC pipe required.

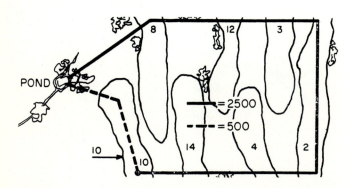

Figure 8–7 Example 3, dead-end vs. loop systems (Adapted from Pira, 1982)

c. Segments 12 to 3 and 14 to 4: Q = 75 gpm, 2.5-in PVC pipe required.
d. Segments 4 to 3: Q = 25 gpm, 1.25-in PVC pipe required.

INTEGRATING PIPE LOCATIONS, PIPE SIZES, AND CONTROLLER SYSTEMS

The irrigation system designer has no preset rules or standard procedures for integrating the pipeline distribution, pipe sizes, and automatic controller system into the total design. The designer must be guided by the design factors found for a particular installation and try alternatives before arriving at an acceptable plan.

In general, the pipeline layout is determined by the physical conditions of the area, including the location of the water supply. The pipe sizes are determined by the system management and pipeline layout. The automatic controller system is determined by the degree of versatility the buyer wants and is willing to pay for and the management flexibility desired.

This can be best explained by reviewing the following hypothetical example and possible solutions. Each solution indicates some of the reasoning and compromises involved as well as some of the advantages and disadvantages of each. The system to be considered is shown in figure 8–8.

Determine the pipeline distributions system, pipe sizes, and automatic controller system for a golf course, using the following design criteria:

1. Fully automatic, single-row valve-in-head sprinklers

2. Number of heads to cover entire area = 100

3. Operate five heads, 20 minutes per head to meet the irrigation cycle and watering schedule

4. Sprinkler head flow = 50 gpm

5. Total flow = 250 gpm

Assume the golf course fairways were divided into five equal zones or areas (with 20 sprinklers per zone) as shown. The water source will be the pond.

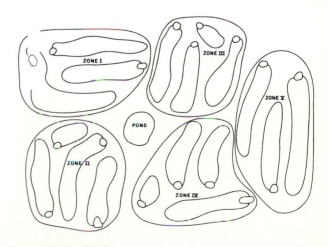

Figure 8–8   Zoning

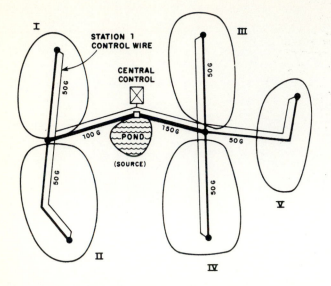

Figure 8–9 Central control without satellites (Adapted with permission from Pira, 1982)

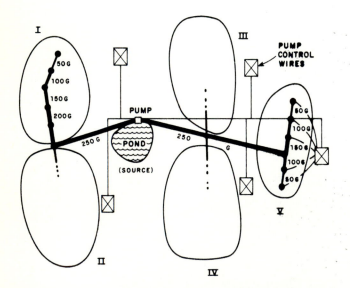

Figure 8–10 Controller in each zone (Adapted with permission from Pira, 1982)

Solution 1

Design the system with a maximum of one head to operate at one time per zone. The automatic controller will be centrally located at the pump house as shown in figure 8–9.

Advantage

The advantage of this solution is the cost of pipe and fittings. Only a relatively short length of supply line is designed to carry 150 and 100 gallons per minute and all submains within each zone are required to handle only 50 gpm.

Disadvantages

The disadvantages of the solution are:

1. Lack of versatility. The operator cannot adjust for different watering needs that may exist in each zone, such as soil conditions, type of turf grass and root zone, thatch, slopes, and traffic.

2. Cost of control wire needed to wire a total of 20 stations.

3. Difficulty of checking whether the system is operating properly (even with the use of a jeep and walkie-talkies).

4. Questionable whether five remote control valves can operate per station due to the length of control wire.

5. Wire size needed to limit the voltage drop.

6. Difficulty of finding control wiring breaks.

Solution 2

Design the system based on running the five sprinkler heads within a zone. The controllers will be located in the field, one controller per zone (see figure 8–10). The areas will be divided into five zones as mentioned. Other controller alternatives include using more than one controller per zone, which may improve the control. Individual head control could be obtained by using five 4-station controllers in each zone. If all five controllers are initiated simultaneously, the sprinklers will have the same result as one controller per zone with each station wired to five heads.

Advantage

The advantages are:

1. Considerable versatility is offered. Each head can be individually controlled to adjust to the different watering needs that may exist in a particular location.

2. Shorter lengths of control wiring.

3. Observation of the area may be possible from the field controller.

Disadvantages

The disadvantages are:

1. Cost of increased pipe sizes, fittings, and installation.

2. No central control.

3. Controller wires must be run back to the pump.

Solution 3

Design the system based on the conditions of solution 2 with a central control at the pump house and one field controller (satellite) for each zone (see figure 8–11). This could most easily be done with one 20-station satellite in each of the five zones. This will yield a need for only 50 gpm per zone.

Advantages

The advantages are:

1. Considerable versatility is offered.

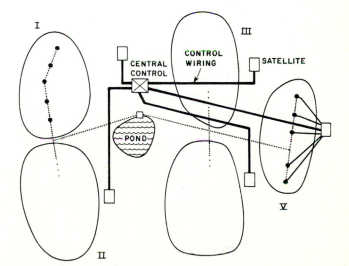

Figure 8–11 Central control with satellite controllers (Adapted with permission from Pira, 1982)

2. Various built-in and optional features for the central-satellite control system. These can be selected to suit the user's wishes.

Disadvantages

The disadvantages are:

1. Each additional field controller and optional feature such as syringing adds to the cost of installation.

2. As the complexity increases, the chances for breakdowns and failures increase.

It is essential for the golf course superintendent to know exactly what the system is designed to do, its versatility, as well as its limitations. Further, he should have a complete set of plans showing the precise locations of pipe lines, valves, control wiring, and heads, as well as the watering program and other instructions.

CONTROL AND PIPING ALTERNATIVES

It is desirable, on automatic systems, to install three or four quick-coupling valves along the fairway and near the green to water trees, shrubs, and rough areas, as well as permit manual watering of critical areas (see figure 8–12). These valves can be of great

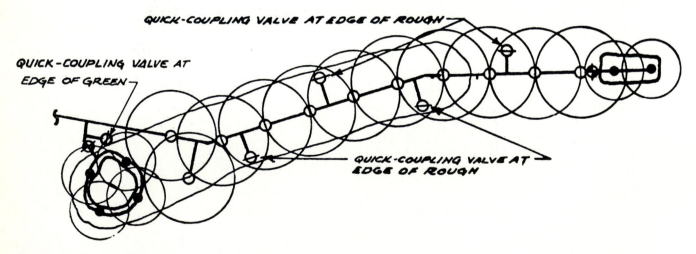

Figure 8–12 Auxiliary quick-coupling valves

help in maintaining the course and add little to the overall cost of the system.

Two-Row System with Two Sprinklers per Valve

In the design of a double-row system, it is more desirable to run the mainline along the side of the fairway. If two fairways run parallel and are relatively close together, the mainline may be run between the two fairways and thus supply both fairways (see figure 8–13). One control valve is generally used to supply two sprinkler heads. However, a separate valve for each sprinkler could be used if desirable and cost is not prohibitive.

Two-Row System with Four Sprinklers per Valve

If small sprinklers are being used, then four sprinklers may be supplied from one control valve. This reduces the cost of the system but also reduces the flexibility of the system (see figure 8–14).

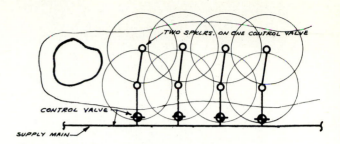

Figure 8–13   Two sprinklers per valve

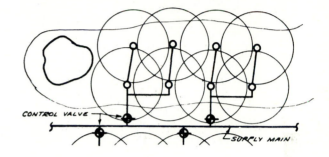

Figure 8–14   Four sprinklers per valve

GOLF COURSE IRRIGATION DESIGN EXAMPLE

This section continues the golf course irrigation design example from chapter 7.

Pipe Layout

Of the two basic methods of pipe layout, the loop system is more difficult to design or analyze precisely. This type of system will be discussed later by comparing it with the easier dead-end system. To size any pipe system, it is necessary to know how many gpms are expected to flow through each section of pipe. For this reason, the dead-end system will be discussed first. It should be used to size pipe for most systems.

The objective of any pipe system is to deliver water to the sprinklers as they are turned on by the controller system. There are an infinite number of ways to lay out a piping system. On golf courses, it is desirable to operate only one valve at a given time on each pipeline. This will make pipe sizing easy and reduce pipe costs, but it will limit the system's flexibility.

Pipeline locations are usually chosen for maintenance purposes. However, remember that pipelines should end in low areas rather than high elevation areas and that main supply lines should connect to sprinkler lines within 10 feet (elevation) of the highest elevation on that line. Figure 8–15 shows a pipeline layout for the fairways of this example. Figure 8–16 shows how these laterals may be connected to the pump by supply mains.

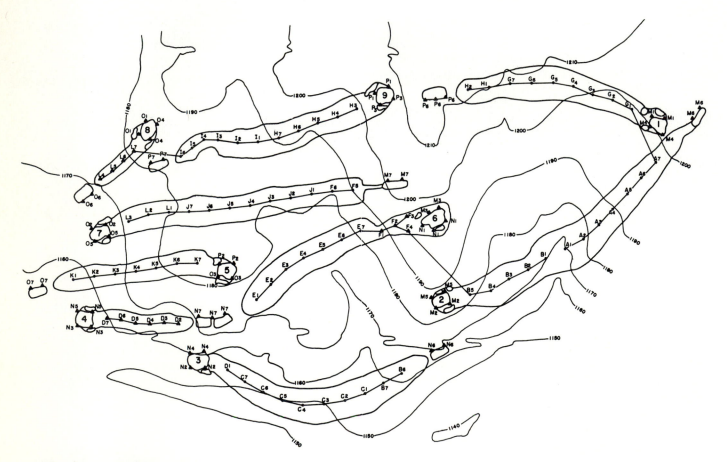

Figure 8–15   Sprinkler supply lines

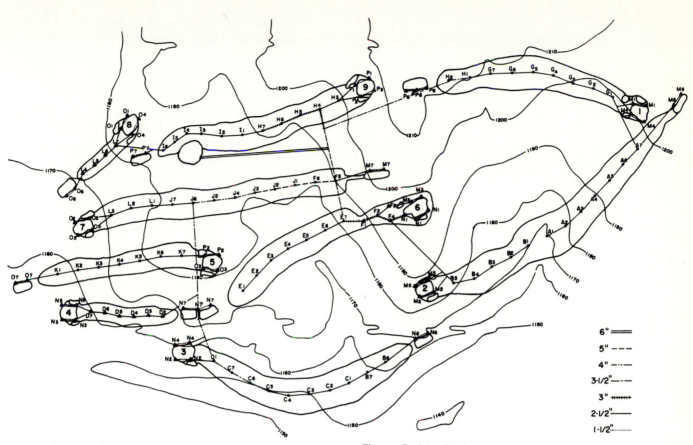

Figure 8–16 Mainline locations and pipe sizes

Pipe Sizing

The key to pipe sizing is to determine the maximum number of gpms expected to pass through each pipe section. With this determined, each pipe section is sized by selecting the smallest pipe that will pass the design gpms at less than 5 fps. As an example, any pipeline that carries a maximum flow demanded by one large fairway sprinkler (78.0 gpm) should be sized as 2.5-inch diameter if schedule-200 PVC pipe is used. This flow situation will cause water to flow through the pipe at a velocity of about 4.7 fps, which is less than the design criteria (5.0 fps); see Appendix B for friction and velocity chart. Pipe sizes are shown on figure 8–16.

Layout System

The dead-end piping system is simple to lay out and easy to size. But as indicated earlier, the loop system offers the advantages of flexibility of operation and smaller pipe sizes. Most systems are laid out and sized as dead-end systems to gain the advantages of easy pipe sizing. After the pipes have been sized as a dead-end system, the single valve fairway pipe, 2½-inch in this case, is used to connect the dead ends in a logical, convenient manner. The goal is to be able to supply any valve from two paths. Maintaining greens and tees if a break should occur anywhere on the course is particularly important. Figure 8–17 shows the final piping systems of figure 8–16 extended to provide this flexibility. Figure 8–18 shows the final pipe sizes calculated with the loop system used from the beginning assuming half of each loop's water travels around the loop in each direction. Figure 8–18 also shows the quick-couplers added to further increase the flexibility.

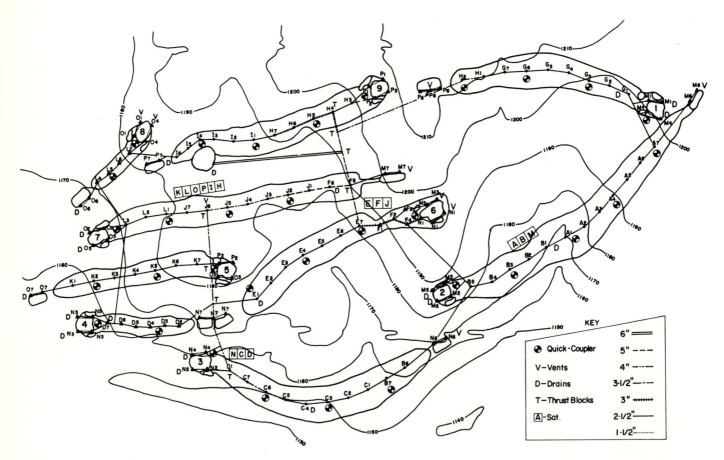

Figure 8–17 Loop pipeline design

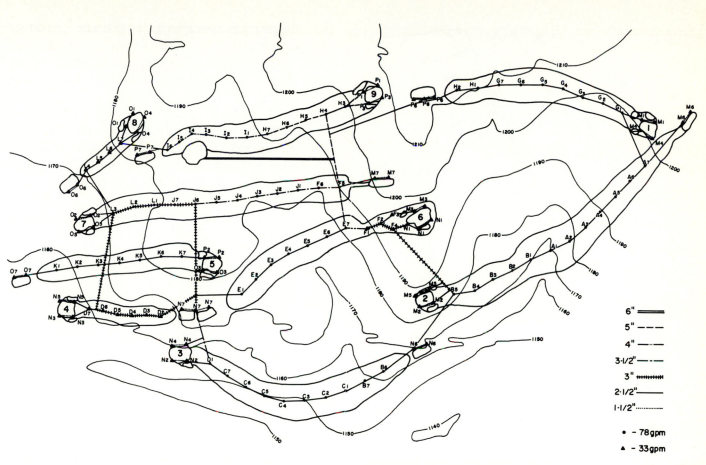

Figure 8–18   Loop pipeline sizes

PROBLEMS

1.   Assign each sprinkler in figure 8–19 to a controller station. Assume a valve-in-head system with individual head control. Use 8-station controllers. How many controllers are required if this is the whole system? What is the flow in each section of pipe? (Ignore greens.)

2.   Assign each sprinkler to a controller station in figure 8–19. Assume a valve-in-hand system with two heads per control station. How many controllers are required if 11-station controllers are to be used? Put sprinklers together that will allow the smallest piping system. What is the flow in each section of pipe?

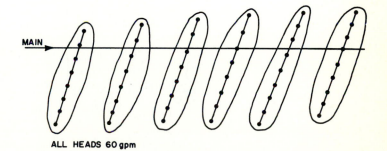

MAIN

ALL HEADS 60 gpm

Figure 8–19

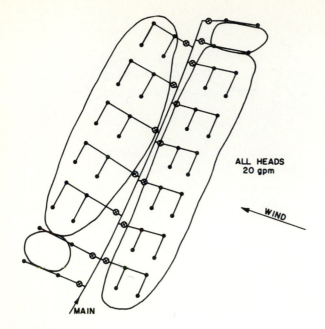

Figure 8–20

3. Assign each sprinkler to a hydraulic controller station in figure 8–19. Each control station can operate up to 10 valves. Keep flow rates small, if possible. Each controller has eight stations. What is the flow in each section of pipe?

4. Assign the valves in the figure 8–20 system to an electric controller with (one valve per station to minimize pipe sizes). Use an 8-station controller. What is the flow in each section of pipe?

5. Can you suggest a modification of the pipe and sprinkler layout to accommodate a prevailing wind as shown in figure 8–20. Assign the valves to 11-station controllers. What is the flow in each section of pipe?

6. Size each pipe section in figure 8–21 with the eight sprinklers shown operating simultaneously. Use PVC-160 pipe and assume each sprinkler discharges 50 gpm.

7. Same as problem 6 for figure 8–22.

8. Assume the pipeline distribution systems were planned as shown in figures 8–23 and 8–24 with

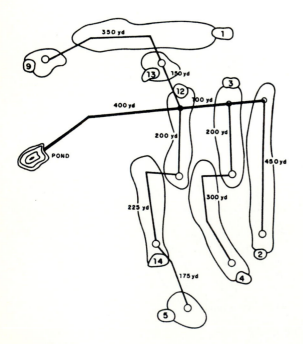

Figure 8–21

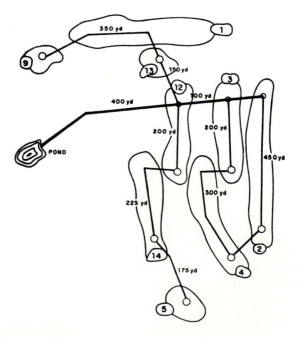

Figure 8–22

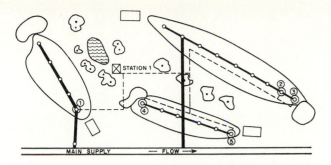

Figure 8–23   (Adapted with permission from Pira, 1982)

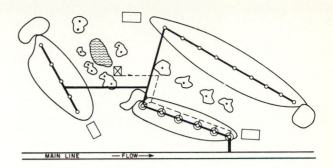

Figure 8–25   (Adapted with permission from Pira, 1982)

the numbered heads operating on the same station of the controller. If each sprinkler discharges 40 gpm, determine the carrying capacity (gpm) that each section of pipeline must handle and size each section of PVC-200 pipe.

9.   Assume that the designs in figures 8–25 and 8–26 are based on running the six heads in each of the fairways. Indicate the flow capacities and pipe sizes for each section of PVC-200 pipe if each sprinkler discharges 40 gpm.

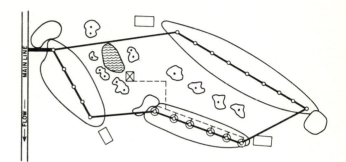

Figure 8–26   (Adapted with permission from Pira, 1982)

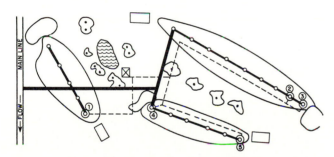

Figure 8–24   (Adapted with permission from Pira, 1982)

Chapter 9

PRINCIPLES
OF HYDRAULICS

Hydraulics is the study of the parameters that influence the pressure within a piping system. These parameters include factors that cannot be controlled, such as the elevation at various locations in the system. It also includes all the energy forms that influence the pressure in the system. These energy forms include friction in the pipes, which robs the energy and decreases the pressure, and the energy input to the system by the pump.

Before attempting to analyze pipe systems and determine pump and power unit selection, it is essential to become thoroughly acquainted with the principles of hydraulics. Hydraulics is nothing more than calculating the total resistance against which the pump must operate. The hydraulic terms used

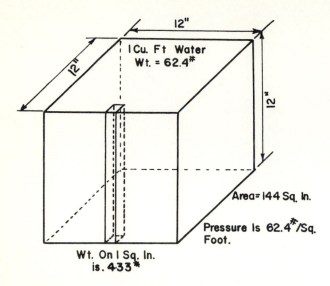

Note: 1 cu ft water weighs 62.4 lbs.

Base area = 144 sq in. Therefore: a pressure of 433 lbs. will be exerted on each square inch.

$$\frac{62.4 \text{ lbs}}{144 \text{ sq in}} = .433 \text{ psi}$$

Figure 9–1   Pressure

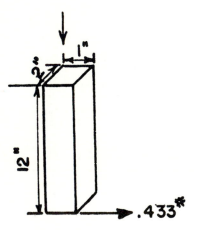

Figure 9–2   Head of one foot

to express this resistance are *pressure* in pounds per square inch (psi) and *friction head* in feet.

PRESSURE

The relationship of pressure and head is explained by the following sequence of illustrations. Figure 9–1 shows that the pressure on each square inch will be dependent only on the weight of the water and not on the area. A column of water one square inch in area and one foot high will exert a force on its base of .433 pounds (see figure 9–2). By applying a pressure of .433 psi, a column of water could be raised one foot high (see figure 9–3). It takes a column of water one square inch in area and 2.31 feet high to exert a force of one pound on its base (see figure 9–4). Therefore, a pressure of one psi could raise a column of water one square inch in area 2.31 feet (see figure 9–5).

The pressure exerted on the base of a column is independent of the shape of the vessel (see figure 9–6). The pressure is only affected by the height of the water column. Figure 9–7 shows that a pressure of .433 lbs will be exerted on each square inch of the base if the column of water is one foot high and 1.0 lb if the water is 2.31 feet high. When water is not moving, pressure is influenced only by the height of water above the point of interest.

Try the following pressure problems:

1.   Fill in the blanks in figure 9–8 with the pressure readings that would be found at the various points of the column of water shown.

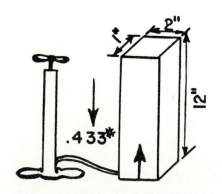

Figure 9–3   Force of 0.433 pounds

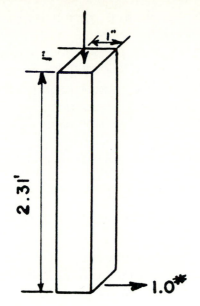

Figure 9–4   Head of 2.31 feet

2.   Fill in the blanks showing the height a column of water can be raised by the following pressures:

     1 psi = _____ feet

    10 psi = _____ feet

    20 psi = _____ feet

    50 psi = _____ feet

  100 psi = _____ feet

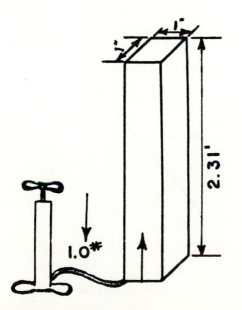

Figure 9–5   Force of one pound

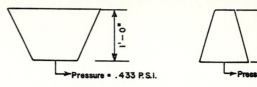

Figure 9–6   Effect of vessel shape on pressure

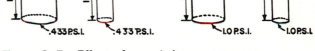

Figure 9–7   Effect of vessel size on pressure

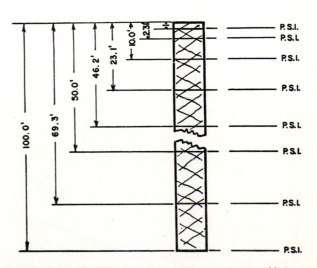

Figure 9–8   Converting heads to pressures. (Adapted from Pira, 1982)

3. Fill in the pressure coming into each house shown in figure 9–9.

4. Using the water pressure tank shown in figure 9–10, determine the following:

    a. At full tank pressure (high limit) water can be elevated _____ feet.

    b. At low pressure limit water can be elevated _____ feet.

    c. What is the faucet pressure located 20 feet above the tank? _____

    d. 80 feet above the tank? _____

5. Using figure 9–11, determine the irrigation pressure as follows:

    a. Assume that the pipe line is used to supply green 1 and green 2. If the pressure at green 1 is 50 psi, what will it be at green 2? _____

    b. If the pressure at green 2 is 50 psi, what is the pressure at green 1? _____

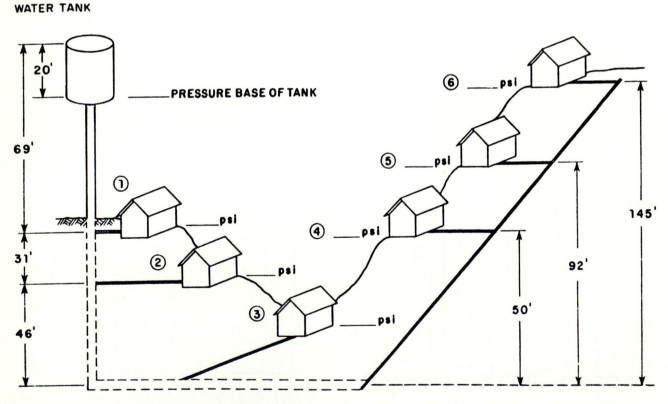

WATER TANK

Figure 9–9 Practical example of converting heads to pressure (Adapted with permission from Pira, 1982)

6. Using figure 9–12, answer the following elevation problems:

   a. Pressure (psi) needed to lift water from the
pond to the highest elevation.

   b. If the pump pressure were 80 psi, what
would the pressure be at the following
locations:
     (1) Green 3?
     (2) Green 7?
     (3) Green 6?
     (4) Green 5?

   c. What is the elevation difference in terms of
psi between the highest and lowest points
of this golf course? _____

   d. Which fairway has the greatest elevation
difference? _____

   e. What would the pressure difference (psi)
be between Green 1 and each of the following greens:
     (1) Green 4?
     (2) Green 10?
     (3) Green 7?
     (4) Green 17?

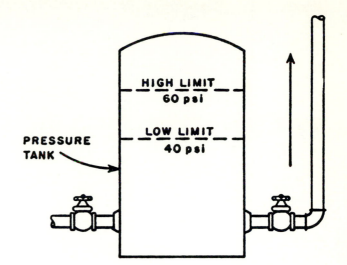

Figure 9–10 Pressure tank

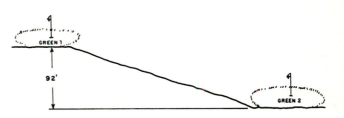

Figure 9–11 Two greens on the same pipeline

FRICTION HEAD

Since water is not merely lifted but flows from one
point to another, friction must be considered. The
movement of any substance from one point to another generates friction, which is a loss that must
be overcome when pumping.

   Friction varies with the following factors:

1. Increases with an increase in velocity.

2. Decreases with increase in pipe diameter.

3. Increases with pipe roughness.

4. Increases with pipe length.

5. Increases with the number of valves.

6. Increases when water changes direction.

   Since friction varies with many factors, engineering information must be utilized when planning a
system.

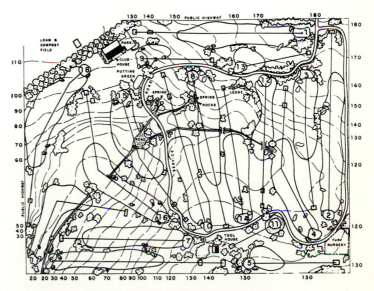

Figure 9–12 Effect of elevation on pressure (Adapted
with permission from Pira, 1982)

Head Loss

Friction or head loss (H_L) can be determined by multiplying the friction factor (F_c) times the length of the pipe (L) or

$$H_L = F_c L$$

The friction factor can be determined from the friction charts in Appendix B if the flow rate (gpm) in the pipeline is known.

Example   A 600-foot length of 2.0-inch diameter PVC 160 pipe is carrying 45 gpm. What is the head loss in this section of pipe?

Solution   From the PVC 160 friction chart (table B–1), find the friction factor (marked psi loss) for the 2.0-inch pipe. For a 45-gpm flow rate, the friction factor (F_c) is 1.08 psi per 100 feet. Therefore,

$$H_L = F_c L$$
$$= (1.08 \text{ psi}/100 \text{ ft}) (600 \text{ ft})$$
$$H_L = 6.48 \text{ psi}$$

Friction Loss for Valves and Fittings

The tables in Appendix B provide friction factors for most pipes used in turf irrigation systems. When water changes direction or when turbulence is introduced, additional friction occurs. The amount of this extra friction can be obtained from figure B–1. This figure is used by finding the fitting or valve on the left column and the pipe size on the right column. By drawing a straight line between the points on the left and right columns the equivalent length of straight pipe is obtained. This equivalent length is added to the actual length of pipe and used in the head loss calculation. For example, an open globe valve in a 2-inch line is equivalent to 55 feet of straight 2-inch pipe. If the glove valve were in a 100-foot length of pipe, the total friction in this pipe would be

$$H_L = F_c (155 \text{ ft})$$

Although friction caused by such changes should be checked, it is usually not necessary to consider the friction in valves and fitting unless a globe valve is present or many fittings are being used.

Problems

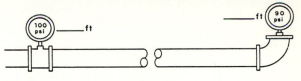

Figure 9–13   Effect of friction

1.   Use table B–8: Friction Loss Characteristics—Asbestos–Cement. Explain or define the following:

   a.   Cause of friction loss in pipes.
   b.   This chart is read in terms of loss of head in _____ per _____ feet of length.
   c.   Assume the pressure at the beginning of the line was 100 psi and a friction loss is 10 psi. Express this in terms of feet (see figure 9–13).

2.   Use Friction Loss Characteristics chart for PVC 200 pipe (table B–2). Find the friction losses. Record answers in both feet and psi for the following:

   a.   200 gpm—distance 1,000 ft using 4-in pipe = friction loss of _____ ft = _____ psi.
   b.   50 gpm—distance 1,000 ft using 2½-in pipe = _____ ft = _____ psi.
   c.   600 gpm—distance 1,000 ft using 6-in pipe = _____ ft = _____ psi.
   d.   100 gpm—distance 750 ft using 3-in pipe = _____ ft = _____ psi.
   e.   350 gpm—distance 1,200 ft using 5-in pipe = _____ ft = _____ psi.

3.   In what terms (pressure loss) and distance are the steel and PVC 315 friction tables based (tables B–3 and B–8)?

   a.   Schedule-40 steel pipe table has friction loss in _____ per _____ feet.
   b.   PVC 315 pipe table has friction loss in __ per _____ feet.

4.   Find the friction loss in psi for both the steel and PVC-315 pipes as follows:

   a.   Carry 25 gpm a distance of 100 feet of 1¼-inch steel pipe _____. PVC _____.
   b.   Carry 100 gpm a distance of 100 feet of 4-inch steel pipe _____.
   c.   Carry 18 gpm a distance of 350 feet of 1-inch steel pipe _____.
   d.   Carry 40 gpm a distance of 50 feet of 2-inch steel pipe _____. PVC _____.
   e.   Carry 200 gpm a distance of 1,000 feet of 4-inch steel pipe _____. PVC _____.

5.   Find the feet of loss to carry 30 gpm a distance of 150 feet of 1½-inch type-L copper pipe. _____.

6. Find the feet of loss to carry 30 gpm a distance of 200 feet in 1-inch rubber hose. _____.

7. Using Figure B–1, Resistance of Valves and Fittings:

    a. Explain what information this chart gives.

    b. Find the "equivalent length of straight pipe" for each of the following valves and fittings:

        (1) Two 4-in globe valves. _____.

        (2) Two 2-in gate valves (open). _____.

        (3) Five standard 6-in elbows._____.

        (4) A sudden contraction 6 in to 3 in. _____.

        (5) Three 3-in standard tees. _____.

8. Find the friction loss (ft) for each pipe section (see figure 9–14):

    a. Suction side. Use 4-inch aluminum pipe:
        Foot valve = _____ ft straight pipe
        45° elbow = _____ ft straight pipe
        90° elbow = _____ ft straight pipe
        Straight pipe = _____ ft
        Total ft straight pipe = _____ ft
        Friction loss = _____ ft

    b. Discharge side. Use 2.0-inch PVC 200 pipe:
        Check valve = _____ ft straight pipe
        1 globe valve = _____ ft straight pipe
        2 standard elbows = _____ ft straight pipe
        2 45° elbows = _____ ft straight pipe
        Straight pipe = _____ ft
        Total ft straight pipe_____ ft
        Friction loss = _____ ft

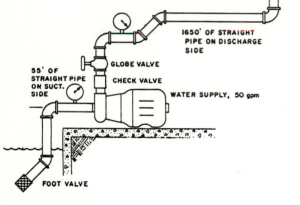

Figure 9–14   Valves and fitting problem (Adapted with permission from Pira, 1982)

ELEVATION, PRESSURE, AND FRICTION

The pressure at any point in a pipeline can be determined if the elevation and the pressure are known at some other point and the head loss between the two points is known. One way of understanding this complex interaction is to use Bernoulli's equation. Bernoulli found that the total energy in a pipe is the sum of the elevation, the pressure, and the velocity energy or

$$Z + P + \frac{V^2}{2g}$$

where Z = elevation in feet

P = pressure expressed in feet of head

V = velocity in ft/sec

g = acceleration of gravity = 32 ft/sec^2

Therefore, the total energy at point A in figure 9–15 is

$$Z_A + P_A + \frac{V_A{}^2}{2g}$$

and the total energy at point B is

$$Z_B + P_B + \frac{V_B{}^2}{2g}$$

By equating the energies at points A and B, we obtain an expression for the energy in the pipeline. We must also account for changes in energy that may occur between points A and B, that is, friction or head loss, (H_L), which removes energy, and a pump input (H_T), which adds energy. Combining all these forms, Bernoulli's equation can be written between points A and B as

$$Z_A + P_A + \frac{V_A{}^2}{2g} + H_T = Z_B + P_B + \frac{V_B{}^2}{2g} + H_L$$

Since in irrigation pipes the velocity is to be less than 5 fps, the $V^2/2g$ term is negligible and these terms can be ignored, this leads to a working equation of

$$Z_A + P_A + H_T = Z_B + P_B + H_L$$

The pump input element is only in the equation if a pump exists between points A and B. Also, in Bernoulli's equation, the water *must* always be flowing from the point on the left side of the equation (here Point A) to the point on the right side of the equation (here Point B). For the pipe system shown in figure 9–15, the elevations are given at points A and B and the pressure is known at point B. The head loss is given as 10 feet. Bernoulli's equation can be applied to determine the unknown pressure (P_A) as follows:

$$Z_A + P_A + H_T = Z_B + P_B + H_L$$
$$600 \text{ ft} + P_A + 0 = 650 \text{ ft} + 100 \text{ psi} (2.31) + 10 \text{ ft}$$
$$P_A = 291 \text{ ft}$$
$$P_A = 126 \text{ psi}$$

Note that H_T was zero since there was no pump between points A and B. This calculation yields the information that a pressure P_A of 126 psi is needed

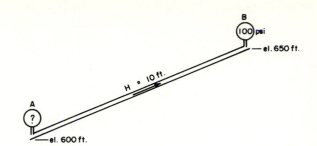

Figure 9–15   Bernoulli principles

at point A if there is to be a 100 psi pressure at point B.

Static Pressure Versus Working Pressure

Since sprinkler performance is directly related to its pressure, it is essential to design the irrigation system on the working pressure (water is flowing), never on static pressure (water is not flowing). Static pressure is a function of the elevation difference, whereas, the working pressure is a function of the elevation difference and friction losses.

Problems

1. Solve the following problem (see figure 9–16), to illustrate the pressure difference that will exist under static and working pressure conditions:

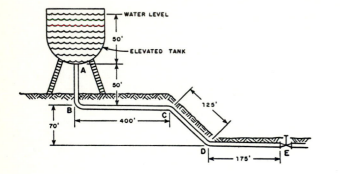

Figure 9–16   Static vs. working pressure (Adapted with permission from Pira, 1982)

a. Calculate static pressure (no water flow) at points A, B, C, D, and E.
Point A = _____ psi
Point B = _____ psi
Point C = _____ psi
Point D = _____ psi
Point E = _____ psi

b. Calculate the working pressure (water flow) at points A, B, C, D, and E. (35 gpm 1½-in PVC 200 pipe)
Point A = _____ psi
Point B = _____ psi
Point C = _____ psi
Point D = _____ psi
Point E = _____ psi

2. Assume the six greens are piped as shown in figure 9–17. The incoming pressure at green 1 is 100 psi. One green is irrigated at a time. Sprinkler flow rate is 50 gpm. Compare the working pressure at each green for 2-in PVC 200 pipe and 2½-in PVC 200 pipe.

PUMP REQUIREMENTS

One of the most important uses for Bernoulli's equation is to compute the energy that must be in-

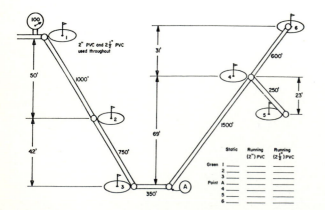

Figure 9–17   Practical example (Adapted with permission from Pira, 1982)

troduced into the irrigation system by the pump. This is done by computing the pump energy (H_T) by writing Bernoulli's equation between the highest and/or most remote sprinkler and the water source. This calculation should be made for the sprinkler set that demands the largest discharge.

Example For the system shown in figure 9–18, compute the total head (H_T) required. The maximum discharge set has five 50-gpm sprinklers and each sprinkler must have at least 80 psi.

Solution To solve for H_T, write Bernoulli's equation from the water source (point A) to the most remote sprinkler (point B) as follows:

$$P_A + Z_A + H_T = P_B + Z_B + H_L$$
$$0 \text{ psi} + 590 \text{ ft} + H_T = 80 \text{ psi } (2.31) + 700 \text{ ft} + 17 \text{ psi } (2.31)$$
$$H_T = 334 \text{ ft}$$

The power requirements can now be computed for the pumping unit that must deliver 250 gpm at 334 feet of head:

$$HP = \frac{Q(gpm)H_T(ft)}{3960(eff)}$$
$$= \frac{(250)(334)}{3960(.7)} = 30HP$$

This calculation assumes a pump efficiency of 70% and an electric motor.

It is often useful to know the pressures desired at the pressure gauges located on the suction (point C) and discharge sides of the pump (point D). The pressure at point C can be computed as follows:

$$P_A + Z_A = P_C + Z_C + H_L$$
$$0 + 590 \text{ ft} = P_C + 600 \text{ ft} + 0$$
$$P_C = -10 \text{ ft}$$

The pressure at point D can be computed as

$$P_D + Z_D = P_B + Z_B + H_L$$
$$P_D + 600 \text{ ft} = 80(2.31) + 700 \text{ ft} + 17(2.31)$$
$$P_D = 324 \text{ ft} = 140 \text{ psi}$$

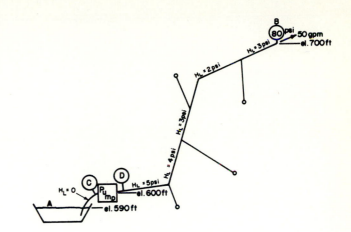

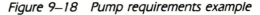

Figure 9–18 Pump requirements example

WATER HAMMER OR SURGE PRESSURE

Water hammer or surge pressure will occur whenever the movement of water in a pipe is stopped either in part or completely. The worst possible condition occurs when it is abruptly stopped, for example, when a valve suddenly closes. This would also happen when water in the mainline moves back toward the pump as the check valve closes.

When the flow of water is stopped instantaneously, the water rebounds, setting up a pressure wave that rushes through the pipe. This pressure wave travels through the pipe until it becomes equal to the pressure moving forward, then it rebounds. This bouncing back and forth continues until the pressure wave or surge dissipates itself. The same principle applies as with dropping a golf ball to the pavement. The ball rebounds with the greatest force after the first bounce and continues until it has no energy left.

The pressure wave that develops depends on the velocity of flow and the rate at which the flow is stopped. Under certain conditions, it can reach proportions that will burst the pipe. In other words, the higher the velocity, the higher the pressure from water hammer. Since the pressure due to water hammer is over and above the working pressure of the system, they must be added.

For example, the theoretical pressure rise due to water hammer in PVC schedule-40 plastic pipe carrying 150 gpm in a 2½-in pipe at a velocity of 10 feet per second is about 190 psi. Therefore, assume working pressure = 100 psi + water hammer, 190 psi, the peak pressure is 290 psi. Higher flow rates would increase the velocity and consequently the water hammer. For this reason it is suggested that pipe sizes are selected which will not exceed a maximum velocity of 5 feet per second.

Control of Water Hammer

The following points should be remembered in controlling water hammer.

In filling a long piping system, the flow should be controlled with a gate valve set to pass about 75% of the operating capacity. When the lines have filled, the gate valve should be opened slowly until full operating pressure is attained. Install check valves designed to close at zero velocity for relatively long lines sloping up and away from the pump as well as shorter lines that slope sharply upward from the pump.

Estimate Potential Mainline Surge Pressure

Consider surge pressures that may damage the mainline piping system when designing your sprinkler system. Surge pressure or water hammer occurs in a mainline pipe when the flow of water in that pipe is suddenly stopped. The magnitude of the surge pressure depends upon several factors:

1. The initial velocity of flow in feet per second.

2. The length of time it took to stop the flow of water in the pipe.

3. The length of the mainline pipe between the point where the flow first stopped and the first entrance connection into the source of water.

The total pressure subjected to the mainline pipe during a surge condition is equal to

$$P_{Total} = P_o + P_s$$

where P_{Total} = total system pressure during a surge (psi)

P_o = the operating pressure at the time of the surge (psi)

P_s = the surge pressure: an increase in pressure over and above the existing operating pressure at the time of the surge (psi)

The easiest method to use when estimating the magnitude of the surge pressure is to use either the accompanying nomograph shown in figure 9–19 or the following formula:

$$P_s = \frac{V \times L \times .07}{t}$$

where V = original velocity of flow at time of surge (ft/sec)

L = the length of the straight mainline pipe that extends between the water source and the point in the mainline (valve or pump location) where the flow was stopped (feet)

t = the approximate time it required to stop the flow of water (seconds) (i.e., time to close the valve)

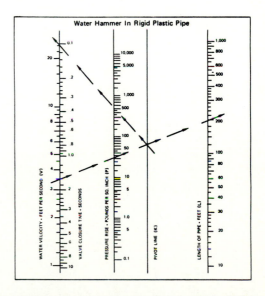

Water Hammer In Rigid Plastic Pipe

Figure 9–19 Surge pressure nomograph (Taken from Rain Bird, 1967)

How to Use Nomograph

1. Locate the flow velocity (ft/sec) on the velocity index lines (v).

2. Locate the length of the pipe affected on the pipe length index line (L).

3. Connect these two points with a straight line.

4. Locate the intersection of the straight line and the pivot index line (K).

5. From the intersection of the straight line and the pivot index line, project a straight line intersecting the appropriate point on the valve closing time.

6. At the intersection of this second line and the pressure increase index line (P), read the approximate increase in pressure due to a surge condition.

7. Add the pressure increase to the existing line pressure to obtain the total pressure at the time of surge.

GOLF COURSE IRRIGATION DESIGN EXAMPLE

Compute H_T for the system shown in figure 8–16. The total head for this system should be based on the required pressure at either the highest point X with the fairway sprinklers running or the most distant point Y with the fairway sprinklers running.

Total head required when point Y or A_1 is running is computed by determining the discharge in each pipe section when the number 1 station on controllers A, B, C, D, E, and F are on (see figure 9–20). Now write Bernoulli's equation from the source (point S to point Y) as follows:

$$P_S + Z_S + H_T = P_Y + Z_Y + H_{L_{S-Y}}$$

The head loss between points S and Y is the sum of the head losses in each section:

> From Y to H_1; 78 gpm in 1,700 ft of 2.5-in PVC 200 pipe
> From H_1 to 5-in; 78 gpm in 800 ft of 3.5-in PVC 200 pipe
> From 5-in to 6-in; 78 gpm in 50 ft of 5-in PVC 200 pipe
> From 6-in to pump; 421 gpm in 600 ft of 6-in PVC 200 pipe

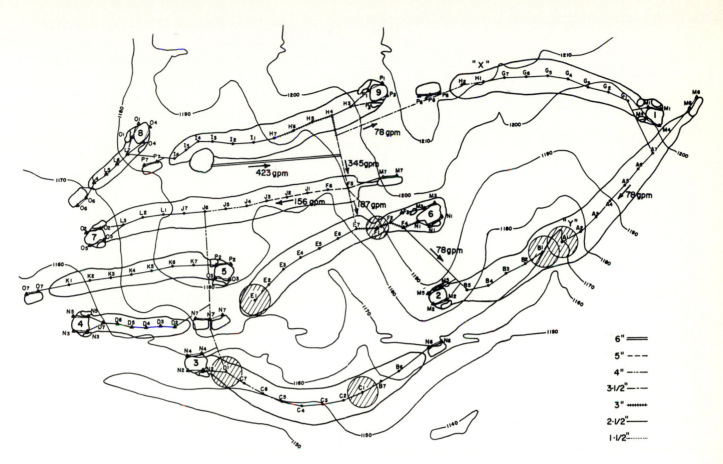

Figure 9–20   Analysis of points X and Y

Therefore, the head loss between S and Y is:

    (1.36 psi/100 ft) (1,700 ft) = 23.1 psi
    (0.27 psi/100 ft) (800 ft)   = 2.1 psi
    (0.05 psi/100 ft) (50 ft)   = 0.0 psi
    (0.52 psi/100 ft) (600 ft)   = <u>3.1 psi</u>
        Total   28.3 psi

Therefore, the total head (H_T) is

$$0 + 1185 \text{ ft} + H_T = 90 \text{ psi } (2.31) + 1,170 \text{ ft} + 28.3 \text{ psi } (2.31)$$
$$H_T = 285.3 \text{ ft}$$

Recalculating the total head for the highest point (H_1) when the number 1 station on controllers G, H, I, J, K, and L are running yields head losses of

    H_1 to 5-in; 78 gpm in
    800 ft of 3.5-in PVC 200 = 2.1 psi
    5-in to 6-in; 156 gpm in
    50 ft of 5-in PVC 200   = 0.1 psi
    6-in to pump; 468 gpm in
    600 ft of 6-in PVC 200   = <u>3.8 psi</u>

Or, H_T equals

$$0 + 1185 \text{ ft} + H_T = 90 \text{ psi } (2.31) + 1210 \text{ ft} + 6.0 \text{ psi } (2.31)$$
$$H_T = 246.8 \text{ ft}$$

Since the energy required to properly run point Y is greater, the pump must deliver 285 feet of head.

PROBLEMS

1. Compute the head loss for 55 gpm flowing through 555 feet of 2-in PVC 40 pipe.

2. Compute the total head loss for a pipeline consisting of the following three sections. All sections of the pipe carry 60 gpm.

    a.   500 feet of 3-in copper (L)

    b.   325 feet of 2½-in copper (L)

    c.   1000 feet of 2-in copper (L)

3. A pipeline has three sprinklers (these lines are often called laterals). Each sprinkler discharges 10 gpm. Compute the pressure drop due to friction only (1) if all three sprinklers run at one time and (2) if only sprinkler C is running (see figure 9–21).

4. A pump with a working pressure of 100 psi is located at an elevation of 400 feet. A 60-gpm sprinkler is located at an elevation of 250 feet and there is 700 feet of 2-in PVC-315 pipe between the pump and the sprinkler. When the sprinkler is not running what is the pressure at the sprinkler? What is the pressure at the sprinkler when it is running?

5. Compute the pressure at gauge B in psi. (See figure 9–22.)

6. Compute the pressure at gauges A and B in psi if the pressure at gauge C is 50 psi. (See figure 9–23.)

7. In figure 9–24 the pressure at gauge C is 60 psi. Compute the pressure at sprinkler A and sprinkler B. What is the pressure at pipe intersection D?

8. In figure 9–24 sprinklers A and B are selected to discharge 45 gpm at a pressure of 60 psi. What is the required pressure at gauge C if both sprinklers

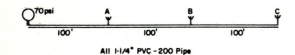

All 1-1/4" PVC - 200 Pipe

Figure 9–21

Figure 9–22

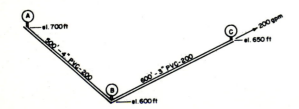

Figure 9–23

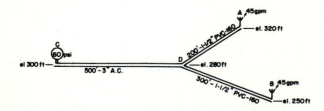

Figure 9–24

are to operate at the design conditions simultaneously?

9.   In figure 9–23 the pressure at gauge B is known to be 80 psi. What is the pressure at gauges A and C?

10.   What is the pressure in psi at the base of the 80-foot high water tower?

11.   A pressure tank has a pressure of 100 psi. How high will water rise in a vertical tube leaving the tank?

12.   Complete the following table:

1 psi   = _____ feet
1 foot   = _____ psi
20 psi   = _____ feet
40 feet = _____ psi
100 psi = _____ feet
150 feet = _____ psi

13.   What is the pressure in psi at the bottom of a 20-foot deep lake?

14.   What is the pressure in psi at the surface of a 30-foot deep lake?

15.   What is the pressure at sprinkler B if the pressure at sprinkler A is 80 psi (see figure 9–25). Each sprinkler discharges 75 gpm.

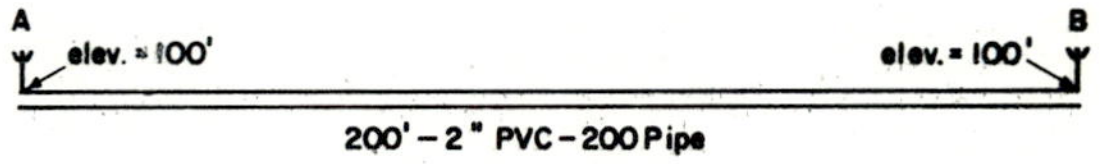

16.   Determine the friction loss in feet and psi for 200 gpm flowing through 1,000 feet of 4-inch AC pipe.

17.   Determine the friction loss in feet and psi for 50 gpm flowing through 1,000 feet of 2-inch PVC 40 pipe.

18.   Determine the head loss in psi for 90 gpm flowing through 500 feet of each of the following types of 3-inch pipe. Compare the results. Which has the most friction? The least?

Pipe	H_L
PVC 160	_____
PVC 200	_____
PVC 315	_____
PVC 40	_____
galvanized steel 40	_____
copper-L	_____
AC	_____

A   elev. ≈ 100'   elev. ≈ 100'   B

200' – 2" PVC – 200 Pipe

Figure 9–25

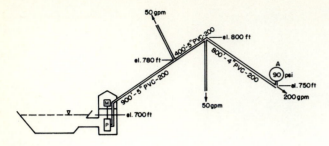

50 gpm

el. 800 ft

400'-5" PVC-200

el. 780 ft

800'-4" PVC-200

A

90 psi

900'-5" PVC-200

M

P

el. 700 ft

50 gpm

el. 750 ft

200 gpm

Figure 9–26

19. Sprinkler A in figure 9–26 requires 90 psi. Based on the flow values given, compute the required H_T for this system.

20. Compute the head loss in psi for a swing joint containing the following: three 90-degree standard elbows, one globe valve, one open gate valve, and four feet of 1½-inch PVC 40 pipe. The sprinkler on this swing joint discharges 60 gpm.

Chapter 10

PUMPS

A pump is a mechanical device that imparts energy to a fluid. Pumps are commonly required on golf course irrigation systems to lift water from a source to the sprinklers. The energy imparted to the water by the pump must be sufficient to overcome the elevation differences on the course, to overcome the friction in the piping system, and to deliver the water to each sprinkler at the desired operating pressure.

TYPES OF WATER SUPPLIES

Water required to supply a turf irrigation system will usually come from one of several sources—municipal water supply, surface pond or reservoir, or wells.

Municipal Water Supplies

When the areas to be irrigated are located near municipal water supplies, it is often possible to buy water from the supplier. Water from municipal systems is high-quality water and will usually be delivered to the property boundary at a certain pressure. This pressure represents energy the irrigation pumping system does not have to add to the water. Municipal water, if available, will be delivered in a main that has a limited capacity. It will not be possible for the irrigation system to draw water more rapidly than the supply main can deliver it. In addition, the municipal supplier may establish limited rates and volumes that may be taken by the golf course. These limits are established to protect the other users on the system.

Surface Ponds

Surface water runoff from local watersheds can often be collected and stored in a pond and then used to supply the irrigation system. Figure 10–1 gives estimates of the volume of water that can be expected to run off one acre of land each year for the United States. These numbers need to be reduced by the amount of seepage expected through the pond bottom and the amount of evaporation expected from the pond surface. In most areas, the combined seepage and evaporation losses will be about 40% to 60% of the pond volume. Water from surface runoff is usually relatively poor quality, often containing sediment, nitrogen, and phosphorus from urban or agricultural areas in the watershed. Therefore, storage ponds must have extra capacity to hold any sediment settling from the inflow water. Any plant nutrients may cause algae and other water plants to grow, especially during warm weather.

If the area to be irrigated is near a stream fed by a large watershed, it is often possible to simply draw water from the stream without building a pond to store the water. It may be necessary to get a permit to use stream water from your state water management bureau. The permit ensures that other users on the stream are not affected by your withdrawing water. In addition, make sure there is sufficient water in the stream. An 18-hole golf course

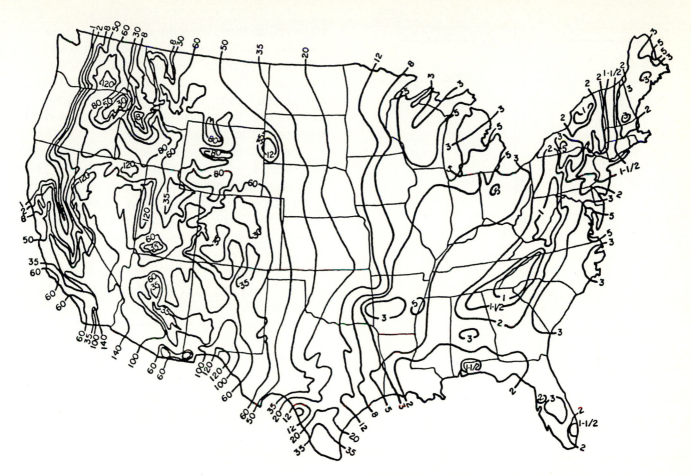

Figure 10–1 Approximate watershed area, in acres, required to impound 1.0 acre-foot of water each year (Taken with permission from Hamilton and Jepson, 1940)

may need up to 1,500 gallons per minute for as much as 10 hours per night. A large stream will be needed to supply this amount.

Wells

Groundwater is often used as a source of water for turf irrigation. Groundwater is generally of good quality and if the watertable is relatively near the surface it is often desirable to use groundwater as a primary or secondary source. Groundwater is removed from the ground by drilling a well into the water-bearing strata and installing a pump in the well. Because of the physics of lifting water, wells are often classified into two categories: shallow wells and deep wells. A shallow well is one in which the water level in the well is within 25 feet

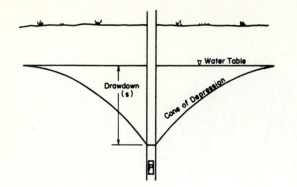

Figure 10–2   Well hydraulics

of the soil surface when the water is being pumped from the well. Shallow wells have the advantage of being able to place the pump on the soil surface and have the pump suck or lift the water from the well. Deep wells have a pumping water level greater than 25 feet from the soil surface and must have the pump placed in the well.

The hydraulics of a well are quite complex and the reader is referred to Davis and DeWiest (1966) or Freeze and Cherry (1979) for a detailed treatment of this topic. Figure 10–2 is a schematic of the water levels within the geologic structure while a pump is drawing water from the well. The cone of depression is produced when water is removed from the well bore by the pump causing the water level in the well to drop. This drop in the well water level means the water surrounding the well is at a higher elevation than the water in the well and the gravitational water in the soil begins to flow into the well bore. As this continues, the distance between the original watertable and the water level in the well (drawdown) increases, forming a large cone of depression. At some point the drawdown reaches a point of equilibrium where the water is flowing into the well at the same rate it is being pumped from the well. This equilibrium usually occurs after 24 to 48 hours of continuous pumping at a constant flow rate. One reason for pump testing a well is to determine the capacity of the well. The specific capacity (S_c) of a well is the pump discharge (Q) in gpm divided by the drawdown (s) in feet at equilibrium or

$$Sc = \frac{Q}{s}$$

In other words, the specific capacity is the flow rate per foot of drawdown. If the maximum drawdown is known, the maximum pump rate for the well can be established as

Qmax = Sc (Smax)

The maximum drawdown is usually assumed to be the distance from the original water table (before pumping) to the point about 10 feet above the pump.

If the irrigation system requires more water than can be pumped from the well, it will be necessary to find secondary sources of water or to pump the ground water into a surface storage, such as a pond, for long periods, then repump the stored water into the irrigation system. It is not unusual to use a surface storage pond with a well because the multiple demands of the irrigation system often lead to multiple pump systems that cannot be installed in one well.

In recent years it has become common to use treated municipal waste water as a water source for turf systems. Because the effluent is produced continuously at the treatment plant and irrigation only occurs as needed, it is common to use a storage pond to hold the effluent until it is needed.

TYPES OF PUMPS

Pumps are generally categorized into two basic types, based on the method by which energy is imparted to the fluid. In positive displacement pumps, the fluid is physically displaced by mechanical devices such as pistons, cams, plungers, gears, diaphragms, or helical rotors. Pumps of this type are not commonly used for pumping irrigation water. Fertilizer injection pumps or sprayer pumps are, however, often positive displacement pumps and thus provide accurate control of the amount of liquid injected or applied.

The second type of pump is one where the energy is transferred by centrifugal force, viscous forces, or momentum. This type of pump includes irrigation pumps such as centrifugal and vertical turbine pumps. Within these categories the size, shape, speed, number of stages, and mode of operation may vary significantly. In general, there are sufficient models or combinations of pumps to permit proper selection of a pump or group of pumps to meet any irrigation need. Most of the nonpositive displacement pumps can operate over a range of conditions where the discharge will vary as the operating head fluctuates. Much of the material in the following section was taken from Jensen (1980).

Centrifugal Pumps

A centrifugal pump has one or more impellers fastened to a rotating shaft that turns inside a vo-

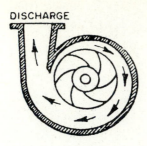

Figure 10–3 Schematic of a centrifugal pump

lute case (see figure 10–3). Water enters the eye of the impeller and is forced outward along the vanes of the impeller by centrifugal force caused by the rotating impeller. The centrifugal force is converted to energy and thus pressure as the water flows out the discharge port. If the discharge from one impeller flows to the eye of another impeller where it undergoes a second increase in energy, the pump is called a multistage pump. Actually, this is no different from placing one pump after another pump on one pipeline, such as a booster pump. Pumps arranged this way are said to be in series.

Generally, the impellers are fixed onto the driveshaft, which is then coupled to a drive unit, electric motor, or engine. Because of their compactness and construction, centrifugal pumps are often stocked as completely assembled units that only require a hookup to the section and discharge pipes. Centrifugal pumps are usually located above the water source. Water enters the pump through a suction pipe and it is usually necessary to prime the pump to remove air bubbles in the pump and suction pipe. Because the need to prime centrifugal pumps is an inconvenience to automatic controlled turf irrigation systems, these pumps are used less than the turbine pumps discussed in the following section.

Turbine Pumps

Turbine pumps are often used to extract water from wells or raise it from rivers, lakes, or sumps. Both the standard vertical turbine and the submersible turbine impart energy to the water by rotating an impeller inside a bowl (see figure 10–4). In a multistage vertical turbine, several of these bowl assemblies are directly coupled together so the flow from the lower impeller moves directly to the next impeller above. This is actually the same as having independent pumps in series.

The impellers are directly fixed to a shaft, known as a line shaft. The line shaft of a vertical turbine extends vertically upward and is coupled to the motor or gearbox resting on the floor of the pump house. Most turf irrigation systems are connected to vertical turbine pumps, which draw water from a surface water source.

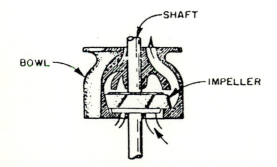

Figure 10–4 Bowl assembly for turbine pump

The submersible turbine is the same pump driven by an electric motor located below the pump in a well. These units are more commonly used in wells in which they usually pump water from the well to the surface storage.

SYSTEM ENERGY RELATIONSHIPS

As shown in chapter 9, the total energy required to operate any irrigation system can be calculated from the Bernoulli equation. The total energy or head (H_T) is made up of five components, as shown in figure 10–5. Each component should be evaluated since this represents the energy the pump will be asked to overcome.

Suction Head

Suction head is the distance between the water level of the source and the pump. If the source is a surface pond, the water level is the pond surface. The suction head is usually constant at any time but may change over the season if the level in the storage pond drops.

Discharge Head

Discharge head is the distance between the pump and the highest elevation sprinkler running at any given time. For most systems this is a constant, but with golf courses this may change every time the sprinkler set changes. For planning purposes the sprinkler with the highest elevation should be used. However, others should be examined to know how the discharge head will vary throughout the watering period.

Well Drawdown

Well drawdown was defined as the distance from the water table to the water level in the well. This changes as the discharge changes. For most golf course systems the source is a surface pond

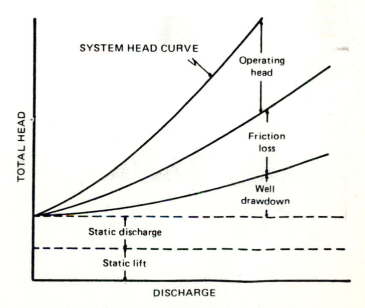

Figure 10–5 A system head curve illustrating the parameters that contribute to the curve (Taken with permission from Jensen, 1980)

and the drawdown is zero. If the water is being pumped from a well into the watering system without an intermediate pond in between, the drawdown must be computed, from the specific capacity, for each pump discharge.

Friction Head

Friction head is the amount of energy needed to overcome the friction in the system for each discharge head. Computing friction head in detail would require a great amount of work. Typically on golf courses, only the friction between the pump and the highest-elevation sprinkler is considered. Note also that since the highest sprinkler changes each set, the friction may also change.

Operating Head

Operating head is the pressure head required to run each sprinkler. For most golf courses this will be one of two or three sprinklers, depending on whether a green, tee, or fairway sprinkler is operating. Again, the highest-elevation sprinkler is used for this calculation.

System Head

System head is the sum of the suction head, the discharge head, the well drawdown, the friction head, and the operating head (see figure 10–5). This is the total energy needed as a function of the system discharge. Many times the system head (H_T) is computed for only one or two critical runs. However, it is important that the maximum energy condition be determined so the pump chosen to meet that condition will properly function for all sets. Changes in the system head that may occur over the life of the system should also be considered. These changes are often minor but can be significant. They include changes in pipe friction as the pipe ages or changes in the water level of the source, especially if a well is used.

PUMP CHARACTERISTIC CURVES

Pumps have certain well-defined properties. These properties vary between types of pumps, manufacturers, and models. Most manufacturers publish information about each pump's performance. These relationships are known as the pump's characteristic curves. There are four basic curves for each pump. Each is a function of system discharge and will be described in the following sections.

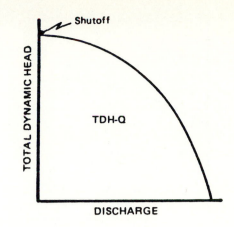

Figure 10–6   Total head versus discharge (Adapted with permission from Jensen, 1980)

Total Head Versus Discharge

The total head curve relates the head produced by the pump to the discharges (see figure 10–6). Generally, the head has a maximum at zero discharge and decreases as the discharge increases. This is perhaps the most important characteristic curve since it has the same dependent and independent axes as the system head relationship. Pump selection is accomplished by superimposing the system head curve on the total head curves for various pumps. The point at which the two curves intersect is the performance point.

Efficiency Versus Discharge

A pump's efficiency is defined as the output work divided by the input work. The output work is the work the pump does on the liquid, often called the water power (WP), where

$$WP = \frac{QH_T}{3,960}$$

and Q is the discharge flow rate in gpm and H_T is the total head of the system in feet. The input work is the work required to drive the pump. The pump efficiency varies with discharge as shown in figure 10–7. Efficiency is zero at zero discharge and increases as discharge increases to a maximum point and then decreases. It is desirable to choose a pump in which the performance point is at or near the peak efficiency. Most new pumps are chosen with the performance point just to the right of the peak efficiency so the slight decrease in discharge

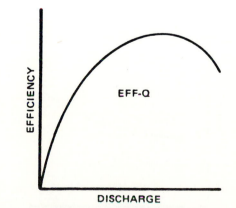

Figure 10–7   Efficiency versus discharge (Adapted with permission from Jensen, 1980)

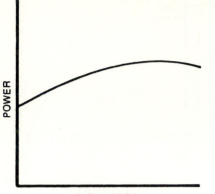

Figure 10–8 Power versus discharge (Adapted with permission from Jensen, 1980)

with time (wear of pump components) will cause a slight improvement in efficiency.

Power Versus Discharge

The power versus discharge relationship is obtained by computing the required power requirement from total head (H_T), discharge (Q), and the pump efficiency. Most manufacturers include the results of this calculation on the published pump curve. If plotted alone it generally looks like figure 10–8. The required power increases as the discharge increases to a maximum near to but not identical to the point of maximum efficiency. If the discharge continues to increase, the power required will remain at or just below the maximum. For some pumps the power requirement continues to increase.

Net Positive Suction Head Versus Discharge

The last characteristic curve is the net positive suction head required (NPSHR) versus discharge. The NPSHR is the amount of energy required to move water into the eye of the impeller and is a function of the pump design (see figure 10–9). It is a value determined by the manufacturer from laboratory tests and is a function of pump speed, impeller shape, liquid properties, and discharge rate. If sufficient energy is not present in the water on the intake side of the pump to move the fluid into the eye of the impeller, the water will vaporize and pump cavitation will occur. Cavitation must be avoided since it physically destroys the pump (Jensen, 1980). Note the NPSHR generally increases as the discharge increases.

To assure that the required energy is available, the net positive suction head available (NPSHA) must be determined. The available head is a function of the system in which the pump operates and can be calculated for all installations. If the NPSHA does not exceed the NPSHR, the pump will cavitate. The NPSHA can be computed as follows:

NPSHA = (barometric pressure) − (suction head) − (friction loss in the suction pipe) − (vapor pressure of the water)

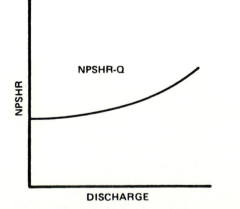

Figure 10–9 Net positive suction head required versus discharge (Adapted with permission from Jensen, 1980)

Under normal turf irrigation, the barometric pressure will be about 34 feet. (If the elevation is more than 2,000 feet above sea level, check the normal barometric pressure for your area). The suction head is the elevation of the pump minus the elevation of the water source in feet. The friction loss in the suction line will usually be approximately zero and the vapor pressure is usually less than 1.0 foot. Therefore, the NPSHA can be summarized as

$$\text{NPSHA} = 34 \text{ ft} - \text{SH (ft)} - 0 - 1.0 \text{ ft}$$
$$\text{NPSHA} = 33 - \text{SH (ft)}$$

Although the NPSHA should be checked for all pumps, it is especially important for centrifugal pumps that are usually located above the water source (positive SH).

COMBINATIONS OF PUMPS

Individual pumps are often combined in various ways to produce different desired outputs. The two methods of combining pumps are in series or parallel.

Pumps in Series

Two or more pumps may be connected and operated in series (see figure 10–10). Pumps in series are connected so the discharge from the first pump or stage is piped into the inlet side of the second pump or stage. Each stage adds more energy to the water. Pumps are placed in series where it is necessary to increase the head but not the discharge rate.

Multistage turbine pumps

A multistage turbine pump consists of single stages connected in series. The same discharge passes through all stages and each one adds additional head to the water. For two pumps operating in series, the combined head is equal to the sum of the individual heads for each specific discharge (see figure 10–11). The combined total head versus discharge curve can be determined by adding the heads for each pump at several fixed discharges.

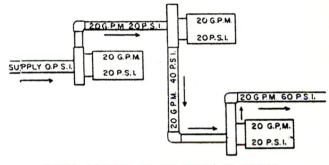

THREE 20 G.P.M., 20 P.S.I. PUMPS IN SERIES
EQUALS 20 G.P.M. AT 60 P.S.I.

Figure 10–10 Pumps connected in series (Adapted with permission from Toro, 1972)

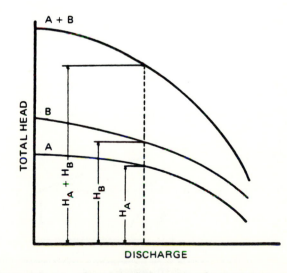

Figure 10–11 Characteristic curve of total head versus discharge for two pumps operating in series (Adapted with permission from Jensen, 1980)

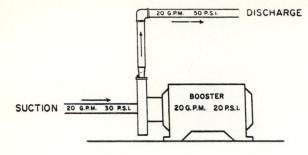

Figure 10–12   Booster pump

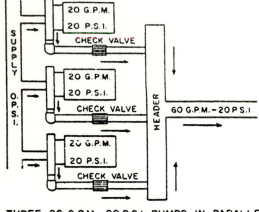

THREE 20 G.P.M., 20 P.S.I. PUMPS IN PARALLEL
EQUALS 60 G.P.M. AT 20 P.S.I.

Figure 10–13   Pumps connected in parallel

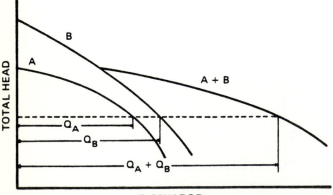

Figure 10–14   Characteristic curve of total head versus discharge for two pumps operating in parallel (Adapted with permission from Jensen, 1980)

Booster pumps

A booster pump can be used on a line of inferior pressure or in a large irrigation system where compensations are necessary for pressure losses due to elevation. Booster pumps usually are of the centrifugal type. A booster does as its name implies, boosts the pressure. If the pressure at a certain point in a system is 30 psi at 20 gpm and the system requires 50 psi at 20 gpm at that point, a booster pump rated at 20 psi at 20 gpm can be installed in the line (see figure 10–12).

Pumps in Parallel

Two or more pumps may be operated in parallel (see figure 10–13). A typical example would be where two or more pumps draw water from a single pump sump and the individual flows discharge into a single pipeline. Pumps are often operated in parallel where the system requires a wide variation in discharges at approximately the same head. Watering of parks or golf courses often requires pumps in parallel.

To properly select pumps to operate in parallel, it is necessary to develop their combined operating curves. Since pumps operating in parallel cause the output discharge to be the summed discharges from the operating pumps, the combined total head curve is obtained as in figure 10–14. Note the output head does not change, just the discharge.

COMPLETE PUMPING SYSTEM

A pumping system for a golf course irrigation system is often a complex combination of pumps and accessories. On a large turf system the pumping system is often looked upon to provide water for a combination of needs such as supplying water fountains on the course, syringing greens and/or tees, or supplying water to grow the turfgrasses. These needs are very different in discharge rate and pressure required. To help overcome the problems associated with operating a large irrigation pump when small volumes of water are needed, such as when a golfer takes a drink or when one sprinkler is used to syringe a small area, two additional pieces of equipment are often added to the pump system. These are a jockey pump and a pressure tank. As we shall see in a later section, the main pumping system must be designed and selected to supply the evapotranspiration water for greens, tees, and fairways. The jockey pump and pressure tank are used to supply low flows.

Pressure Tanks

Pneumatic pressure tanks are often used where there is a wide variance of discharge requirements. The pressure tank will relieve the pump from turning on for a short period of time when a low discharge demand is made. The tank acts as a pressurized reservoir of water with expanding air forcing water out of the tank to fulfill low and infrequent water demands. Most pressure tanks are located on the discharge line from the pumps and are often used to control the pumping system as described here. The pressure tank volume should be equal to or greater than the water discharged by the pumping system in 10 minutes under maximum discharge conditions. Undersized tanks cause the pumps to run frequently. Large tanks are usually mounted vertically; small tanks are often installed horizontally. The air-to-water ratio should vary from one-third to one-half over the range of operating pressures. Various features are available for maintaining the air to water ratio in pneumatic tanks.

An alternative to a pressure tank in a system where the demand varies widely is recirculation using a pressure relief valve. Recirculation means taking the water supplied by the pump in excess of the water demanded by the system and dumping it back into the supply. The water should be dumped back into the reservoir. Just repiping it back to the inlet can cause the water to severely heat when the demand is small, making the recirculating water volume large.

Jockey Pumps

At times a small jockey pump is used to replenish the pressure tank if low demands exist for a period longer than that for which the tank can provide.

A jockey pump should be sized to provide the discharge and pressure required to operate one

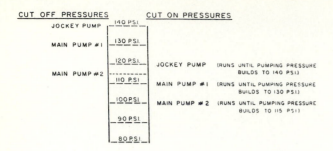

Figure 10–15 Example of pump switching (Adapted with permission from Toro, 1972)

quick-coupler sprinkler or one green or tee sprinkler used in syringing. When the jockey pump is combined with a pressure tank, the pressure tank is often used to control the entire pumping system. An example, shown in figure 10–15, would be to have the jockey pump activate, by way of a pressure switch, at a given pressure such as 120 psi. It would continue to run until the pressure tank is replenished to 140 psi.

If the demand were greater than the jockey pump, the pressure would continue to decrease until it reached the low limit of the pressure switch of the main supply pump. At that point the main pump would activate. If more than one main pump is used, each additional pump would be activated in turn as the pressure continues to drop.

PUMP SELECTION

After the pumping requirements have been computed, it is necessary to find or select a pump or pumps to deliver the needed water at the desired pressure. This is usually accomplished by contacting a pump dealer or manufacturer and discussing your needs. It is often desirable, especially for planning purposes, to be able to make a preliminary pump selection. This preliminary pump selection can often be made by obtaining the pump catalogs from several companies. Then, by looking under the types of pump desired, the selection can be made. Many pump companies, however, do not publish all the data for all of their pumps and it will be necessary to discuss your needs with the dealer.

When the pump catalogs have been obtained, look under centrifugal or turbine, depending on the physical arrangement at the pump house. Then, by consulting the beginning of the appropriate section, you should find a complex figure called a composite curve. This composite curve gives data on the limitation and performance range of each model. By plotting your total head and discharge on the composite curve, you should find several models listed that will probably be appropriate for your system. If none seem to fit, try a different company. A set of sample composite curves is shown in figure 10–16. After one or more potential models have been identified, turn to the performance data for these pump models. The data should also be in the

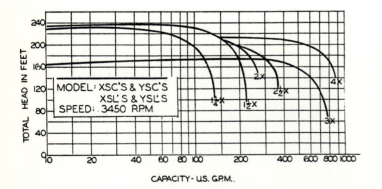

Figure 10–16 Composite curves (Adapted with permission from ITT Marlow, 1980)

pump catalog. The performance data on pump curves for each model will be considerably more complex than the individual pump characteristic curves shown in figures 10–6 through 10–9. This is because the total head, efficiency, power, and NPSHR data are all combined on one plot (see figures 10–17 through 10–20). Note also that each of these pump curves contains the characteristic data for that particular pump model. However, since each pump may have more than one size impeller, the characteristic data are included for several standard impellers. Therefore, there are usually three to five total head curves, one for each impeller on each pump curve. The efficiency data are drawn as a series of lines representing discrete efficiencies. The power data are also shown as a series of nearly straight lines representing discrete input power requirements. The NPSHR data may be on the pump curve or may be plotted separately on an adjacent graph.

The procedure for selecting a pump is to plot the system performance data (maximum points or complete curves) on each of the pump curves that may be sufficient for your system as selected from the composite curves. Then look for the pump model where the performance point is nearest the peak efficiency or slightly to the right of peak efficiency. When this has been found, determine the impeller size and the power required to get your performance. Always choose the impeller size above the performance point. Impellers can be ground to any size by the manufacturer at an extra

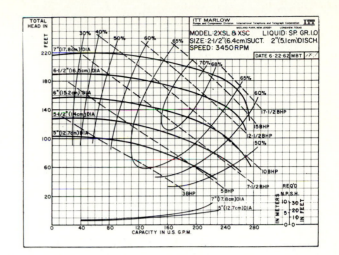

Figure 10–18 Model 2 XSC&L pump (Adapted with permission from ITT Marlow, 1980)

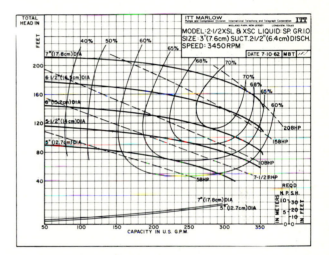

Figure 10–19 Model 2½ XSC&L pump (Adapted with permission ITT from Marlow, 1980)

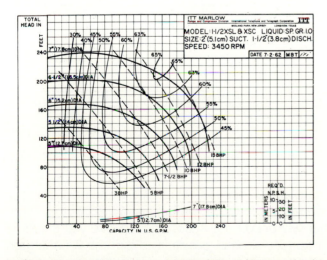

Figure 10–17 Model 1½ XSC&L pump (Adapted with permission from ITT Marlow, 1980)

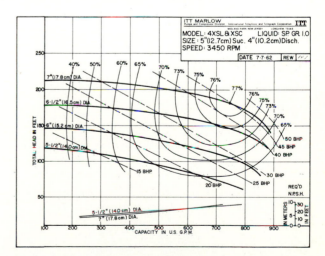

Figure 10–20 Model 4 XSC&L pump (Adapted with permission from ITT Marlow, 1980)

cost. One of the impeller sizes given on the pump curve is usually selected.

The power required should be calculated and increased by about 10% to prevent overloads, which can occur if too many sprinklers are operated at one time or if a pipe is broken. The following example will show the selection procedure.

Example   Select a pump for the following conditions: $H_T = 195$ ft and total gpm $= 200$.

Solution

1. Referring to the composite curve chart, figure 10–16, select all the models capable of meeting the conditions given:
   a. 1½ XSC&L—3,450 prm
   b. 2 XSC&L—3,450 rpm
   c. 2½ XSC&L—3,450 rpm
   d. 4 XSC&L—3,450 rpm

2. Record and analyze the information in the following chart. Select the pump model that best meets the requirements for the conditions given.

Pump model	Efficiency %	Required NPSH	Impeller size	BHP	RPM
1½X					
2X					
2½X					
4X					

GOLF COURSE IRRIGATION DESIGN EXAMPLE

From the results of chapter 7, table 7–1, and chapter 9, we know the pump will have to pump 468 gpm at 285 feet of head. We must now select a pump. None of the pumps examined in this chapter will deliver the head required. We will therefore introduce another possibility. From the Worthington pump catalog, the composite curves for a closed impeller centrifugal pump are shown in figure 10–21. The "X" shows that a 4 × 3 × 8 D-800 pump should do a good job. The pump performance curve for the 4 × 3 × 8 pump is shown in figure 10–22. The desired design point falls directly on the 8.00-inch impeller curve. Therefore, at a discharge of 468 gpm, the pump would deliver 285 feet of head. The pump efficiency will be about 74.5%, and a 50-HP electric motor should be used.

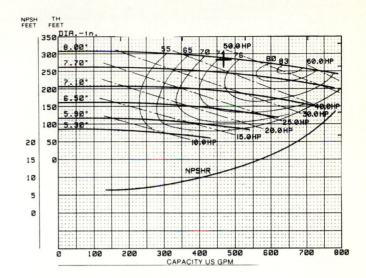

Figure 10–22 *Performance curve (Taken with permission from Worthington, 1983)*

PROBLEMS

1. The well in figure 10–23 was pump tested at 100 gpm for 24 hours. After 24 hours, the drawdown was 30 feet. What is the maximum pump rate if the elevation of water in the well may not drop below 550 feet?

2. Figure 10–24 is a typical centrifugal pump curve. Determine the following from information obtained from the curve:

   a. Diameter of the discharge side of pump.
   b. Diameter of the suction side of the pump.
   c. Diameter of pump housing.
   d. Recommended operating speed.
   e. Peak efficiency.
   f. Power requirement, when pumping 120 gpm at 475 feet of head.

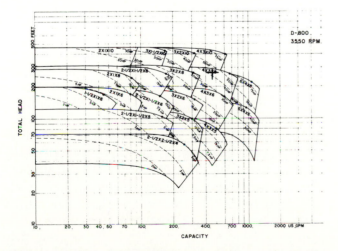

Figure 10–21 *Composite curve (Taken with permission from Worthington, 1983)*

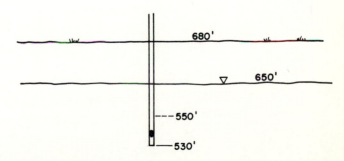

Figure 10–23

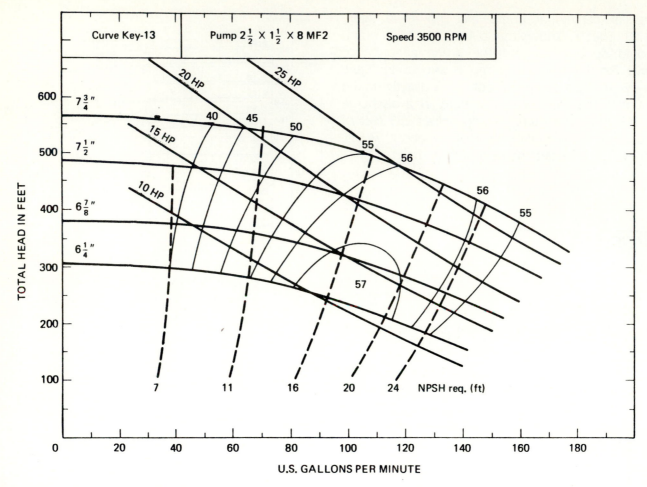

Figure 10–24 Typical centrifugal pump curve

g. Impeller size required to pump 130 gpm at 350 feet of head.

h. Net positive suction head required when pumping 100 gpm at 350 feet of head.

i. Maximum suction lift when pumping 70 gpm at 450 feet of head.

j. If pump is sized to deliver 80 gpm at 450 feet of head using a 7½-inch impeller, what is the efficiency? The HP requirement? If this same pump is later used to pump 140 gpm, what will be the operating head? The new efficiency? The HP requirement? If this pump is used to pump 40 gpm, what will be the operating head? The efficiency? The HP requirement?

Chapter 11

FINAL CONSIDERATIONS

There are several aspects of a complete watering system that have not been discussed to this point. These include thrust blocks, drains, and vents. Several scheduling concepts will also be discussed in this chapter.

THRUST BLOCKS

Thrust and Anchorage

When a pipeline changes direction, the water in the pipe exerts a force or thrust as it attempts to continue in a straight line. This thrust must be coun-

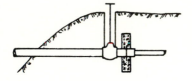

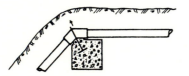

Figure 11–1 Typical thrust block details (Adapted with permission ASAE, 1983–84)

teracted by an equal force or the pipe will come apart. In many cases such as small pipes, the soil packed around the pipe absorbs the force. In other cases, thrust blocks must be installed.

In soft, unstable soils, thrusts can be resisted in two ways. Either connect the pipe to solid foundations with corrosion-resistant tie-rods or remove the soft material and replace it with ballast large and heavy enough to resist the thrusts.

Where a fitting is used to make a direction change, anchor the fitting to a concrete thrust block designed to key into undisturbed soil and heavy enough to resist upward and outward thrust (see figure 11–1). This is done because the new-placed backfill may not have sufficient holding strength.

Required Thrust-Block Area

Assume that the block is to hold against the horizontal thrust at a 90° bend in a 14-inch pipe. Further assume that the pipeline will be pressure tested at 200 psi. The soil, for this example, is sand.

First, check table 11–1. Find the 14-inch pipe size. Move to the 90° bend column and find 22,650 pounds for each 100 pounds per square inch of water pressure. Since we are working on a total test pressure of 200 pounds, double 22,650, making the total 45,300 pounds.

Next, determine the bearing capacity of sand. Table 11–2 provides bearing load data. If the bear-

Table 11–1 Thrust at fittings in pounds for each 100 psi of water pressure (Adapted with permission from ASAE, 1983–84)

Pipe size (in)	90° bend	45° elbow	Tees & dead ends
1½	415	225	295
2	645	350	455
2½	935	510	660
3	1,395	755	985
4	2,295	1,245	1,620
6	4,950	2,680	3,500
8	8,375	4,540	5,930
10	13,000	7,000	9,150
12	18,200	9,850	12,900
14	22,650	12,260	16,020
16	28,440	15,380	20,110

Table 11–2 Safe soil bearing loads (Adapted with permission from ASAE, 1983–84)

Soil	Safe bearing load (lbs/ft²)
Muck, peat and similar	0
Soft clay	1,000
Medium clay—can be spaded	2,000
Coarse and fine compact sand	3,000
Sand and gravel cemented with clay	4,000
Sound shale	10,000

ing capacity of compact sand is 3,000 pounds per square foot, the total force (45,300 lbs) divided by 3,000 gives the area needed of 15.1 square feet. A bearing area of 4 foot×4 feet (16 sq ft) would be appropriate (see figure 11–2).

DRAINS

In areas where cold winter weather may cause parts of the irrigation system to freeze, it is necessary to drain the water from all parts of the system. It is common practice to connect a large air compressor to the main discharge line near the pump and pump compressed air through the pipelines to allegedly remove the water. This practice will not drain water from pipes.

The preferred procedure is to gravity drain as much of the water from the system as possible. This is done by placing a valve, usually a gate valve, at the lowest elevation on the irrigation system (generally near the pump house). However, this one valve will rarely drain all of the pipe lines. There will be places on the system that have higher pipe on either side of a low spot. There will also be sections of the system that may terminate in a downhill direction away from the pump.

Drains must be located on all low spots so all gravitational water in the irrigation system can drain. After all drains have stopped flowing, water will still be held in small openings by capillarity, especially in sprinklers and valves. This water will never flow from these small crevices and additional energy is needed to dry the system. Therefore, after

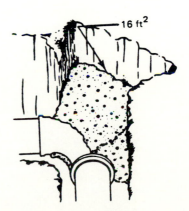

Figure 11–2 Required thrust area

water has stopped flowing from the drains, the drains should be closed. An air compressor should be connected near the pump and air should be forced through all the lines. To dewater all valves and sprinklers, each sprinkler should be turned on just as if irrigation were to occur. As a final safety measure, the sprinklers should be turned on a second time. All drains, except those located such that surface water could enter the empty pipe from the outside, should be opened for the winter.

VENTS

Vents are used to release air trapped in the pipeline during the process of filling the system, usually in the spring. If air is trapped in a line, it may increase the probability of water hammer occurring when the sprinklers are turned on. To prevent breakage of pipe due to trapped air, vents should be placed at the high spots on each pipeline and located so the air can always travel upward along a pipe to a vent. On golf courses, sprinklers are often located on these high spots and can serve as vents. When sprinklers are not located on high spots, a valve should be placed to vent air.

IRRIGATION SCHEDULING

It is possible to use some type of soil moisture meter as an indicator for scheduling irrigation. Moisture meters are being successfully used for this purpose in various applications. However, meters are not practical to use on golf courses.

A survey of methods available to measure soil moisture showed the following main categories as (a) chemical, (b) electrical, (c) gravimetric, (d) lysometers, (e) nuclear, (f) penetrometer, (g) tension, (h) thermal, and (i) miscellaneous. Of these, only the tension method appears to offer a solution to the moisture measurement problem. This method is commercially available and has received fairly wide acceptance.

Tensiometer

Tensiometers work on the principle that a partial vacuum is created in a closed chamber when water moves out through a porous, ceramic tip to the surrounding soil. The tension is measured by a water manometer, a mercury manometer, or a vacuum gauge. In all cases, the purpose is to determine the amount of tension that the soil is able to exert on the water contained in the unit. As the soil dries, it has a greater affinity for the water and draws it from the unit. As the soil water level increases, water flows back into the unit and reduces the vacuum. A tensiometer can only measure a tension of about 0.8 atmospheres.

A tension of about 1.0 atmosphere is generally regarded as the lower limit of water easily available to plants. Therefore, the tensiometer is suited to this range of soil moisture measurement. The vacuum (tension) gauge is generally calibrated in centibars instead of atmospheres. One atmosphere of 14.7 psi is equal to 100 centibars where 0 centibars $= 0$ psi $= 0$ atmosphere (saturation); 100 centibars $= -14.7$ psi $= 1.0$ atmosphere.

The range of the tensiometer is suited to turfgrass irrigation. Areas such as golf courses that would commonly have compacted soil conditions and a reading of 70 to 80 centibars indicates a dry condition.

Automatic control with moisture sensors can be effective if used under the right conditions and in the proper manner. However, in large areas, such as golf courses, where watering conditions may differ not only from fairway to fairway but within the fairway itself, it is difficult to select a typical site to install sensors that are representative of all areas.

Operation

The tensiometer tube is filled with water through the fill cap (see figure 11–3). The ceramic tip is placed in the soil at the desired sensing depth. The moisture level selector is manually positioned at the optimum soil moisture level. As the soil moisture is depleted, water is pulled from the tensiometer through the ceramic tip, creating a vacuum that registers on the indicating needle. When the indicating needle contacts the moisture level selector, a switch

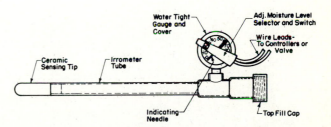

Figure 11–3 Tensiometer

is closed allowing the next scheduled watering cycle to operate.

Installation

A minimum of two tensiometer instruments should be used in conjunction with each controller. However, as many tensiometer locations as necessary can be used in parallel. One tensiometer should be installed with the tip in the feeder-root zone of the plant and the second tensiometer with the tip at a deeper depth, in the tap-root zone of the plant. The tensiometer locations are then wired in parallel to the controller. This allows for shallow sensing to control the application of water according to the daily use of the plant. It also allows deeper tensiometers to control tap-root moisture as the moisture is gradually depleted.

The tensiometer either allows an irrigation cycle to start when the turf is too dry or prevents an irrigation cycle from starting when the turf has sufficient moisture. Therefore, the watering times on each station should be properly adjusted for differences in watering application rates or soil moisture requirements of the sprinklers involved on the controllers.

Type of Grass

Watering practices must also be adjusted to the requirements of the predominating grass on the fairway. Some kinds of grasses will thrive at lower level of available soil moisture than others. The Fescues and Kentucky Bluegrass, for example, can grow on drier soils than the Bentgrasses and do not require as frequent watering.

Further, the cool weather grasses such as the Fescues and Bluegrasses grow slowly during periods of high temperature and cannot be forced into rapid growth by watering. The principle effect of frequent heavy watering of these grasses during hot weather is to stimulate rapid weed development.

IRRIGATION SYSTEM DESIGN

The superintendent must know exactly how the irrigation system is designed, its versatility, its water application rate, its limitations, and so on. The system must be programmed to apply the correct amount of water to meet these needs. For these reasons, it is common practice in the design and sales of automatic irrigation systems to merely provide their customers with a watering tool. The tool is designed to provide a specified number of inches of water or precipitation per week when used as directed.

The superintendent is the soil and turfgrass management expert. Therefore, it is his duty to apply this tool to the fullest advantage. *Nothing can substitute for the operator's experience, common sense, and good judgment in planning a watering schedule.*

INSTALLATION DETAILS

Figures 11–4 through 11–10 provide detailed information on the proper installation and construction of various components of the irrigation system.

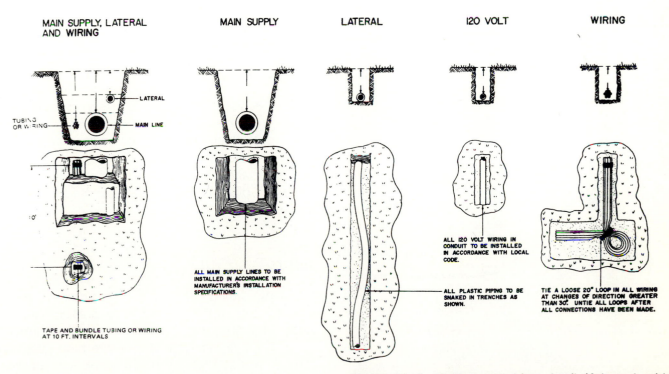

Figure 11–4 Typical trenching detail (Adapted with permission from Rain Bird, 1974)

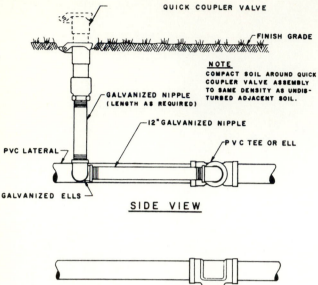

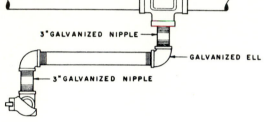

Figure 11-5 Quick-coupler valve detail (Adapted with permission from Rain Bird, 1974)

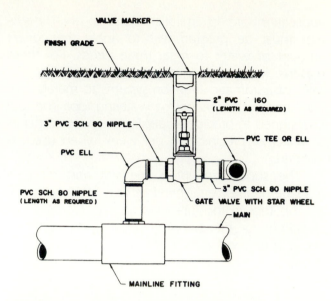

Figure 11-7 Main to lateral detail with gate valve (Adapted with permission from Rain Bird, 1974)

GOLF COURSE IRRIGATION DESIGN EXAMPLE

This example has carried you through most of the steps of an irrigation system design. Only a few details remain.

Thrust Blocks

It is seldom worthwhile to size individual thrust blocks. You should be aware, however, that as the pipes get larger, thrusts at direction changes get larger. Therefore, in typical mineral soils it is usually not necessary to thrust block pipes smaller than 3.5 inches in diameter. Larger lines should be thrust-blocked.

Vents

In the spring when the pipe system is being filled for the summer season, air pockets will develop in high spots of the pipe lines. Normally, there is a sprinkler located near the high spot that can be used as a vent. When a sprinkler is not present on a high spot, a valve should be installed that can be used to vent the air in the pipes.

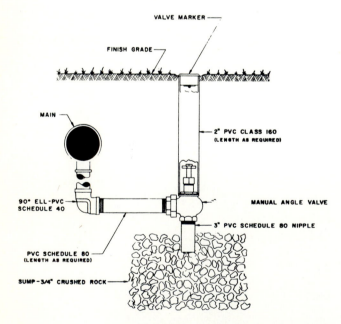

Figure 11-6 Manual drain valve assembly detail (Adapted with permission from Rain Bird, 1974)

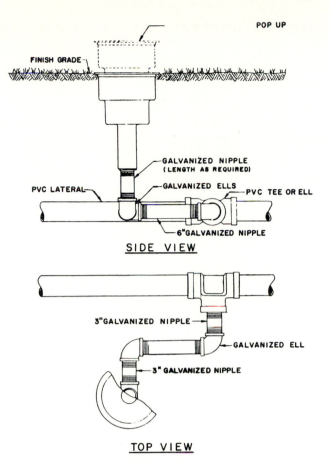

SIDE VIEW

TOP VIEW

Figure 11–8 Swing-joint riser assembly detail (Adapted with permission from Rain Bird, 1974)

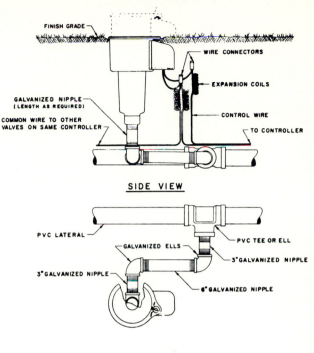

SIDE VIEW

TOP VIEW

Figure 11–9 Electric valve-in-head detail (Adapted with permission from Rain Bird, 1974)

Drains

All pipes of an irrigation system should be drainable by gravity. Therefore, valves must be placed in all low areas to drain the system. After gravity drainage, compressed air can be blown through each sprinkler to remove thin films of water.

PROBLEMS

1. Determine the thrust force caused by the water flowing through a 6-in diameter tee if the line pressure is 100 psi.

2. Determine the thrust force caused by water flowing through a 4-in diameter 45°-elbow if the line pressure is 70 psi. What size impact area is re-

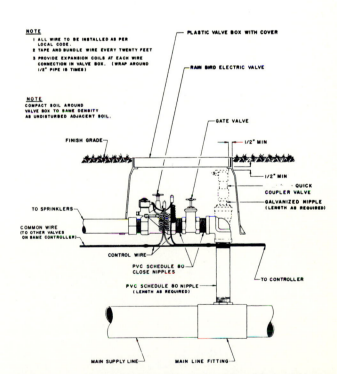

Figure 11–10 Solenoid valve detail (Adapted with permission from Rain Bird, 1974)

quired to counterbalance this thrust force in a soft clay soil?

3. Determine the thrust force caused by water flowing through a 6-in diameter 90°-elbow if the line pressure is 120 psi. What size impact area is required to counterbalance this thrust force in a fine compacted sand soil?

4. Why are vents needed in an irrigation system? When can sprinklers be used as vents? When are sprinklers inappropriate vents?

5. Describe the procedure for draining (for winter) an automatically controlled golf course irrigation system.

6. Why would quick-couplers be needed on an automatic irrigation system?

Part Two
DRAINAGE

Chapter 12
INTRODUCTION

Land drainage has been practiced in some form since man began to till the soil. Records show that as early as 400 BC Egyptians employed drainage principles to improve agricultural production of the Nile Valley. Greek and Roman writers refer to the application of agricultural drainage in those nations during their prime. The development and utilization of drainage practices and principles were described by English and French writers of the 1600s.

Drainage in the United States dates back to the early 1800s. In 1835 the first subsurface drain tile were laid on the farm of "the father of tile drainage," John Johnston, a Scotchman living in Geneva, New York. In 1848, the first subsurface drain tile installation machine was imported from England and, 10 years later, 856 acres of Central Park in New York City were successfully drained. The rec-

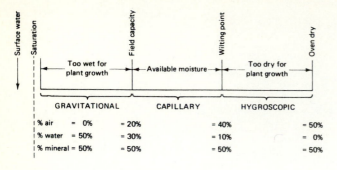

Figure 12–1 Soil-water continuum

reation demands of our ever-increasing population have created the need for larger, more numerous and better quality recreational areas. Removal of excess surface and subsurface water is required to establish and maintain high quality turf.

SOIL-WATER RELATIONSHIPS

A bulk, grab sample of natural topsoil is about 45% mineral and about 5% organic matter. The remaining 50% by volume is water and air in varying proportions. Figure 12–1 is a soil-water continuum representing all of the possible soil moistures. The right end of the continuum represents an oven-dried soil. An oven-dried soil contains no water and all of the pore spaces are filled with air.

The left end of the continuum represents a saturated soil. At saturation, all of the air in the soil has been replaced by water so that 100% of the pores are filled with water. Soil existing at either extreme of the continuum cannot support healthy turf.

Between the extremes of the continuum, any soil moisture can exist, filling all or part of the soil's pore space. Field capacity is that moisture content existing after a soil has been saturated and is left to drain under the influence of gravity for 24 hours. The objective of subsurface drainage is to reduce the moisture content of a soil to field capacity.

NECESSITY FOR DRAINAGE

Capillary moisture is essential to the maintenance of good soil characteristics and healthy turf. Gravitational moisture, and in many cases surface runoff, constitute excess water that is detrimental to the turf. This excess water retards plant growth by producing the following effects:

1. It excludes air from the root zone, preventing a healthy root atmosphere.

2. It provides an environment conducive to water-loving disease organisms such as pythium.

3. It causes anaerobic conditions that may result in reducing soil minerals that are toxic to turfgrass roots.

4. It delays use of the area for recreation activities and management practices.

5. It increases winter killing and frost heaving of turf.

6. It prevents beneficial bacterial activity from converting nitrogen and other plant nutrients to forms that can be easily used by turfgrasses.

7. It results in denitrification and loss of nitrogen needed by the turfgrass.

8. It may result in wet wilt of turfgrasses.

9. It softens soil leading to compaction in high traffic areas and it may cause soft areas where mowers and other vehicles may get stuck.

10. In the case of surface runoff, it erodes fertile soil, carrying nutrients, and in some cases turf, from the site. The loss of soil may take place from an entire surface area or gullies may form, rendering large turfed recreation areas worthless.

Therefore, gravitational water must be removed from the soil if healthy turf growing conditions are to exist. Surface runoff must be removed from all turf areas such that erosion will not occur and water will not be retained in surface depressions. The process of removing gravitational water from within the soil is subsurface drainage. The actual methods that may be employed to accomplish surface and subsurface drainage will be discussed in detail in the following chapters.

BENEFITS OF DRAINAGE

The following sections discuss the benefits of surface and subsurface drainage.

Surface Drainage

Benefits that occur due to the controlled removal of surface water by surface drainage systems are:

1. Erosion control. Soil erosion is influenced by
    a. Rainfall or irrigation intensity.

b. The physical and chemical properties of the soil.
c. Antecedent soil moisture.
d. Vegetative cover on the soil.
e. The slope of the land.
f. The length of the land slope.

In regions where recreation areas are often located on steep slopes and where high-intensity summer rains are common, excess water must be removed under controlled conditions to prevent erosion.

2. Removal of surface water. Excess rain or irrigation water will naturally flow to areas of lower elevation. If these natural depressions contain soils with a high clay content or have a relatively impervious, hard pan layer that restricts vertical water movement, the excess water may remain ponded, causing poor aesthetic conditions as well as destroying turf. Surface drainage structures can prevent these undesirable conditions and can often be located so they will not interfere with the planned recreational use.

Subsurface Drainage

Removal of gravitational water from the soil profile provides many benefits. These benefits are often inconspicuous because they occur within the soil and the root zone of the turf. They are often more important, however, to turf production than those occurring due to surface drainage. The benefits of subsurface drainage include:

1. Improved trafficability. When a soil becomes very wet (especially as it approaches saturation) it becomes liquid and loses its ability to support weight. This is evidenced by soil not being able to support vehicles or people. The removal of gravitational water helps the soil retain the strength properties and structure required on recreation areas.

2. Timeliness of maintenance operations. This benefit is closely related to benefit 1. The emphasis here is on timing. Subsurface drainage systems start removing gravitational water as soon as the moisture content exceeds field capacity. This means that

reclamation, mowing, and use can be started earlier in the spring because the soil has been drained and can support equipment and people. Continued removal of excessive soil water during the recreation season permits extended, more intensive use, resulting in increased revenue.

3. Helps the soil warm earlier in the spring. Water requires about five times as much heat as dry soil to produce the same temperature change. Therefore, a turf area that has less soil moisture will warm faster in the spring than a poorly drained area. This permits earlier turf growth and winter recovery.

4. Provides increased aeration in the root zone. Air is necessary in the root zone for healthy turf growth. Removal of gravitational water from the root zone by subsurface drainage will permit increased circulation of air and soil gases.

5. Deepens the root zone. Figure 12–2 shows the progression of root development during the spring and summer seasons under conditions of drained and undrained land. Note that for turf grown in undrained land, root development is restricted during the spring because the gravitational water level (often called the water table) is near the soil surface. When the water table drops during the summer, increasing the available root zone, the poorly developed root system can not use the additional soil volume. On the other hand, for drained land, the root system is encouraged to develop to much greater depths during the fall and spring because the subsurface drain has lowered the water table. When the water table returns to its natural summer lower level, the turf can extract water and plant nutrients from a much larger soil volume. The mechanical action of the deep penetrating roots breaks up the subsoil and encourages development of soil structure. This increased root development also provides improved drought resistances during periods of inadequate soil moisture.

6. Increases the supply of available plant food. Subsurface drainage provides two mechanisms by which the supply of plant food is augmented. The first was discussed in benefit 5. The second is caused by the increased presence of air in the root zone. Many plant nutrients must change in their

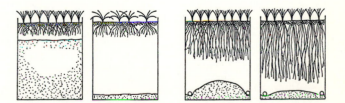

Figure 12–2 Interaction between root development and subsurface drainage

chemical form during the period between when they are applied to the soil until they become available to the plants. One example is nitrogen. Much of the nitrogen applied to the soil as fertilizer must be acted upon by aerobic bacteria that require air, specifically oxygen, to break down the nitrogen from its original state to nitrate-nitrogen, which is the form best used by the turf.

7. Decreases the damage due to freezing. Soil with little or no gravitational water does not freeze easily because of the lack of water to freeze and the insulation effect of the air in the soil. Frost heaving is the result of soil water expanding as it freezes. Drained soils have less water to freeze and frost heaving is less of a problem.

8. Removed toxic salts. In arid, irrigated areas where salts often build up in the soil due to the evaporation of irrigation water, excess irrigation water removed from the soil as gravitational water through subsurface drain lines transport these dissolved salts from the soil-water system. Fertilizers, herbicides, and so on may also be removed with gravitational water.

9. Increased water retention and decreased runoff. A subsurface drainage system will keep soil at least as dry as field capacity most of the growing season. This provides a natural reservoir in the soil. When fields are drained, a larger percentage of rain water enters the soil where it can be stored and used by plants, reducing runoff and erosion.

Proper drainage converts a cold, damp soil into a warm, easily managed soil. It usually helps the soil retain fertilizers and rain water, thereby helping to put the soil into the necessary physical condition for producing maximum quality turf. It has been demonstrated that the increased quality and use of turfgrasses derived from drainage will pay for the cost of drainage.

PROBLEMS

1. Why is the need for adequate drainage (especially subsurface drainage) often increased when an irrigation system is added to a golf course?

2. Explain or show the effect of good subsurface drainage on root system development. What is the effect of irrigation on root system depth?

3. Sketch the soil-water continuum. Show what water is removed by surface and subsurface drainage what water is needed for crop growth.

4. What are the benefits of surface drainage?

5. What are the benefits of subsurface drainage?

Chapter 13

SLOPES, GRADES, AND ELEVATIONS

Before studying soil drainage, it is essential to understand the fundamentals of determining and establishing slopes, grades, and elevations.

SLOPES

Few areas on the earth's surface are horizontal or level planes. In most situations this can be seen by the eye. However, the eye is often not a reliable guide to the direction of fall and gives no information about the magnitude of the fall.

The deviation from a horizontal plane is called slope. This may be expressed in several ways, but it

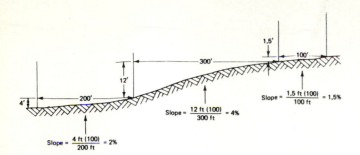

1.5'

300'

100'

12'

$$Slope = \frac{1.5 \text{ ft} (100)}{100 \text{ ft}} = 1.5\%$$

200'

4'

$$Slope = \frac{12 \text{ ft} (100)}{300 \text{ ft}} = 4\%$$

$$Slope = \frac{4 \text{ ft} (100)}{200 \text{ ft}} = 2\%$$

Figure 13–1 Determining slope from elevation difference and distance

always indicates the vertical rise or fall that occurs for a given horizontal distance. It may be expressed as feet per foot, feet per hundred feet, meters per hundred meters, and so on. It is commonly expressed as feet of vertical rise or fall per 100 feet of horizontal distance, which is referred to as percent slope. Mathematically, percent slope can be determined by multiplying the feet of vertical rise or fall by 100 and dividing by the horizontal distance in feet. This is illustrated in figure 13–1.

GRADES

When slopes are referred to in connection with drainage, they are usually called grades, a term normally applied to a single line or direction rather than an area or surface. For instance, we speak of the grade of a drain line or the grade of the bottom of a diversion.

Almost all drainage-related structures are constructed to some planned grade and located at some desired elevation. Subsurface drains and drainage channels must be constructed at planned grades so the water will flow in the direction desired and at velocities that will not cause erosion.

ELEVATIONS

The elevation of a point on the earth's surface is the vertical distance between that point and some accepted datum plane. In topographical work, mean sea level is commonly used as this datum plane, (e.g., the mountain is 2,200 feet above mean sea level). When drainage structures are considered, the absolute elevation is not important and an assumed elevation, commonly 100.0 feet, is used as a starting elevation. This starting point is called a bench mark. The bench mark can be any permanent, accessible point, such as a mark on the foundation of a building, a large stone, the corner of a wall, a culvert, a bridge, or even a wooden stake if the work is to be completed in a few days. The bench mark should not be disturbed during construction.

LEVELING

Elevations are determined with leveling instruments that establish level planes. These level planes are used as references from which the desired elevations are determined. Many types of leveling instruments have been improvised and developed. Leveling can be done using a simple carpenter's level or line level if the slope of the line is not critical. As the desire for precision increases, more sophisticated equipment is required to produce the desired results. A hand level or abney level will give accurate results as long as the line of sight does not exceed 100 feet. Larger projects will require the use of a tripod level.

Line Level

A line level is a small level bubble enclosed in a metal case, which can be hooked over a taut string. With the string tied to a stake or held to the ground at one point and adjusted until it is level, the difference in elevation between the string and the ground can be measured with a rule as shown in figure 13–2. The line level must be placed near the center of the string so any sag in the string will not cause false readings. This method is suitable for distances up to 50 feet where great precision is not required.

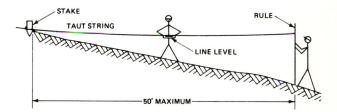

Figure 13–2 Measuring elevation difference with a line level

Carpenter's Level

A carpenter's level can be supported on a flat surface, adjusted to level, and used to determine elevation differences. Sights are provided on some makes, but, if not, they may be readily improvised as illustrated in figure 13–3. Be sure the top of both sights are centered and exactly the same distance from the bottom of the level. Line and carpenter's levels are suitable for rough slope measurements.

Hand Level

The hand level is a telescope with cross-hairs and a level bubble. It is ordinarily hand held, as

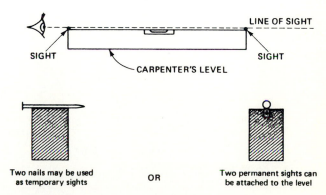

Figure 13–3 Measuring elevation difference with a carpenter's level

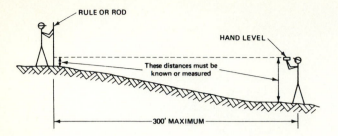

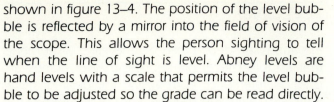

Figure 13–4 Measuring elevation difference with a hand level

shown in figure 13–4. The position of the level bubble is reflected by a mirror into the field of vision of the scope. This allows the person sighting to tell when the line of sight is level. Abney levels are hand levels with a scale that permits the level bubble to be adjusted so the grade can be read directly.

The hand level is used by resting the level on a four- or five-foot long stake. If a uniform grade is to be laid out, a 100-foot horizontal distance is measured, and the hand level sighted to the top of a second stake that is equal in length to the height of the first stake plus the vertical fall due to the grade.

Tripod Levels

Tripod levels are composed of a telescope, containing a horizontal cross-hair, and a frame that can be adjusted so the telescope tube will remain level in all directions. The frame and telescope are mounted on a tripod, which holds the instrument steady and level. These instruments vary in cost from $100 for a farm level to $800 or more for an engineer's level. The cost, of course, depends on the refinements, accessories, and precision of the instrument.

The most inexpensive type of tripod level, the farm level, is adequate for most turf drainage work. Contractor's levels and engineer's levels are excellent and provide lines of sight up to 500 feet in length. A tripod level is always used in conjunction with a leveling rod. The latter is used to measure the distance from the line of sight to the bottom of the rod located on the ground.

To find the difference in elevation between two points with a tripod level, set the instrument about half way between the two points and adjust the level so the bubble is centered regardless of horizontal direction sighted (see figure 13–5). Hold the rod vertically with the zero-end of the rod at the bottom, on point A. Sight at the rod through the level telescope and read the rod at the horizontal cross-hair location (0.4 feet). Then hold the rod on point B, sight at the rod, and read the rod (2.5 feet). The values read with the rod located on points A and B are the vertical distances from the bottom of the rod to the horizontal plane of the telescope. If

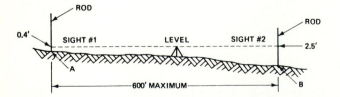

Figure 13–5 Determining elevation difference with a tripod level

the elevation of point A is 100.0 feet, the elevation of the line-of-sight through the level is 100.4 feet. The elevation of point B is, therefore, 2.5 feet below the line-of-sight, or 97.9 feet. If the two rod readings are subtracted, the result is the difference in elevation between points A and B, or 2.1 feet.

If the two points of interest are so far apart that it is difficult to read the rod (about 500 feet for a farm level, about 600 feet for a contractor's level, and about 1,000 feet for an engineer's level), or if there are trees or other obstructions between the two points, the level must be relocated several times as shown in figure 13–6. (Rod readings are shown at each rod location.)

To determine the elevation of point #2 relative to point #1, the elevation of each intermediate turning point (TP) must first be determined. First, assume the elevation of point #1 to be 100.0 feet. The elevation of the initial line-of-sight is 2.0 feet above the known point #1, or 102.0 feet. TP #1 is 6.5 feet below the line-of-sight and has an elevation of 95.5 feet. The tripod level is then moved from its initial location to a location where the rod, still located on TP 1, can be seen when the level is properly adjusted and ready to use.

In the example, this relocation of the level placed the instrument such that the new line-of-sight was 3.2 feet above TP 1. Adding 3.2 feet to the elevation of TP 1 (just determined to be 95.5 feet) yields a new elevation of the line-of-sight, 98.7 feet. This procedure can be repeated as often as required until the rod can be seen when placed on the point-of-interest, here point #2. If this example is continued, we find the elevation of TP #2 to be 93.2 feet, the elevation of TP 3 to be 90.3 feet, and the elevation of point #2 to be 85.6 feet. The difference in elevation between point #1 and point #2 is, therefore, 14.4 feet.

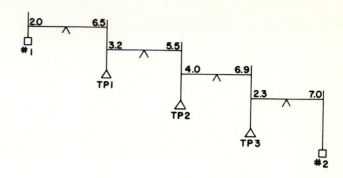

Figure 13–6 Determining elevation difference using turning points

PROBLEMS

1. Define slope.

2. If two points are 200 feet apart horizontally and 10 feet apart vertically, what is the slope in percent of a line between these points?

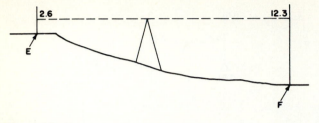

Figure 13–7

3. A drain line has a grade of 3%. If two points of interest along the drain are 400 feet apart, what is the elevation difference between the two points?

4. A par three (200 yd) hole has a drain line along the rough that drains the tee and green. If the elevation difference between tee and green is 25 feet, what is the slope of this fairway?

5. Determine the elevation difference between points E and F in figure 13–7.

Chapter 14
SURFACE DRAINAGE

Surface drainage has been defined as the controlled removal of surface runoff resulting from precipitation, irrigation, spring thaws, or hillside seeps. This excess water flowing over the surface is the primary cause of soil erosion. Excess surface water will accumulate in surface depressions. If these surface depressions are underlaid by low-permeability soils, the excess surface water may remain in these areas for long periods. These poorly drained areas will be slow to recover in the spring and difficult to mow and manage due to poor trafficability throughout the season. In more severe cases where water remains ponded for more than a day, turf will not survive, creating areas that cannot be used and are not aesthetic.

There are two basic philosophies that can be used to alleviate surface drainage problems. In cases where water naturally flows to depression areas, the water can be diverted from the depressions through surface drainage channels lined with turf to natural outlets before it reaches the depression. If surface runoff cannot be diverted before it reaches the depressions, it will be necessary to provide a path through which the surface runoff can safely flow from the depression. As previously mentioned, natural seepage and evaporation are generally too slow and not recommended. Surface water can also be removed by encouraging vertical percolation through the soil. This method is commonly used on golf course greens where the natural soil medium is radically modified to provide rapid drainage. It may be necessary to construct a drainage channel to provide a gravity flow path where surface water can flow to a natural outlet. In areas of extremely flat terrain, it may become necessary to channel surface water to a subsurface sump where it can be pumped to an outlet. Many types of surface drainage structures and techniques are commonly used in the turf industry. These practices will be discussed after the rainfall-runoff process, which supplies the surface drainage water, is examined in the next section.

RAINFALL-RUNOFF

The process that creates runoff from any land surface is very complex. The runoff process is usually stimulated by precipitation, but may be caused by warming temperatures if water is frozen on a watershed in the form of ice or snow. Water falling as precipitation encounters the vegetation and does not contribute to the useful water needed for plant and animal agriculture. Most of this water evaporates back to the atmosphere after the storm. Water, which does reach the soil surface, will either infiltrate into the soil, be stored on the soil surface and infiltrated at a later time, or flow over the land surface to an adjacent site where it is again exposed to the total complement of possible destinations. The purpose of this section is to develop an understanding of the factors that influence the runoff process and to learn to estimate the peak rates of runoff to be expected from small, specific watersheds.

Time of Concentration

A watershed's time of concentration is defined as the duration of rainfall required before all areas of the watershed are contributing runoff at the outlet location. One of the more popular and easy-to-use models for approximating a watershed's time of concentration is given by Kirpich (1940) as

$$t_c = 0.0078 \, L^{0.77} S^{-0.385}$$

where L is the length of the watershed from the outlet to the most remote or highest point and S is the slope of the watershed between the most remote or highest point and the outlet in feet/foot. The solution to this equation has been summarized in table 14–1. Where flow occurs in defined channels with known velocities, the travel time for these reaches should be based on the flow velocity.

Rainfall Intensity

As long as precipitation continues, it is easy to envision how larger and larger portions of a watershed will contribute runoff water to the outlet. If it continues to rain longer than the watershed's t_c, the rate of runoff will continue at the rate that occurred at t_c. For this reason, one of the assumptions required to estimate runoff rates is that rainfall duration be set equal to t_c. This is done because from

Table 14–1   Time of concentration for small watersheds

Maximum length of flow (ft)	t_c (min) (S = %)								
	0.1	0.5	1.0	2.0	4.0	7.0	10.0	15.0	20.0
100	4	2	2	1	1	1	1	1	0.5
300	9	5	4	3	2	2	2	1	1
500	13	7	6	4	3	3	2	2	2
1,000	23	11	9	7	6	4	4	3	3
2,000	39	20	16	12	9	8	7	6	5
4,000	66	33	27	21	16	13	11	10	9
6,000	91	46	37	29	22	18	15	13	12
8,000	114	57	47	36	27	22	19	16	15
10,000	134	67	55	42	32	26	23	20	17
20,000	234	117	94	72	55	45	39	33	30
40,000	390	210	161	123	94	76	66	57	51

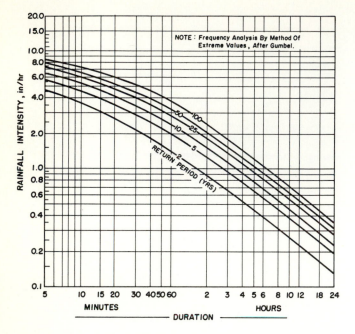

Figure 14–1   Rainfall intensity-duration data for St. Louis, Mo. (Redrawn with permission from U.S. Weather Bureau, 1955)

a historical record perspective we know that short-duration storms tend to have higher intensities and longer storms have lower intensities (see figure 14–1). Since it can be reasoned that intensity directly influences the runoff rate, the higher intensities will produce the larger runoff events. It can also be seen from figure 14–1 that rainfall intensity in St. Louis is related to return period. Return period is the design period. For example, if you want to build a structure that is to last 10 years, the structure should be designed based on the largest intensity expected in a 10-year period or a 10-year return period. Design rainfall intensity is not constant across the entire United States. Therefore, it is necessary to adjust the St. Louis intensities given in figure 14–1 by multiplying them times the geographic location factor given in figure 14–2.

Example   Determine the 25-year design rainfall intensity for a watershed in northern New York State that has a maximum flow length of 2,000 feet and an average slope of 2.0%.

Solution   The time of concentration (t_c) is obtained from table 14–1 as $t_c = f(L = 2,000$ ft, $S = 2.0\%) = 12$ minutes. Since the duration of the design storm is assumed to be equal to t_c, the design duration is 12 minutes. Figure 14–1 shows the design rainfall intensity in St. Louis (i_{SL}) = f(duration = 12 min, return period = 25 yr.) = 5.8 in/hr. The design intensity in northern New York state is determined by multiplying i_{SL} times the location factor R from figure 14–2, or

$$i_{NY} = i_{SL}R$$
$$= (5.8 \text{ in/hr})(0.6)$$
$$i_{NY} = 3.5 \text{ in/hr}$$

Influence of Soil, Vegetation, and Slope

Integrating the influence of the various soils, soil covers, and slopes into a runoff prediction model can be approached in many ways. One should realize that more permeable soils such as sands will infiltrate water more rapidly than heavier soils such as clays. Therefore, watersheds containing sandy soils will produce less severe runoff events based on the same rainfall as watersheds with loams or clays.

Figure 14–2   Rainfall intensity location factor (Redrawn with permission from Hamilton and Jepson, 1940)

Table 14–2   Runoff coefficients for agricultural areas

Topography and vegetation	Soil texture		
	Open sandy loam	Clay and silt loam	Tight clay
Woodland			
Flat 0–5% slope	0.10	0.30	0.40
Rolling 5–10% slope	0.25	0.35	0.50
Hilly 10–30% slope	0.30	0.50	0.60
Pasture			
Flat	0.10	0.30	0.40
Rolling	0.16	0.36	0.55
Hilly	0.22	0.42	0.60
Cultivated			
Flat	0.30	0.50	0.60
Rolling	0.40	0.60	0.70
Hilly	0.52	0.72	0.82

Note: Taken with permission from Schwab et al., 1971.

The influence of vegetation is twofold. One, the denser and larger the vegetative cover, the more rain will be intercepted and not reach the soil surface. Two, the presence of deep-rooted vegetation tends to improve soil structure, which increases infiltration.

The interaction of slope, land use, and soil type on runoff is summarized in tables 14–2 and 14–3. The runoff coefficient (C) is defined as the ratio of the peak runoff rate to the rainfall intensity. From a practical standpoint, C can be viewed as the percentage of rain that becomes runoff and therefore varies from 0.0 to 1.0 (as a decimal), where 0.0 indicated no runoff regardless of the intensity or duration and 1.0 indicates 100% runoff such as would be expected from a roof or parking lot.

Since most watersheds consist of more than one soil with multiple land uses and slopes, it is necessary to average the effect of each of the various areas. This is done by applying a weighted average over the entire watershed in the following form:

$$C = \frac{A_1 C_1 + A_2 C_2 + A_3 C_3 + \ldots A_n C_n}{A_1 + A_2 + A_3 + \ldots A_n} = \frac{\Sigma AC}{\Sigma A}$$

This formula, where C_i = runoff coefficient for area A_i, can be applied in a tabular form as shown in the following example.

Example Determine the runoff coefficient for a 30-acre watershed made up of the following land uses:

1. 15 acres of playground on 7% sloping silt loam soil.

2. 10 acres of park on 3% sloping sandy loam soil.

3. 5 acres of woodland on 15% sloping clay soil.

This problem can be solved by completing the following table:

Part	Area (A)	×	C	=	CA
1	15		0.28		4.2
2	10		0.18		1.8
3	5		0.60		3.0
	$\Sigma A = 30Ac$				$\Sigma CA = 9.0$

$$\text{or } C = \frac{\Sigma CA}{\Sigma A} = \frac{9.0}{30} = \frac{0.30}{-}$$

Table 14–3 Runoff coefficients for urban areas

Type of drainage area	C
Business	
Downtown areas	0.83
Neighborhood areas	0.60
Residential	
Single-family areas	0.40
Multiunits, detached	0.50
Multiunits, attached	0.68
Suburban	0.33
Apartment dwelling areas	0.60
Industrial	
Light areas	0.65
Heavy areas	0.75
Parks, cemeteries	0.18
Playgrounds	0.28
Railroad yard areas	0.30
Unimproved areas	0.20
Streets	0.83
Brick	
Drives and walks	0.80
Roofs	0.85
100% impervious surface	1.00

Note: Taken with permission from Chow, 1962

The CA column is obtained by multiplying the area column times the C column as shown for part 1 as $15 \times 0.28 = 4.2$.

Rational Formula

The many factors that influence the peak runoff rate have been combined into the rational formula:

$$Q = CiA$$

where Q is the peak runoff rate in cfs expected once in the design period (return period), C is the runoff coefficient, i is the design rainfall intensity in inches per hour adjusted for geographic location, and A is the watershed area in acres. Each of the factors has been discussed and can be applied to obtain the peak runoff rate. The units in the rational formula are correct as follows:

$$\frac{ft^3}{sec} = None \times \frac{in}{hr} \times Ac \times \frac{hr}{3,600 \ sec} \times \frac{43,560 \ ft^2}{Ac} \times \frac{ft}{12 \ in}$$

The unit conversions for Ac-in/hr to ft³/sec (cfs) equal approximately 1.0.

Example Determine the peak runoff rate expected once every 25 years for a 15-acre watershed in central Georgia. The highest elevation on the watershed is 1,050 feet and the outlet elevation is 1,000 feet. The length of flow is 1,000 feet. The watershed has the following land uses:

1. 5 acres; tight clay forest; 20% slope

2. 5 acres; sandy loam golf course; 2% slope

3. 5 acres; club house

Solution To solve this problem, first determine the slope and length that can be used to obtain the t_c.

$$S = \frac{\Delta Elev}{L} = \frac{1,050 - 1,000}{1,000} = 0.05 \ ft/ft = 5\%$$
$$t_c = f(L,S) = \underline{5 \ min}$$

Assuming the duration (D) equals t_c, then the intensity in Georgia, from figure 14–1, for a 25-year storm is

$$i_{SL} = f(D,T) = 7.2 \ in/hr.$$
$$i_G = i_{SL} \ R = (7.2 \ in/hr.) \ (1.2) = 8.6 \ in/hr$$

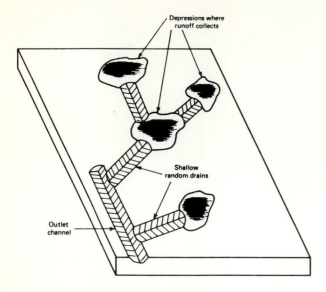

Figure 14–3   Random drain system

The runoff coefficient is computed as follows:

Part	A	×	C	=	CA
1	5		0.60		3.0
2	5		0.28		1.4
3	5		1.00		5.0
	15				9.4

$$\text{or } C = \frac{9.4}{15} = 0.63$$

The peak runoff rate will be

$$Q = CiA$$
$$Q = (0.63)\ (8.6\ \text{in/hr})\ (15\ \text{Ac})$$
$$\underline{Q = 81\ \text{cfs}}$$

RANDOM DRAINS

When depressions are scattered in an area and it is not desirable or possible to remove the depressions, random drains should be considered as a method of surface drainage. Random drains are channels that are excavated between depressions and the outlet, as illustrated in figure 14–3. The depth of cut for these drains is usually limited to three feet and the length should be kept short.

To prevent interference with recreation activities, triangular-shaped channels (see figure 14–4) are used with side slopes as flat as 10:1 (horizontal:vertical). The drainage channels should be maintained in turf and there is no reason to remove these areas from use except during a runoff event. The grade of the bottom of the channel in the direction of flow should follow the natural lay of the land. Random drains will not normally be used on recreation areas but may be useful on golf courses. On golf course fairways, short channels could carry water from a depression to the rough areas where an established outlet channel may or may not be required. Generally, the slope of a drainage channel should not exceed 2% slope.

Design Considerations

The grade of a random drain is determined by the elevation difference and distance between the

(a) TRAPEZOIDAL

(b) TRIANGULAR

Figure 14–4   Channel cross-sectional

point where the water enters the channel and the discharge point. Since the objective is to drain a surface depression, the drain elevation at the depression must be at least as deep or slightly deeper than the depression. The discharge point should be above the normal water level where the drain enters a stream or other natural water course.

In the example shown in figure 14–5, a depression collects water during rainfall events. The lowest point of the depression is marked as 0+00 on the plan view. It is desired to provide a drain so that water will be free to flow by gravity from the depression to the stream channel about 350 feet away. The first step in the layout and design is to select a logical location for the drain. The centerline location chosen is shown on the map. If the centerline had been selected a few feet to the south, the depth of cut would have been slightly smaller, but the drain would have been longer.

After the location has been selected, a survey of the lay-of-the-land from the start of the drain to the outlet should be obtained. One of the leveling techniques discussed in chapter 13 will provide the elevation at each desired point along the line. Fifty to 100 feet is usually selected as the distance between points-of-survey along the centerline, where elevations will be determined relative to a local benchmark.

After the elevation at each point-of-survey is determined, these elevations should be plotted as shown in figure 14–6 (Note: it is not necessary to determine sufficient information from the survey to produce a complete topographic map as shown in figure 14–5. However, if a good topographic map exists, it may be possible to read elevations along the centerline instead of running a survey.) The plotted profile should show the lay-of-the-land from the depression's lowest elevation to the outlet channel or stream.

It is now possible to select a drain elevation at the depression, which in the example was selected to coincide with the elevation of the depression bottom, 41.6 feet. The discharge end of the drain must be located above the stream's normal water level and in this example it could be even higher. In the example the drain coincides with the existing ground elevation at station 3+00, 39.6 feet. This is equivalent to a 2-foot drop from 0+00 to 3+00, or a 0.67% slope. The elevation of the existing ground

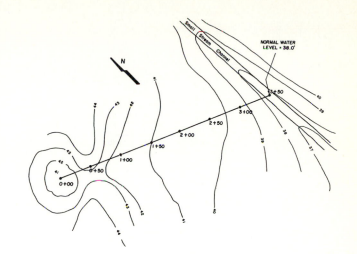

Figure 14–5 Depression example

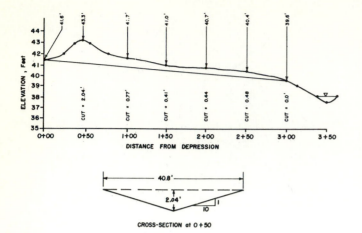

Figure 14–6   Finished cross-section

can be determined from the plotted profile as shown in figure 14–6. The cut required at the drain centerline to establish the 0.67% slope is also shown.

The only remaining requirement is to select the side slope. Since the drain should fit into the existing terrain as well as possible, a 10:1 side slope will be used. The finished cross-section at the 0 + 50 station is shown in figure 14–6. The drain will be the widest at the maximum cut. For instance, at station 2 + 00, the drain will be 0.44 feet deep and 8.80 feet wide at the top. This drain could be maintained in the same grasses as the surrounding areas.

Outlet Channels

Outlet channels are used to carry water collected in random drainage systems and diversions (to be discussed later) to natural discharge points. They may also be used as discharge points for subsurface drainage systems. This type of channel often has a subsurface drain laid in its bottom to remove low flows and to help maintain the turf in the channel. In some cases, it is desirable to line an outlet channel with nonerosive materials such as riprap, asphalt, or concrete, but this is seldom required in small drainage areas. In large channels or curved channels, it may be necessary to protect the banks with riprap, concrete, asphalt, masonry walls, gabions, or inflatable concrete blankets (see figure 14–7).

Outlet channels may have a trapezoidal or a triangular shape as shown in figure 14–4 or may be a natural swale with a good vegetative cover. In the case of a trapezoidally shaped channel, the bottom width is usually determined by the width of the equipment that will be used for construction and maintenance and varies from two to eight feet. As a general rule, channel side slopes steeper than 1:1 should never be used on channels unless the soil is very stable or banks are stabilized. On light, sandy soils, the channel side slopes should not be steeper than 3:1.

Outlet channels are usually designed with sufficient capacity to carry the maximum discharge ex-

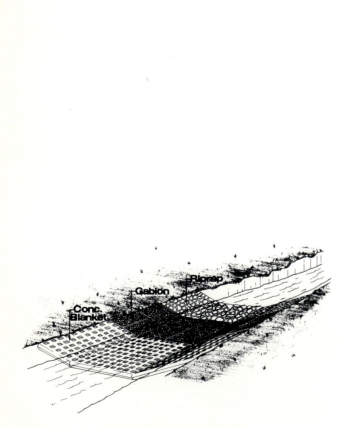

Figure 14–7   Outlet channel protections

pected in a 10-year period. This peak discharge must be removed at a velocity that will not cause erosion in the channel or from its banks. Sedimentation in the channel can be prevented by keeping the velocity above two feet per second. Velocities as great as six feet per second will not erode a channel lined with dense turf.

The velocity and flow rate in outlet channels depend upon all the previously discussed design variables: channel cross-sectional shape and area, grade, and roughness of the channel lining. Because of the complexity involved in designing an outlet channel, the design should be done by an engineer. For small systems, the nomograph in figure 14–8 can be used. This nomograph is developed from Manning's equation and assumes a trapezoidal cross-section with 4:1 side slopes, a design velocity of 3 fps, and a Manning roughness coefficient of 0.04. The nomograph yields bottom width and total depth, where the total depth includes 0.3 feet of freeboard. The required input data are design discharge in cfs, and slope in the direction of flow in ft/ft.

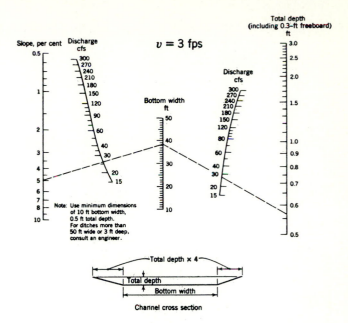

Figure 14–8 *Nomograph for trapezoidal cross-sections with a velocity of 3 fps (Taken with permission from Schwab et al., 1971)*

SOIL MODIFICATION

There are situations, especially on large recreation areas and golf course greens, where it is not convenient or desirable to alter the shape of the land surface to achieve surface drainage. In the case of greens, the surface contour, shape, and location are chosen to provide challenging golf, and the removal of surface water, either from excess irrigation or rain, is secondary. If surface water cannot be made to flow downslope, off the surface, the only realistic alternative is to modify the soil so that water can rapidly percolate downward through the soil profile. This usually means removing the natural soil to a depth of a foot or two and replacing it with a mixture of sand, soil, and peat. The natural soil and peat are used to provide a medium that can retain some available water and plant nutrients and sustain plant growth. The sand is used to provide a solid base that will not change with time, to resist compaction, and to provide a porous medium that will permit the rapid natural vertical percolation of surface water.

Soil modification is an appropriate method of surface drainage. However, any time water is quickly moved underground, an outlet must be provided for its removal from the soil medium. Soil modification as a surface drainage method must, therefore, be accompanied by a well-designed and properly installed subsurface drainage system that will remove the water entering the soil profile. Subsurface drainage systems will be discussed in chapter 15.

TERRACES

The primary purpose of terracing in a drainage context is to move surface runoff water from sloping areas to an outlet channel without causing erosion. Terracing, as a means of controlled drainage, has been practiced since the beginning of agriculture. Because terraces have been used for a long time, and since there are many types of terraces, there is often confusion as to what constitutes a well-designed terrace. To be certain we are all thinking of the same structure, a brief discussion of the various types of terraces will follow. Bench terraces and tile outlet terraces are the two types of terraces that have been used in turf drainage.

Bench Terraces

Bench terraces are used to divide very steep hillsides into a number of level or nearly level strips or benches constructed on the contour around a hill. These benches are separated by nearly vertical walls of rock or heavily vegetated banks.

The usefulness of bench terraces is limited by high construction costs, exposure of subsoil, and their being too small for the efficient use of large maintenance equipment. There are situations, however, especially around commercial buildings or homes, where bench terraces can be used to reduce erosion and create an aesthetically appealing landscaped area.

Tile Outlet Terraces

A tile outlet terrace collects runoff water behind an embankment located on the contour around a hillside. The water is impounded and channeled toward the deepest locations long the terrace, usually near the center. A riser pipe located in the deepest part of the terrace is connected to a subsurface drain line that is the only method of removing water from the terrace. These terraces provide flood peak reduction, erosion control, and surface water management. The subsurface drains are usually designed to discharge any water collected in the terrace within a 12-hour period. Normally, the entire terrace is maintained in grass. These terraces provide a safe method of surface drainage and, if located and designed with care, can provide interesting hazards on golf course fairways.

DIVERSIONS

In areas characterized by short, irregular slopes, such as found in many eastern turf areas, diversions are frequently placed to divert water away from a specific area such as neighboring fields or adjacent turf or landscaped area. Diversions often carry large quantities of surface runoff and are shaped as shown in figure 14–9. The entire structure, including channel, ridge, and back slope, as well as a 20-foot strip above the channel, should be maintained in turf to prevent erosion of the ridge and scouring of the channel. The grass lining permits channel grades of up to 2%, which helps increase the water carrying capacity. Diversions can be sized by using figure 14–8.

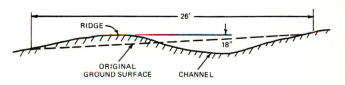

Figure 14–9 Cross-sectional view of a typical diversion

PROBLEMS

1. Determine the time of concentration for a watershed having a high elevation of 987 feet and an outlet elevation of 915 feet if its length is 1,200 feet.

2. Determine the design rainfall intensity to be expected for watersheds having the following times of concentrations:

    a. $t_c = 30$ min; 10-year return period in St. Louis, Mo.

b. $t_c = 10$ min; 10-year return period in State College, Pa.

c. $t_c = 5$ min; 5-year return period in southern Ohio.

d. $t_c = 2$ min; 2-year return period in western Wisconsin.

3. If a watershed has the following land uses, what is the runoff coefficient?

a. 5 acres; 4%; cultivated silt loam
b. 10 acres; 2%; playground
c. 5 acres; 8%; apartment area
d. 5 acres; 1%; parking lot

4. What is the peak runoff rate expected once every 10 years from a 2,000-foot-long watershed having a high elevation of 1,521 feet and a low elevation of 1,421 feet? The watershed is located near State College, Pa., and the land uses follow:

a. 15 acres; pasture; 8%; tight clay
b. 25 acres; cultivated; 3%; silt loam
c. 10 acres; woodland; 25%; sandy loam

5. For the surface drainage system shown in figures 14–5 and 14–6, determine the depth of cut at each 50-foot station if the ditch has a grade of 0.8%. Assume the ditch has an elevation of 41.5 feet at station 0 + 00.

6. A trapezoidal outlet channel is to carry 30 cfs down a 2% slope. Use the nomograph in figure 14–8 to size the channel. What will the velocity be?

7. A diversion diverts the water from a watershed have a peak runoff rate of 20 cfs. If the diversion has a 2% slope, what size trapezoidal channel is needed in the diversion?

8. Describe the purpose of a diversion.

Chapter 15

SUBSURFACE DRAINAGE

INTRODUCTION

Subsurface drainage has previously been defined as the removal of gravitational water from the soil. At times, especially when discussing drainage of turf areas, the distinction between surface and subsurface drainage is not clear. For instance, on a golf green a modified soil is used to encourage the removal of surface water, but this surface drainage technique immediately creates a situation where the surface water, now underground, must be removed by subsurface drainage. Other examples also exist where turf is drained by moving surface water into gravel-filled trenches, creating a subsurface drainage problem that is greater than the original surface drainage problem. This chapter will attempt to discuss the various types of subsurface drainage, their design, and proper installation.

TYPES OF DRAINAGE SYSTEMS

Subsurface drainage systems are classified by the arrangement of the drains in the field. The slope and terrain of the area also affect the type of system to be used.

Random Drains

The random system is illustrated in figure 15–1a. This system is used to drain several locations in an otherwise well-drained area. These wet areas may be springs, surface depressions, greens, and so on.

Springs may be drained most effectively by running the drain line directly to the place where water is intercepted 1.5 to 2.5 feet below the soil surface. The drain line should be installed for a distance of 5 to 10 feet beyond the spring outlet and covered with about a foot of gravel.

A surface depression may be drained by subsurface drainage if the drain line can be installed at least a foot below the lowest point in the surface depression and not excessively deep in the higher land through which the drain has to pass to reach an outlet. A permeable backfill, such as gravel, should be placed over the section of the drain in the depression to aid in rapid removal of water. Surface water, wherever possible, should be diverted using surface drainage techniques to prevent it from reaching depressions.

Gridiron System

The gridiron system, illustrated in figure 15–1b, is used to drain areas with uniform slopes. In this system, a single main is located along one edge of the area and laterals direct water to the main from one side. It is usually more economical to place the main along the shorter side of the area because (a) fewer large drain pipes are required; (b) the total length of drain pipe will be less; (c) fewer initial

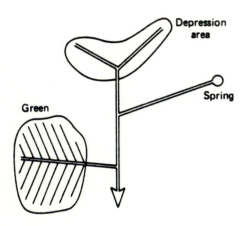

(a) RANDOM

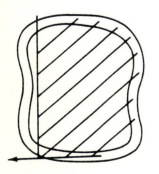

(b) GRIDIRON

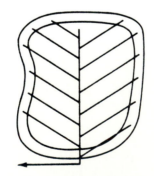

(c) HERRINGBONE

Figure 15–1 Types of drainage systems

placements of the ditching machine are required; and (d) fewer junctions are required.

The gridiron system is commonly used where an entire area requires drainage. The gridiron system may be the best drainage system for a large recreation area if the area slopes in one direction. It is also used for greens and the tubing under prescription athletic turf (see chapter 16). Golf course fairways and rough areas could be drained using the gridiron system if systematic drainage is desired.

Herringbone System

The herringbone system, illustrated in figure 15–1c, is used to drain swale areas. Water flows toward the swale in laterals connected to the main from both sides. The main is located in the lowest part of the swale. The herringbone system is the least economical of the systems because a larger area along the main is drained by both the main and the laterals. The most common application of the herringbone system is the drainage of putting greens.

Interceptor Drains

Interceptor drains, shown in figure 15–2, are used for draining areas made wet by hillside seepage. Much of the drainage on golf courses is of this type. Hillside seepage occurs when the soil on a hillside is underlain by a tighter, less permeable layer that restricts vertical water movement. Precipitation on the soil surface percolates downward through the previous surface soil until it reaches the tighter layer, which may be a clay hardpan; or a vein of slate, coal, or shale; or a clayey subsoil. The water flows laterally over this less pervious layer until it emerges at the soil surface forming a hillside seep. A seep may occur anywhere along a slope, wetting the area below it.

Hillside seeps may also be caused by a regional or perched water table encountering the soil surface. The most likely place for a water table to appear at the soil surface is near the intersection of a steep slope and a flatter slope. This phenomenon most commonly occurs at the base of large hills and flatter valleys. It is also a common problem on golf courses. A seep can often be found where el-

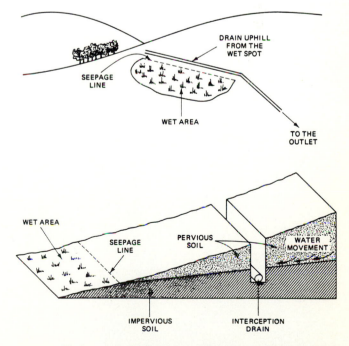

Figure 15–2 Two views of an interceptor drain system

evated greens meet the surrounding land area. Wet seep areas are also common on approaches where the fairway slopes downhill toward the green, which is slightly elevated. In this case, the approach may be wet because some irrigation water is retained in the green base materials, and a seep may be caused in the same approach area from a surfacing water table on the fairway side.

A hillside seep area may be drained by a subsurface drain line laid across the hillside nearly perpendicular to the slope and above the seep zone. The purpose of the subsurface drain line is to intercept the water flowing on the slowly permeable layer or the water table before it appears at the soil surface, much like a diversion is used to intercept surface runoff. In cases where several seeps exist on one hillside, the upper line of seepage should be intercepted first to help eliminate other seep areas farther down the slope.

The placement of the interceptor drain can best be determined by digging test holes when most of the area is ready for use, but the seep area is still too wet. By observing the water level in the test holes a day after they are dug, the position of the water table or the water flowing over the tight layer in the ground can be located. The drain line should be installed where the water table is 1 to 2 feet below the soil surface. The trench should be dug to approximately a 2.5-foot depth. The trench, therefore, will extend below the water table. If the trench is backfilled to the depth of the water table with coarse stone, the water will easily enter the drain. In the case of lateral flow over an impervious layer, the seep should be eliminated. In the case of a water table intersecting the soil surface, this one drain may or may not completely solve the problem. If not, additional interceptor drains may be needed farther down the slope.

SUBSURFACE DRAIN PIPE

Concrete Tile

Concrete tile are classified according to physical test characteristics as standard-quality, extra-quality, and special-quality. Standard-quality tile should be satisfactory for most drainage work in nearly neutral soils. In alkali or acid soils, special-quality tile made with cements having specific chemical characteristics should be used. Extra-quality tile is resistant to damage by freezing and thawing. Concrete tile should not be used in mining areas where the soil water contains high concentrations of sulfates.

Clay Tile

Clay tile are available in standard-quality, extraquality and heavy-duty classes. As with concrete tile, standard-quality clay tile is satisfactory for most drainage systems. Clay tile may be made of either shale or surface clays. When manufactured from surface clays, tile are normally not affected by the action of soil acids, but they are likely to be damaged by exposure to frequent freezing and thawing. Tile made from shale are less porous and more resistant to deterioration from freezing and thawing.

Corrugated Plastic Tubing

Corrugated plastic tubing has become the most popular type of subsurface drain line, nearly replacing concrete and clay tile. The corrugated plastic tubing is made of polyethylene plastic and is resistant to damage by acid soils and frost. It has 0.25-inch deep corrugations that give it strength, especially when installed with proper lateral support. The water enters the tubing through small slots spaced around the circumference of the tubing. The tubing is manufactured in long, continuous lengths ranging from 500 feet for 2-inch diameter tubing to 250 feet for 4-inch diameter to 20 feet for 8-inch or larger tubing. Four-inch tubing commonly comes in 250-foot rolls that weigh about 70 pounds (see figure 15–3). New installation procedures have increased the advantage of plastic tubing by reducing the installation cost by 50% under traditional installation techniques. These new techniques will be discussed in a later section.

INLETS

Subsurface drain lines are located, designed, and installed assuming that all of the gravitational water carried by the subsurface drain pipe will freely enter

Figure 15–3   Corrugated plastic tubing

the pipe, drop by drop, at hundreds of locations along the length of the pipe. Contractors, manufacturers, and laymen have been concerned about making the slots or entry holes in the corrugated plastic tubing large enough to permit the proper amount of water to enter. These concerns are unfounded.

The use of slotted drainage tubing in sandy soils has caused some concern. Fine textured (heavy) soils adhere or stick together in aggregates so the soil particles do not easily enter the drain pipe. Sandy soils do not stick together and individual sand particles can pass through the slots into the tubing and may eventually clog the pipe. This problem has been partially solved by developing a sock-type covering (called a filter fabric), which is placed around the tubing. The filters are usually oil-based products, woven to form a cloth material that removes soil particles while permitting water to enter the tubing. These filters do not significantly restrict the flow of water into the tubing.

There are two common methods of delivering surface water to subsurface drainage systems. The simplest kind of inlet, a blind inlet, is constructed by backfilling a subsurface drain line with gravel or crushed rock. This material is pervious enough to allow water to enter the drain line very rapidly, but the gravel may become filled with silt in a short time. Also, large amounts of silt may enter and eventually plug the drain line. Blind inlets are economical to install and may be satisfactory for small areas for a few years. They operate best when constructed by backfilling the drain trench with a gradation of gravel and rock, the coarser material at the bottom near the pipe followed by gradually finer material as the trench is filled. Filter fabric material can also be used to line trenches before stone is inserted.

Greater quantities of surface water can be drained by installing an open or surface inlet structure in the drain line as shown in figure 15–4. Many materials may be used in the construction of surface inlets and the inlet may be round, square, or any other convenient shape.

The following guidelines should be observed when planning and constructing surface inlets:

1. The inlet must be constructed of durable material. Materials satisfactory for the inlet are brick,

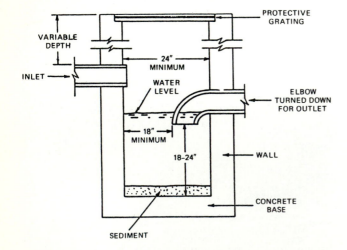

Figure 15–4 Surface inlet installed in a subsurface drain line

stone, concrete, sewer tile, metal pipe, and many others. Wood is unsatisfactory because of its short life.

2. For collecting sediment, the bottom of the structure should be at least 18 inches to 24 inches below the outlet to provide for sediment collection.

3. A protective grating should be placed over the top to prevent large objects and debris from washing into the basin and to protect against possible injury to humans.

4. When the inlet is installed in a subsurface drain line, the incoming drain must be at an elevation higher than the outlet.

5. The surface inlet should be equipped with an elbow turned down at the end of the outlet pipe, as illustrated in figure 15–4, to prevent debris from washing into the drain.

OUTLETS

The drain outlet, where the subsurface line comes to the soil surface to discharge water, is usually the weakest part of the drainage structure. If a subsurface drainage outlet is to function without the need for repair and reconstruction, it must be designed to be resistant to the following common causes of failure:

1. Clogged outlet. The outlet must be kept clear of weeds and debris that may cause the discharged water to pond and back up into the outlet. Outlets should receive maintenance at least one each year.

2. Dead rodents or animal nests. Rodents and other small animals often crawl into the outlet to build nests if the outlet is an open pipe.

3. Broken or crushed pipe. Since the drain pipe is closer to the soil surface at the outlet than at any other location, the drain may be broken or crushed by heavy equipment.

4. Deterioration of tile due to freezing. Clay and concrete tile absorb small amounts of water. When the soil freezes to the depth of the tile, the water absorbed into the pipe will freeze and expand, breaking the pipe.

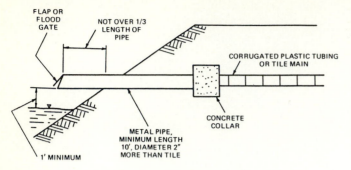

Figure 15–5 Metal pipe outlet for subsurface drainage systems

5. Displacement of tile. Individual clay or concrete tile are only 12 inches long and they can be displaced easily.

6. Erosion of soil from the outlet. Water flowing from the outlet may cause erosion and cause the pipe to move out of alignment.

The best method of constructing subsurface drain outlet to prevent failure due to the items previously listed is shown in figure 15–5. Instead of extending the tile or plastic tubing to the discharge point, a section of metal pipe 10 to 15 feet in length is used to carry the water from the point where sufficient cover is available to the discharge point. The outlet pipe should be equipped with a flap as shown in figure 15–5 or some type of rodent guard to keep small animals out of the drain. The outlet should be connected to the subsurface drain line by a concrete collar. The collar helps to anchor the outlet pipe and prevents movement. The outlet should be the same size or larger than the main line coming to the collar and the outlet should discharge at least one foot above the normal water level in the outlet ditch or stream. A small portion of the metal pipe should extend from the bank to help prevent bank erosion.

A concrete head wall, similar to the one shown in figure 15–6, may be used in place of the metal outlet pipe. The head wall is usually less desirable because of the concrete forming required for its construction.

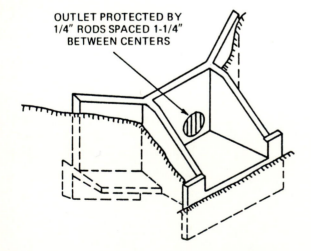

Figure 15–6 Concrete head wall for subsurface drain outlet

DEPTH OF DRAIN LINES

Subsurface drain lines are usually placed between 1.5 and 4.0 feet below the soil surface. This placement allows for at least 1.0 foot of soil cover. The minimum depth of cover recommended when clay or concrete tile are used is 2.0 feet. The primary concern is to provide sufficient protection for the tile to prevent breakage when crossing the lines with heavy maintenance equipment. Corrugated plastic drain tubing was developed about 1965. If properly installed with sand or gravel surrounding the tubing, this tubing can support heavy loads without the protection of 2.3 feet of cover. The drain tubing has made it possible to place subsurface drain lines on slowly permeable hardpans, claypans, and fragipans even if located within 15 inches to 18 inches of the soil surface.

Generally, subsurface drains should be placed deeper in light, sandy soils than in heavy soils. The slow percolation of water in heavy soils may prevent water from reaching the drain lines if they are placed too deeply.

It is common when draining turf areas to place drain lines within 1.5 feet of the soil surface. Drains under golf course greens are usually covered with about 1.5 feet of media. Drains in and around athletic fields seldom have more than 1.0 foot of cover. It should be remembered, however, that a soil cannot be drained (i.e., have the gravitational water removed) to a depth below the drain lines.

SPACING OF DRAIN LINES

When using the gridiron or herringbone systems in heavy clay soils, it may be necessary to space laterals as close as 30 to 40 feet apart for adequate drainage. In contrast, drain lines may be spaced as much as 200 or more feet apart in light, sandy soils. In clay loam soils, a spacing of 50 to 60 feet is common.

Depth and spacing of drains are closely related. It is necessary to place drains deeper for wide spacings than for narrow spacings. In sandy soil it may be possible to use a 200-foot spacing, but a depth of at least 4.0 feet should be used. In tighter soils, drains may be spaced only 40 feet apart, but only 2.0 feet from the surface. There is no uniformity of spacing in the random drainage system.

SIZE OF DRAIN LINES

Subsurface drains must carry all water delivered to it by the soil. Factors that affect the size of drains are (a) the grade (the steeper the grade the faster water will flow through the pipe); (b) the area contributing water to the system; and (c) the ease with which water will percolate through the soil to the drain, often called the drainage coefficient (DC).

Establishing Grades
of Subsurface Drains

Subsurface drain lines are small open channels that convey water under the influence of gravity. If the water in a drain line is expected to flow to the outlet, it must be conveyed in a pipe that flows from a point of higher elevation to a point of lower elevation. If a section of a pipe is lower than the section closer to the outlet, the water will pond in the low section. This will cause any sediment in the water to settle and collect in the bottom of the pipe. When the low section is below the desired grade by the diameter of the pipe, the drain will eventually fill completely with sediment. This will cause the line to fail. This failure can also be caused by having a high section of pipe that allows the on-grade section to fill with sediment prior to the high section.

It is very important that the grade of all drain lines be planned and that the drain lines are installed at the design grade. In the past it was nearly impossible for contractors to keep trenching machines exactly on grade. This fact lead to 4- or 5-inch diameter pipe being the minimum accepted by the Soil Conservation Service. A 4-inch diameter pipe can be off grade by as much as 4 inches and still permit some water to flow.

When drain pipes are to be laid at grades flatter than 1.0%, extreme care must be taken. The minimum grade for mains and laterals is 0.1%. Very flat grades should be attempted only with large pipe laid in a trench dug by an experienced operator.

The maximum grade to be used is ordinarily of little consequence. Field experience indicates that subsurface drain lines have been safely laid on grades up to 20% or more in clay soils. However, maximum grade should not exceed 10% in sandy or loamy soils.

The specific grade selected for a drain line will depend primarily upon the slope of the land being drained. This, however, need not be the only controlling factor. It may be possible to dig the trench deeper to establish grade if the land is nearly level or to place the laterals across the slope if the land is rather steep.

The easiest method of establishing a design grade is to place the drain the same distance below the soil surface at both the upper and lower ends of the lateral. A straight grade line is then established between the two end points as illustrated in figure 15–7. Each point along the grade line should be checked to be sure there is sufficient cover. Another method of establishing grade is known as digging-for-grade (see figure 15–8). This method is to start deep at the outlet end and trench with less depth of cut as the far end of the tile line is approached.

The grade for the main must be established such that the main is deep enough for all laterals to discharge into it. When possible, the elevation of the lateral should be about one-half the diameter of the main higher than the elevation of the main at the point where the two join. If this is not possible, the elevation of the lateral must be at least as high as the main.

When establishing the grades of a subsurface drain systems, it is best to start at the outlet and establish the grade of the main. After the grade of the main has been established, start at the main to establish the grade of each lateral.

Design and Field Layout

After the decision has been made to install subsurface drainage in an area, the outlet has been located, and the main and laterals have been located, a line-of-levels must be run along each anticipated drain line. The results of this leveling survey should be elevations determined at 100-foot intervals or closer along each line. These ground elevations for each line should be plotted as shown in figure 15–9. This is the same procedure discussed in chapter 14. The grade must be established and the depth of cut must be determined for each station.

In the following example, elevations were taken at 100-foot intervals. The elevation of a tree root was assumed to be 100.0 feet. The elevation at each 100-foot station is shown in figure 15–9. The problem is to find a grade that will cause the water in the drain to flow. The drain must have at least 1.0 feet of cover and the depth of cut should not exceed 3.0 feet.

First, determine the vertical fall of the earth's surface between the ends of the planned drain line.

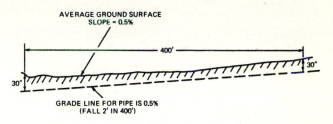
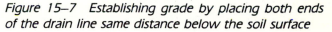

Figure 15–7 *Establishing grade by placing both ends of the drain line same distance below the soil surface*

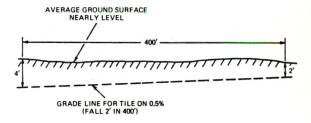

Figure 15–8 *Digging for grade*

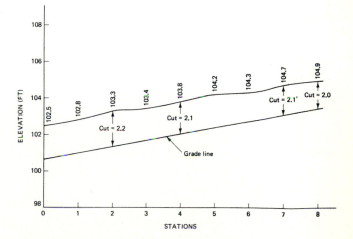

Figure 15–9 *Plotting field elevation*

Subtract the lower elevation (station 0) from the higher elevation (station 8) (104.9 ft − 102.5 ft = 2.4 ft) to find the difference in elevation of 2.4 feet. Divide the total fall by the number of 100-foot stations, which in this case is 8 (2.4 ft/8 = 0.30 ft/100 ft). This will give you the fall of 0.30 feet per 100 feet that should occur between each station.

Second, the elevation of the bottom of the drain line should be established at each station starting with the outlet, station 0. To make calculations easier, a value of six inches or 0.5 feet is usually allowed for the diameter of the pipe in the trench. This means that to get an average depth of cover of 1.5 feet, the ditch should be 2.0 feet deep. Therefore, using a cut of 2.0 feet subtracted from the ground elevation at the outlet, the elevation of the bottom of the trench at station 0 is determined. Calculations for grade elevation and cut are summarized in table 15–1 for this example. The elevation of the trench bottom at each successive station can be determined by adding the desired fall per 100-foot section (0.3 feet) to the elevation of the previous station (100.5 ft + 0.3 = 100.8 ft).

Third, determine the depth of cut required. The depth of cut required at each station to cause the bottom of the trench to be the design grade line is the difference between the ground elevation and the grade elevation. A few of the cuts are shown in figure 15–9.

If you find when calculating the depth of cut that at one or more stations the drain is either too deep or too shallow, it may be necessary to break

Table 15–1 *Example problem illustrating a method of determining a grade line, depth of cut, and target height for a substance drainage system*

Station	Ground elevation (ft)	Grade line elevation (ft)	Cut (ft)
0	102.5	100.5	2.0
1	102.8	100.8	2.0
2	103.3	101.1	2.2
3	103.4	101.4	2.0
4	103.8	101.7	2.1
5	104.2	102.6	2.2
6	104.3	102.3	2.0
7	104.7	102.6	2.1
8	104.9	102.9	2.0

grade. To do this, simply adjust the figures so the drain is at the desired depth at the station where it was either too shallow or too deep. Then work from that point toward the higher point at one grade and from that point toward the lower point at a different grade. In complex terrain, it may be necessary to break grade several times.

Finally, when all the grades have been calculated and the depth of the drain is satisfactory, proceed to lay out these grades in the field. Use some type of marker as a gauge for determining when the trench is at the proper depth. The type of marker will vary, depending on whether the trenching is to be done by hand or by machine and depending on the type of grade control equipment on the machine. The grade stake commonly used when digging trenches by hand or backhoe is shown in figure 15–10a and the type commonly used when trenching with a machine shown in figure 15–10b.

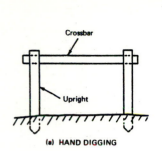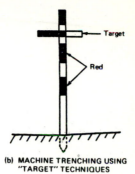

Figure 15–10 Grade stakes

Area to be Drained

The second consideration is the area that will contribute drainage water to each drain line. This is usually a simple matter of either measuring the area of land between the midpoint of the laterals on a gridiron or herringbone system or knowing the area of a whole system flowing into a main (i.e., several laterals under a green all converge to a main that carries the water to an outlet).

Rate of Drainage

After the grade of the drain line and the number of acres to be drained have been determined, it is necessary to establish the rate at which the water will be delivered to the drain. Two methods are used to establish the drainage coefficient (DC). If the drain line is truely a subsurface drain, the hydraulic conductivity of the soil dictates the maximum DC. There is no point in designing a pipeline to carry more water than the soil can deliver to it. Large recreation parks with high water tables, golf course fairways, and other turf areas where modified soil is typically not used are areas that may require subsurface drainage. The DC typically used for these soils is about 1.0 inch per day. Here the DC is the maximum depth of water removed from the soil each day. This rate is equivalent to lowering a water table about 12 inches to 18 inches per day.

The second method used to establish a DC is the expected precipitation rate. On greens, sand-trap areas, athletic fields, and so on, it is desirable to remove precipitation as rapidly as it falls. The method also assumes that the soil (modified) will deliver the water to the drains as rapidly as it falls. If the soils are suitably modified and it is necessary to remove rain water quickly, this method may be applied. The suggested DC for this case is one inch to four inches per hour. Use one inch per hour if water may remain on the soil surface for a short period after a storm. Use four inches per hour if very rapid removal of water is desired and the soil will support this high rate as in sand traps or drainage from gravel filled trenches. Two inches per hour should be adequate for most greens. One or two inches per hour is good for tees.

Design Charts

Figures 15–11 and 15–12 are provided to aid in the proper sizing of drain lines. Figure 15–11 is for clay or concrete tile and figure 15–12 is for corrugated plastic tubing. The use of these figures will be illustrated by using the example shown in figure 15–13.

Figures 15–11 and 15–12 are similar and in fact differ only in the friction or resistance to flow for the clay and concrete versus the corrugated plastic. The plastic has about 50% more friction than the smooth clay pipe. To use either design chart, the area to be drained is located in the column above the selected DC. The designation of the DC and the area fix the expected flow rate that must be carried. For instance, a DC of 2.0 inches per hour from a 10,000 ft² green would be equivalent to about 200 gallons per minute, read on the left side of the design chart. The slope of the drain line is found on the bottom of the chart. Therefore, the main draining a 10,000 ft² green with a 2.0% slope would require a 6-inch diameter pipe. See figure 15–12 for the design

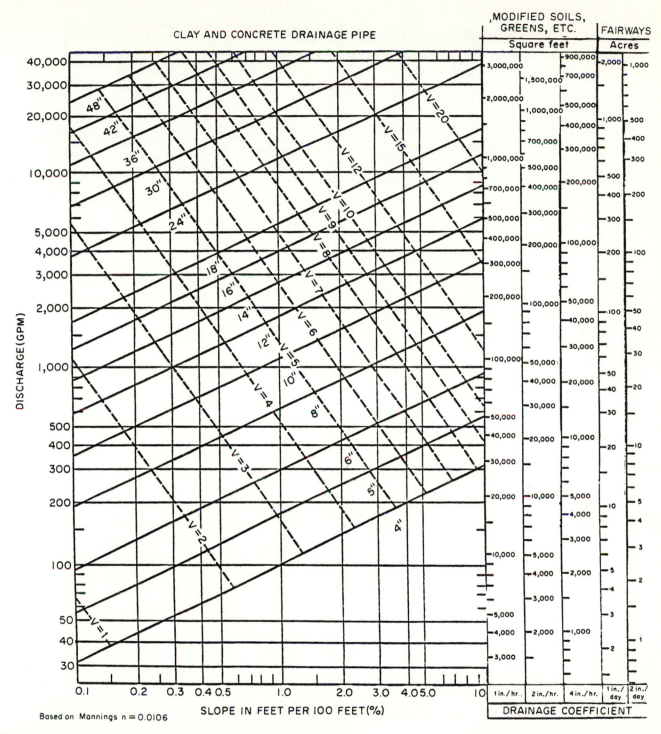

CLAY AND CONCRETE DRAINAGE PIPE

Based on Mannings n = 0.0106

Figure 15–11 Design chart for clay and concrete drainage pipe

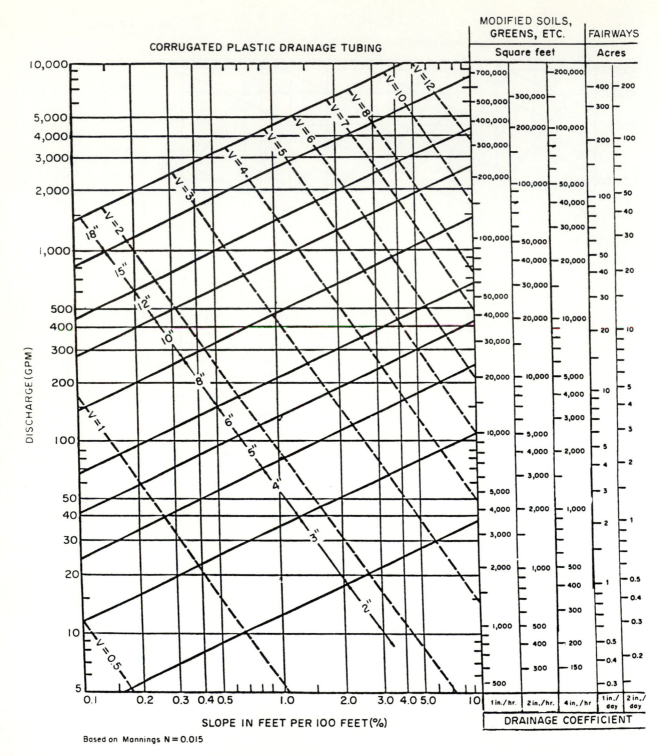

Figure 15–12 Design chart for corrugated plastic drainage tubing

point. By a similar procedure, if you knew the design discharge was to be 200 gpm and the drain had a 2.0% slope, the same design point is reached, 6-inch pipe.

Example The example shown in figure 15–13 consists of several sections to be drained, each connected to a single pipeline.

Solution

1. Greens
   a. Laterals—DC = 2 in/hr, each line 1,000 ft² @ 1.0% slope. Figure 15–12 = 3-inch laterals in greens.
   b. Submains—Up to 4 laterals each; DC = 2 in/hr, 4,000 ft² @ 1.0% slope. Figure 15–12 = 5-inch submains in greens.
   c. Green Discharge Pipe—DC = 2 in/hr, 8,000 ft² @ 1% slope. Figure 15–12 = 6-inch mains (80 gpm).

2. Sand Traps. DC = 4 in/hr, 500 ft² each @ 1% slope. Figure 15–12 = 3-inch for one trap/line (23 gpm). Figure 15–12 = 4-inch for two traps/line (46 gpm).

3. Fairways. DC = 1 in/day, 0.3 Ac @ 1% slope. Figure 15–12 = 2-inch tubing (6 gpm).

4. Interceptor Drain. Even if a DC should be established, the area drained is unknown. Most designers will simply install 4-inch drains as the interceptor drain. This probably is an over design.

5. Main to Gravel Trench. The main to the gravel trench must carry all the water discharged from the various areas feeding it. The best way to handle this design is by adding the gpms expected from each submain. The numbers in parentheses by the pipe sizes are these discharges in gpm. The summation of these discharges is 516 gpm, which on a 1% slope requires a 10-inch main.

6. Gravel-filled Surface Drain. To carry all the surface drainage water from a 1-acre area is equivalent to a DC of 4 in/hr from an area of 43,560 ft², which requires a 15-inch pipe (1,800 gpm).

7. Main Beyond the Gravel Trench. The total gpm is 2,300 gpm, which requires a 15-inch pipeline.

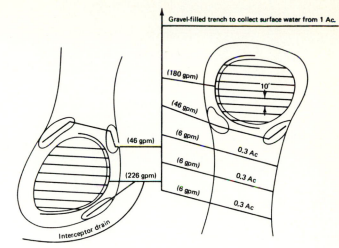

Greens: DC = 2 in/hr each with 8,000-ft² area.
  Laterals are spaced 10 feet apart and drain a 1,000-ft² area.
  Green area includes the collars.

Sand: DC = 4 in/hr each with 500-ft² area.
Fairways: DC = 1 in/day each lateral with 0.3 Ac.
Surface drain: DC = 4 in/hr.

All drains have 1.0% slope.
Use corrugated plastic pipe.
Size all drains.

Figure 15–13 Example for sizing drainage lines

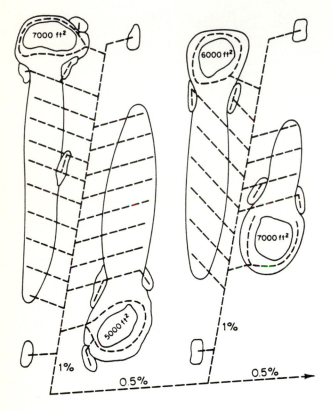

Specifications:

1. Sand traps = 500 ft² each

2. Each lateral drain = 0.2 Ac

3. Each tee = 4,000 ft²

4. Greens feed into apron drains

5. Lateral slope = 2%

6. Mains as shown

7. Fairway DC = 2 in/day

8. Green = 2 in/hr

9. Traps = 4 in/hr

10. Aprons drain 5,000 ft² @ 2 in/hr

Figure 15–14   Example for sizing pipes

NOTES:

1. Generally, individual drainage areas such as greens should be discharged into natural watercourses or surface drainage channels as quickly as possible. This practice could eliminate much of the large pipe needed in the example problem.

2. The drainage of large surface areas through subsurface channels such as the gravel-filled trench should be avoided if possible. The undersizing of such drains often leads to severe washouts during high-intensity storms. These washouts often remove gravel and pipe from the trench.

TIME OF INSTALLATION

Drainage problems are most evident in the spring when the soil is nearly saturated from snow melt and spring rains. The decision to install drainage structures is most often made during this time because the wet areas are visually evident and most turf managers realize the loss of revenue occurring from delays in turf area usage. While the wet period is not the time to actually install drainage structures, many types of drains, especially interceptor drains, require preliminary planning during this period. The surveys and design for most drainage systems can occur anytime during the year, but installation should be attempted only during the driest periods. Installation of drains in wet fields, especially fields with standing water, can result in additional problems.

PROBLEMS

1. Why are approaches often wet areas of a golf course? How can this problem be corrected?

2. As a superintendent, how rapidly would you like to remove rainwater from a green? What is this equivalent to in terms of drainage coefficient?

3. Size all subsurface drainlines on figure 15–14. Use plastic tubing.

4. Explain or show how filter fabric might be used to increase the life of a slit trench. Could filter fabric

be used to replace pipe in a subsurface drainage system? How?

5.   A subsurface drainage system is to drain 4 acres at 2 in/day and 1,000 ft^2 at 1 in/hr. What size plastic drain is needed if the drain has a 1.0% slope? What size clay pipe will carry the same water?

6.   The runoff from a 2-acre parking lot is drained through a surface inlet. What flow rate can be expected and what size plastic pipe is needed to carry this flow down a 1% slope? Use a 2-year return period.

Chapter 16

SPECIAL APPLICATIONS

GREENS

Proper drainage of putting greens is essential. Soil is usually modified to facilitate surface drainage of the green (see figure 16–1). The top foot of the green is usually a mixture of topsoil and sand in varying proportions. This modified growth medium is chosen to provide several functions, one of which is drainage. The topsoil mixture should be able to resist compaction and still drain water from the putting surface, either from precipitation or excessive irrigation, to the gravel base below. One must remember, however, that water reaching the gravel zone requires removal. In a few sandy soils it is possible

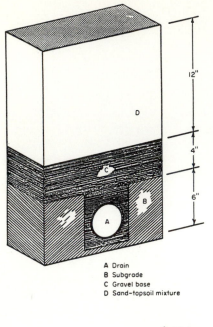

A Drain
B Subgrade
C Gravel base
D Sand–topsoil mixture

Figure 16–1 Soil modification

to get sufficient vertical drainage through the subgrade to dispose of this surface water. Most soils require that a subsurface drainage system be provided at the bottom of the gravel zone to remove excess water. The drain lines should be laid in a pattern adapted to the contour of the green. Gridiron or herringbone systems are common patterns for this. The drain lines are usually spaced 4 feet to 10 feet apart and should be placed on about a one percent slope. The drain lines should be laid on the subgrade before the gravel is placed. Mainlines carrying water from greens should be discharged into another pipeline, into a surface drainage channel, or into a natural drainage swale.

FOOTBALL, SOCCER, AND FIELD HOCKEY FIELDS

Figures 16–2, 16–3, and 16–4 show the layout of typical football, soccer, and field hockey fields, respectively. Drainage of these fields is provided by crowning the center of the field higher than the side lines. Subsurface drains are installed along each side of the field to provide an outlet channel for surface water flowing from the field. For conven-

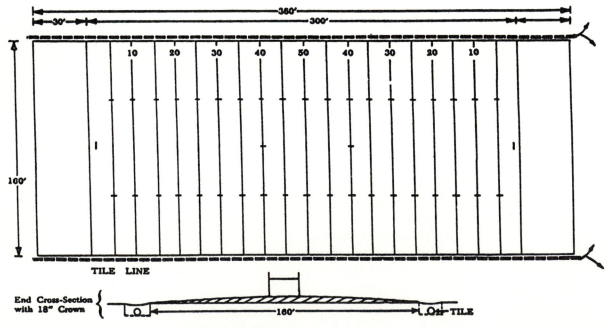

Figure 16–2 Football gridiron showing end section and tile lines

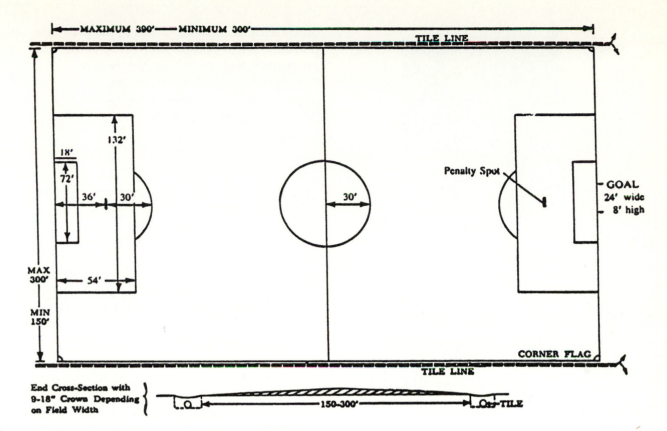

Figure 16–3   Soccer field showing end section and tile lines

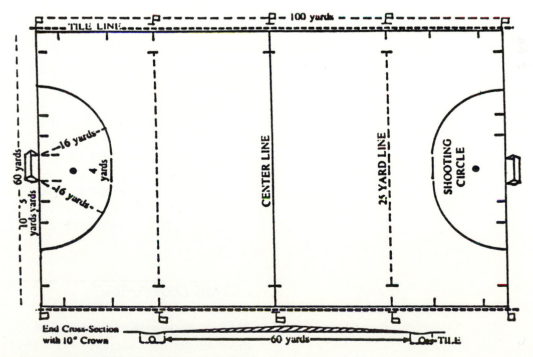

Figure 16–4   Field hockey field showing end section
and tile lines

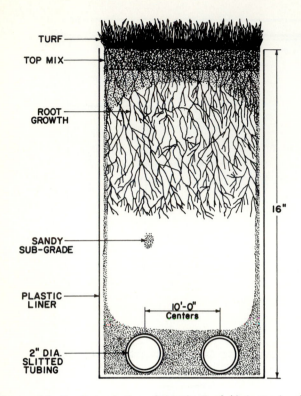

TURF

TOP MIX

ROOT GROWTH

16"

SANDY SUB-GRADE

PLASTIC LINER

2" DIA. SLITTED TUBING

10'-0" Centers

Figure 16–5 Prescription Athletic Turf (Adapted with permission from Hancor, 1977)

tional fields, subsurface drains in the field serve little purpose since compaction makes the soil less permeable and, therefore, the field less drainable. Surface drainage water is usually delivered to the subsurface drains either by several surface inlets placed along the field or by a blind inlet along the length of the side line.

PRESCRIPTION ATHLETIC TURF

The development of Prescription Athletic Turf (PAT) has altered the theories on drainage of many athletic fields, especially high-use fields in stadiums. PAT is a complete irrigation and drainage system (see figure 16–5). Irrigation water is made available to the root zone by pumping water into the drain tubing and developing a water table under the turf. When sufficient water has been applied, the drain tubing, spaced about 10 feet apart, is drained. Excess precipitation is also removed through the drain tubes. Vacuum pumps connected to the drain lines accelerate the drainage rate. During precipitation events, especially if they occur during play, the vacuum created in the drain tubes literally sucks water downward through the sandy subgrade into the drains.

BASEBALL FIELDS

Draining baseball fields is a bit more complex, since the field is not the typical rectangular shape. Subsurface drains are usually provided along the foul lines and beyond the skinned area as shown in figure 16–6. The outfield should also be drained with a gridiron or herringbone system. A PAT system would remove excess precipitation.

HOME DRAINAGE

Poor drainage and lack of proper water management are constant sources of concern to the homeowner. Wet basements and soggy spots in a lawn

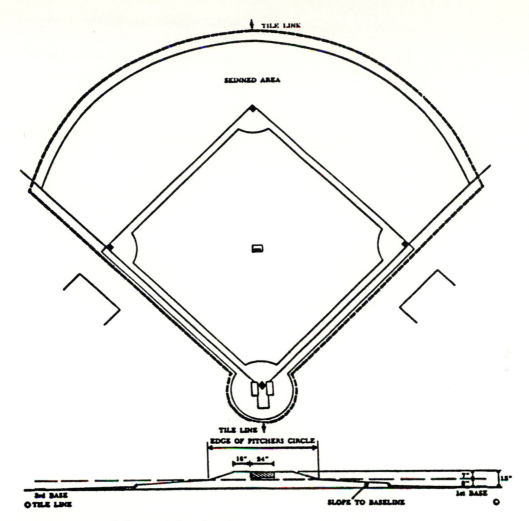

Figure 16–6   Regulation baseball diamond showing design of tile system

can be avoided. The best time to solve home drainage problems is before they start. Select the site for your home with water management in mind. If there is no natural surface drainage, surface drainage most likely will be a problem. If there is a high water table in the area, any home with a basement will literally become a boat and must therefore be watertight. The most satisfactory and cheapest solution is to include the drainage and water management plans with the other construction plans. If you already own a home or plan to buy one, improper planning for drainage at the time of construction may have created problems requiring expensive solutions.

Improper roof drainage is the most common

cause of wet basements. In general, roof drainage water should be discharged away from the house to a natural channel, street, or dry well (see figure 16–7a). If permitted to discharge near the foundation, it will percolate along the foundation wall, probably find a weak spot in the joint between the foundation and the basement floor, and seep into the basement.

The next most common cause of wet basements is the lack of foundation drains (see figure 16–7c). Often foundation drains are not included when the house is built because natural outlets are

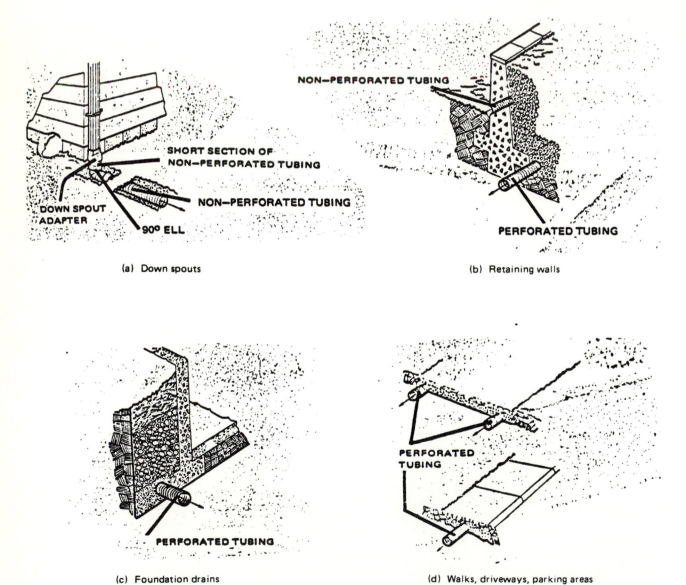

(a) Down spouts

(b) Retaining walls

(c) Foundation drains

(d) Walks, driveways, parking areas

Figure 16–7 (Adapted with permission from Hancor, 1977)

not available. Such a lot should probably not have a house built on it unless the soil is very deep and well-drained.

Retaining walls, driveways, and walks are often in need of frequent repair due to improper drainage (see figures 16–7b and 16–7d). Improperly drained soil below or along side of an impermeable wall, walk, or driveway will expand when the soil water freezes, damaging the structure.

Appendix A

SPRINKLER
PERFORMANCE DATA

Data presented in this appendix are reprinted with permission from Rain Bird, 1982; Toro, 1983; Royal Coach-Buckner, 1983; Weather-Tec, 1983.

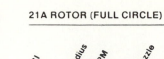
21A / 31A / 41-51A

These **full circle impact rotor pop-up sprinklers** are designed for irrigating large areas of turfgrass. Highly dependable service for a wide range of irrigation applications such as greenbelt areas, athletic fields, parks, golf courses, cemeteries, etc. Constructed of tough corrosion-resistant materials with only two moving parts for reliable operation even in sandy conditions.

41-51A-VIH-E

This **full circle Stopamatic® valve-in-head electric rotor pop-up sprinkler** is designed to allow individual control for irrigating large areas of turfgrass. Highly dependable and ideal for such applications as irrigating golf course greens, or where conversion from a quick coupling valve system with little disruption of the turfgrass area is necessary. Constructed of tough corrosion-resistant materials with only two moving parts for reliable operation even in sandy conditions.

Operating Range
*Precipitation Rate:
.33 to .80 ins./hr.
Spacing: 50 to 80 ft.
Pressure: 45 to 100 psi
(Performance depends on operating pressure, spacing and nozzle selected.)

Features
- **2-5/16" pop-up height**
- **Proven impact drive**
- **Straight-through flow**
- **Energy efficient**
- **Solenoid-actuated Stopamatic valve** (24V, 2-watt solenoid)
- **Manual control**
- **Wiper seal**
- **Double-slotted spreader nozzle**
- **Easy to service**
- **Wide choice of nozzles**
- **High strength plastic case**
- **Aluminum cover**
- **Tapered self-flushing valve seat**
- **Nozzle vane**
- **TNT bearing**
- **Optional vandal-resistant cover screws**

- **21A:** For standard nozzle at 60 psi, the highest point of stream is 10' above nozzle at 30' from sprinkler. Adjusting pin is completely out of stream. Nozzle outlet trajectory is 25°.
- **31A:** For standard nozzle at 60 psi, the highest point of stream is 10'6" above nozzle at 32' from sprinkler. Adjusting pin is completely out of stream. Nozzle outlet trajectory is 25°.
- **41-51A:** For standard nozzle at 70 psi, the highest point of stream is 15' above nozzle at 47'6" from sprinkler. Adjusting pin is completely out of stream. Nozzle outlet trajectory is 23°.

21A

31A

21A ROTOR (FULL CIRCLE)

PSI	Radius	GPM	Nozzle	*Precip. ■	*Precip. ▲
40	41	2.8	1/8"	.16	.13
	42	3.5	9/64"	.19	.15
	43	4.4	5/32" ‡	.23	.18
	43	5.3	11/64"	.28	.22
45	41	3.0	1/8"	.17	.14
	42	3.7	9/64"	.20	.16
	43	4.7	5/32" ‡	.24	.20
	44	5.6	11/64"	.28	.22
50	42	3.2	1/8"	.17	.14
	43	3.9	9/64"	.20	.16
	44	4.9	5/32" ‡	.24	.20
	45	5.9	11/64"	.28	.22
55	42	3.3	1/8"	.18	.14
	43	4.1	9/64"	.21	.17
	44	5.2	5/32" ‡	.26	.21
	45	6.2	11/64"	.29	.24
60	43	3.5	1/8"	.18	.15
	44	4.3	9/64"	.21	.17
	45	5.4	5/32" ‡	.26	.21
	46	6.5	11/64"	.30	.24
65	43	3.6	1/8"	.19	.15
	44	4.4	9/64"	.22	.18
	45	5.6	5/32" ‡	.27	.21
	46	6.7	11/64"	.30	.24
70	43	3.8	1/8"	.20	.16
	44	4.6	9/64"	.23	.18
	45	5.8	5/32" ‡	.28	.22
	47	7.0	11/64"	.31	.24
75	44	3.9	1/8"	.19	.16
	45	4.8	9/64"	.23	.18
	46	6.0	5/32" ‡	.27	.22
	47	7.2	11/64"	.31	.25
80	44	4.0	1/8"	.20	.16
	45	4.9	9/64"	.23	.19
	46	6.2	5/32" ‡	.28	.23
	47	7.5	11/64"	.33	.26

41-51A-VIH-E

31A ROTOR (FULL CIRCLE)

PSI	Radius	GPM	Nozzle	*Precip. ■	*Precip. ▲
40	44	6.3	3/16"	.31	.25
	44	7.3	13/64"	.36	.29
	44	8.4	7/32" ‡	.42	.34
	45	9.6	15/64"	.46	.37
45	44	6.6	3/16"	.33	.26
	45	7.8	13/64"	.37	.30
	45	8.9	7/32" ‡	.42	.34
	46	10.2	15/64"	.46	.37
50	45	7.0	3/16"	.33	.27
	45	8.2	13/64"	.39	.31
	46	9.4	7/32" ‡	.43	.34
	46	10.8	15/64"	.49	.39
55	45	7.4	3/16"	.35	.28
	46	8.6	13/64"	.39	.31
	46	9.9	7/32" ‡	.45	.36
	47	11.3	15/64"	.49	.40
60	46	7.7	3/16"	.35	.28
	46	9.0	13/64"	.41	.33
	47	10.4	7/32" ‡	.45	.36
	47	11.8	15/64"	.51	.41
65	47	8.0	3/16"	.35	.28
	47	9.4	13/64"	.41	.33
	47	10.8	7/32" ‡	.47	.38
	48	12.3	15/64"	.51	.41
70	47	8.3	3/16"	.36	.29
	47	9.8	13/64"	.43	.34
	48	11.3	7/32" ‡	.47	.38
	48	12.8	15/64"	.54	.43
75	47	8.6	3/16"	.37	.30
	48	10.1	13/64"	.42	.34
	48	11.7	7/32" ‡	.49	.39
	49	13.3	15/64"	.53	.43
80	48	8.9	3/16"	.37	.30
	48	10.5	13/64"	.44	.35
	49	12.1	7/32" ‡	.49	.39
	49	13.7	15/64"	.55	.44

*Precipitation Rate — inches per hour. Rates based on full circle operation.
■ Square spacing based on 50% of diameter of throw.
▲ Triangular spacing based on 60% of diameter of throw.

‡ Standard Nozzle Size recommended

41-51A ROTOR (FULL CIRCLE)

PSI	Radius	GPM	Nozzle	*Precip. ■	*Precip. ▲
45	51	11.8	11/64"x11/64"	.44	.35
	52	12.7	3/16"x11/64"	.45	.36
	53	13.8	13/64"x11/64"	.47	.38
	56	15.8	7/32"x3/16" ‡	.49	.39
	58	18.1	1/4"x3/16"	.52	.42
	61	20.7	9/32"x3/16"	.54	.43
	64	23.5	5/16"x3/16"	.55	.44
	67	27.5	11/32"x13/64"	.59	.47
	70	31.7	3/8"x7/32"	.62	.50
50	52	12.4	11/64"x11/64"	.44	.35
	53	13.4	3/16"x11/64"	.46	.37
	55	14.5	13/64"x11/64"	.46	.37
	57	16.6	7/32"x3/16" ‡	.49	.39
	60	19.0	1/4"x3/16"	.51	.41
	62	21.7	9/32"x3/16"	.54	.44
	65	24.7	5/16"x3/16"	.56	.45
	69	28.9	11/32"x13/64"	.58	.47
	72	33.3	3/8"x7/32"	.62	.50
55	53	13.0	11/64"x11/64"	.45	.36
	54	14.0	3/16"x11/64"	.46	.37
	56	15.1	13/64"x11/64"	.46	.37
	58	17.3	7/32"x3/16" ‡	.50	.40
	61	19.8	1/4"x3/16"	.51	.41
	64	22.7	9/32"x3/16"	.53	.43
	66	25.8	5/16"x3/16"	.57	.46
	70	30.2	11/32"x13/64"	.59	.48
	73	34.8	3/8"x7/32"	.63	.50
60	54	13.5	11/64"x11/64"	.45	.36
	55	14.6	3/16"x11/64"	.46	.37
	57	15.8	13/64"x11/64"	.47	.38
	59	18.0	7/32"x3/16" ‡	.50	.40
	62	20.7	1/4"x3/16"	.52	.42
	65	23.7	9/32"x3/16"	.54	.43
	68	26.9	5/16"x3/16"	.56	.45
	71	31.4	11/32"x13/64"	.60	.48
	75	36.3	3/8"x7/32"	.62	.50
65	55	14.0	11/64"x11/64"	.45	.36
	56	15.1	3/16"x11/64"	.46	.37
	58	16.4	13/64"x11/64"	.47	.38
	60	18.7	7/32"x3/16" ‡	.50	.40
	63	21.5	1/4"x3/16"	.52	.42
	66	24.6	9/32"x3/16"	.54	.44
	69	27.9	5/16"x3/16"	.56	.45
	72	32.6	11/32"x13/64"	.61	.49
	76	37.7	3/8"x7/32"	.63	.50
70	56	14.5	11/64"x11/64"	.45	.36
	57	15.7	3/16"x11/64"	.47	.37
	59	16.9	13/64"x11/64"	.47	.37
	61	19.4	7/32"x3/16" ‡	.50	.40
	64	22.2	1/4"x3/16"	.52	.42
	67	25.5	9/32"x3/16"	.55	.44
	70	28.9	5/16"x3/16"	.57	.46
	74	33.8	11/32"x13/64"	.59	.48
	77	39.0	3/8"x7/32"	.63	.51

41-51A ROTOR (FULL CIRCLE)

PSI	Radius	GPM	Nozzle	*Precip. ■	*Precip. ▲
75	57	15.0	11/64"x11/64"	.44	.36
	58	16.2	3/16"x11/64"	.46	.37
	60	17.5	13/64"x11/64"	.47	.38
	62	20.0	7/32"x3/16" ‡	.50	.40
	65	23.0	1/4"x3/16"	.52	.42
	68	26.3	9/32"x3/16"	.55	.44
	71	29.9	5/16"x3/16"	.57	.46
	75	34.9	11/32"x13/64"	.60	.48
	78	40.3	3/8"x7/32"	.64	.51
80	57	15.5	11/64"x11/64"	.46	.37
	59	16.7	3/16"x11/64"	.46	.37
	60	18.0	13/64"x11/64"	.48	.39
	63	20.7	7/32"x3/16" ‡	.50	.40
	66	23.7	1/4"x3/16"	.52	.42
	69	27.1	9/32"x3/16"	.55	.44
	72	30.8	5/16"x3/16"	.57	.46
	76	36.0	11/32"x13/64"	.60	.48
	79	41.5	3/8"x7/32"	.64	.51
85	58	15.9	11/64"x11/64"	.46	.36
	60	17.2	3/16"x11/64"	.46	.37
	61	18.6	13/64"x11/64"	.48	.39
	64	21.3	7/32"x3/16" ‡	.50	.40
	67	24.4	1/4"x3/16"	.52	.42
	70	27.9	9/32"x3/16"	.55	.44
	73	31.7	5/16"x3/16"	.57	.46
	77	37.0	11/32"x13/64"	.60	.48
	80	42.7	3/8"x7/32"	.64	.52
90	59	16.4	11/64"x11/64"	.45	.36
	60	17.6	3/16"x11/64"	.47	.38
	62	19.1	13/64"x11/64"	.48	.39
	65	21.8	7/32"x3/16" ‡	.50	.40
	68	25.0	1/4"x3/16"	.52	.42
	71	28.7	9/32"x3/16"	.55	.44
	74	32.6	5/16"x3/16"	.57	.46
	78	38.1	11/32"x13/64"	.60	.48
	81	43.9	3/8"x7/32"	.64	.52
95	59	16.8	11/64"x11/64"	.46	.37
	61	18.1	3/16"x11/64"	.47	.38
	63	19.6	13/64"x11/64"	.48	.38
	65	22.4	7/32"x3/16" ‡	.51	.41
	68	25.7	1/4"x3/16"	.54	.43
	72	29.4	9/32"x3/16"	.55	.44
	75	33.4	5/16"x3/16"	.57	.46
	78	39.0	11/32"x13/64"	.62	.50
	82	45.0	3/8"x7/32"	.64	.52
100	60	17.2	11/64"x11/64"	.46	.37
	62	18.5	3/16"x11/64"	.46	.37
	63	20.1	13/64"x11/64"	.49	.39
	66	23.0	7/32"x3/16" ‡	.51	.41
	69	26.3	1/4"x3/16"	.53	.43
	72	30.2	9/32"x3/16"	.56	.45
	75	34.2	5/16"x3/16"	.59	.47
	79	40.0	11/32"x13/64"	.62	.49
	83	46.1	3/8"x7/32"	.64	.52

81B

This **full circle impact rotor pop-up sprinkler** is designed for irrigating very large areas of turfgrass. Highly dependable and perfect for high flow rate operation in such very large, open turfgrass areas as parks and golf courses. Constructed of tough corrosion-resistant materials with only two moving parts for reliable operation even in sandy conditions.

Operating Range
*Precipitation Rate:
.46 to .91 ins./hr.
Spacing: 82 to 125 ft.
Pressure: 60 to 100 psi
(Performance depends on operating pressure, spacing and nozzle selected.)

Features

- 3-⅜" pop-up height
- Proven impact drive
- Energy efficient
- Heavy-duty retract spring
- Wiper seal
- Heavy-duty brass pop-up assembly
- Easy to service
- Three nozzles for optimum uniformity
- Nozzle vane
- Rugged vinyl-coated cast iron case
- TNT bearing
- Self-flushing inlet screen
- Optional rubber cover

Specifications

- 1½" Female thread
- Dimensions with aluminum cover:
  Overall height — 13½"
  Top diameter — 9¼"
- Dimensions with rubber cover:
  Overall height — 13¾"
  Top diameter 9½"

- **81B:** For standard nozzle at 80 psi, the highest point of stream is 17'6" above nozzle at 67'6" from sprinkler. Nozzle outlet trajectory is 23°.

81B ROTOR (FULL CIRCLE)
Spreader Nozzle is 5/32"

PSI	Radius	GPM	Nozzle	*Precip.■	*Precip.▲
60	82	40.7	11/32"x7/32"	.58	.47
	84	45.6	3/8"x7/32" ‡	.62	.50
	86	51.0	13/32"x7/32"	.66	.53
	89	57.2	7/16"x7/32"	.70	.56
	91	63.3	15/32"x7/32"	.74	.59
	93	69.2	1/2"x7/32"	.77	.62
	97	75.7	17/32"x7/32"	.77	.62
	100	81.5	9/16"x7/32"	.78	.63
	103	96.4	5/8"x7/32"	.88	.70
65	84	42.2	11/32"x7/32"	.58	.46
	85	47.3	3/8"x7/32" ‡	.63	.51
	88	52.9	13/32"x7/32"	.66	.53
	90	59.3	7/16"x7/32"	.71	.57
	93	65.6	15/32"x7/32"	.73	.59
	95	72.0	1/2"x7/32"	.77	.62
	98	78.6	17/32"x7/32"	.79	.63
	102	84.7	9/16"x7/32"	.78	.63
	105	99.9	5/8"x7/32"	.87	.70
70	86	43.7	11/32"x7/32"	.57	.46
	87	49.0	3/8"x7/32" ‡	.62	.50
	89	54.8	13/32"x7/32"	.67	.53
	92	61.4	7/16"x7/32"	.70	.56
	94	67.9	15/32"x7/32"	.74	.59
	97	74.8	1/2"x7/32"	.77	.61
	100	81.5	17/32"x7/32"	.78	.63
	103	87.9	9/16"x7/32"	.80	.64
	107	103.4	5/8"x7/32"	.87	.70
75	87	45.2	11/32"x7/32"	.58	.46
	88	50.7	3/8"x7/32" ‡	.63	.51
	91	56.7	13/32"x7/32"	.66	.53
	93	63.5	7/16"x7/32"	.71	.57
	96	70.2	15/32"x7/32"	.73	.59
	98	77.6	1/2"x7/32"	.78	.62
	101	84.4	17/32"x7/32"	.80	.64
	105	91.1	9/16"x7/32"	.80	.64
	108	106.9	5/8"x7/32"	.88	.71
80	89	46.7	11/32"x7/32"	.57	.46
	90	52.4	3/8"x7/32" ‡	.62	.50
	92	58.6	13/32"x7/32"	.67	.53
	95	65.5	7/16"x7/32"	.70	.56
	97	72.5	15/32"x7/32"	.74	.60
	100	80.4	1/2"x7/32"	.77	.62
	103	87.3	17/32"x7/32"	.79	.64
	106	94.3	9/16"x7/32"	.81	.65
	110	110.4	5/8"x7/32"	.88	.70

81B ROTOR (FULL CIRCLE)
Spreader Nozzle is 5/32"

PSI	Radius	GPM	Nozzle	*Precip.■	*Precip.▲
85	90	48.2	11/32"x7/32"	.57	.46
	91	54.1	3/8"x7/32" ‡	.63	.50
	93	60.5	13/32"x7/32"	.67	.54
	96	67.6	7/16"x7/32"	.71	.57
	99	74.8	15/32"x7/32"	.73	.59
	101	83.2	1/2"x7/32"	.79	.63
	104	90.2	17/32"x7/32"	.80	.64
	108	97.5	9/16"x7/32"	.80	.65
	112	113.9	5/8"x7/32"	.87	.70
90	91	49.7	11/32"x7/32"	.58	.46
	92	55.8	3/8"x7/32" ‡	.63	.51
	95	62.4	13/32"x7/32"	.67	.53
	97	69.7	7/16"x7/32"	.71	.57
	100	77.1	15/32"x7/32"	.74	.60
	103	86.0	1/2"x7/32"	.78	.63
	106	93.1	17/32"x7/32"	.80	.64
	109	100.7	9/16"x7/32"	.82	.65
	112	117.4	5/8"x7/32"	.90	.72
95	92	51.2	11/32"x7/32"	.58	.47
	93	57.5	3/8"x7/32" ‡	.64	.51
	96	64.3	13/32"x7/32"	.67	.54
	99	71.7	7/16"x7/32"	.70	.56
	101	79.4	15/32"x7/32"	.75	.60
	104	88.8	1/2"x7/32"	.79	.63
	107	96.0	17/32"x7/32"	.81	.65
	110	103.9	9/16"x7/32"	.83	.66
	114	120.9	5/8"x7/32"	.90	.72
100	93	52.7	11/32"x7/32"	.59	.47
	94	59.2	3/8"x7/32" ‡	.65	.52
	97	66.2	13/32"x7/32"	.68	.54
	100	73.8	7/16"x7/32"	.71	.57
	102	81.7	15/32"x7/32"	.76	.61
	105	91.6	1/2"x7/32"	.80	.64
	108	98.9	17/32"x7/32"	.82	.65
	111	107.1	9/16"x7/32"	.84	.67
	115	124.4	5/8"x7/32"	.91	.73

*Precipitation Rate — inches per hour. Rates based on full circle operation.

■ Square spacing based on 50% of diameter of throw.

▲ Triangular spacing based on 60% of diameter of throw.

Non-shaded areas in performance charts are recommended for optimum distribution.

‡ Standard Nozzle Size recommended

81B

87

This **part circle rotor pop-up sprinkler** is designed for irrigating very large areas of turfgrass. Highly dependable and perfect for high flow rate operation in such very large, open turfgrass areas as parks and golf courses. Constructed of tough corrosion-resistant materials with only two moving parts for reliable operation even in sandy conditions.

Operating Range
*Precipitation Rate:
.92 to 1.72 ins./hr.
Spacing: 82 to 125 ft.
Pressure: 60 to 100 psi
(Performance depends on operating pressure, spacing and nozzle selected.)

Features
- 3-⅜" pop-up height
- Proven impact drive
- Energy efficient
- Adjustable arc — 20° to 340°
- Precision Jet Tube (PJ™)
- Heavy-duty retract spring
- Wiper seal
- Heavy-duty brass pop-up assembly
- Easy to service
- Straight bore range nozzle and spreader nozzle
- Range nozzle vane
- Rugged viny-coated cast iron case
- Double skirted TNT bearing
- Self-flushing inlet screen
- Optional rubber cover

Specifications
- 1½" Female thread
- Dimensions with alumnium cover:
   Overall height — 13½"
   Top diameter — 9¼"
- Dimensions with rubber cover:
   Overall height — 13¾"
   Top diameter — 9½"
- **87:** For standard nozzle at 80 psi, the highest point of stream is 17'6" above nozzle at 67'6" from sprinkler. Nozzle outlet trajectory is 23°.

87

87 ROTOR

PSI	Radius	GPM	Nozzle	*Precip. ■	*Precip. ▲
60	82	39.1	11/32"x1/4"	1.12	.90
	84	43.6	3/8"x1/4" ‡	1.19	.95
	86	48.8	13/32"x1/4"	1.27	1.02
	89	54.3	7/16"x1/4"	1.32	1.06
	91	60.0	15/32"x1/4"	1.40	1.12
	93	65.5	1/2"x1/4"	1.46	1.17
	97	70.6	17/32"x1/4"	1.45	1.16
	100	78.2	9/16"x1/4"	1.51	1.21
	103	91.4	5/8"x1/4"	1.66	1.33
65	84	40.9	11/32"x1/4"	1.12	.90
	85	45.5	3/8"x1/4" ‡	1.21	.97
	88	50.9	13/32"x1/4"	1.27	1.02
	90	56.2	7/16"x1/4"	1.34	1.07
	93	62.2	15/32"x1/4"	1.39	1.11
	95	68.0	1/2"x1/4"	1.45	1.16
	98	73.4	17/32"x1/4"	1.47	1.18
	102	81.7	9/16"x1/4"	1.51	1.21
	105	94.9	5/8"x1/4"	1.66	1.33
70	86	42.6	11/32"x1/4"	1.11	.89
	87	47.4	3/8"x1/4" ‡	1.21	.97
	89	53.0	13/32"x1/4"	1.29	1.03
	92	59.0	7/16"x1/4"	1.34	1.08
	94	65.2	15/32"x1/4"	1.42	1.14
	97	70.9	1/2"x1/4"	1.45	1.16
	100	76.4	17/32"x1/4"	1.47	1.18
	103	84.9	9/16"x1/4"	1.54	1.24
	107	99.1	5/8"x1/4"	1.67	1.34
75	87	44.2	11/32"x1/4"	1.12	.90
	88	49.2	3/8"x1/4" ‡	1.22	.98
	91	54.9	13/32"x1/4"	1.28	1.02
	93	61.1	7/16"x1/4"	1.36	1.09
	96	67.5	15/32"x1/4"	1.41	1.13
	98	73.2	1/2"x1/4"	1.47	1.18
	101	79.2	17/32"x1/4"	1.50	1.20
	105	88.0	9/16"x1/4"	1.54	1.23
	108	102.4	5/8"x1/4"	1.69	1.36

*Precipitation Rate — inches per hour. Rates based on half circle operation.

■ Square spacing based on 50% diameter of throw.

▲ Triangular spacing based on 60% diameter of throw.

87 ROTOR

PSI	Radius	GPM	Nozzle	*Precip. ■	*Precip. ▲
80	89	46.1	11/32"x1/4"	1.12	.90
	90	51.0	3/8"x1/4" ‡	1.21	.97
	92	56.9	13/32"x1/4"	1.29	1.04
	95	63.4	7/16"x1/4"	1.35	1.08
	97	70.1	15/32"x1/4"	1.43	1.15
	100	75.9	1/2"x1/4"	1.46	1.17
	103	82.2	17/32"x1/4"	1.49	1.20
	106	91.2	9/16"x1/4"	1.56	1.25
	110	106.4	5/8"x1/4"	1.69	1.36
85	90	47.6	11/32"x1/4"	1.13	.91
	91	52.6	3/8"x1/4" ‡	1.22	.98
	93	58.8	13/32"x1/4"	1.31	1.05
	96	65.5	7/16"x1/4"	1.37	1.10
	99	72.5	15/32"x1/4"	1.42	1.14
	101	78.4	1/2"x1/4"	1.48	1.19
	104	85.0	17/32"x1/4"	1.51	1.21
	108	94.2	9/16"x1/4"	1.56	1.25
	111	110.1	5/8"x1/4"	1.72	1.38
90	91	49.2	11/32"x1/4"	1.14	.92
	92	54.3	3/8"x1/4" ‡	1.24	.99
	95	60.8	13/32"x1/4"	1.30	1.04
	97	67.6	7/16"x1/4"	1.38	1.11
	100	74.9	15/32"x1/4"	1.44	1.16
	103	80.9	1/2"x1/4"	1.47	1.18
	106	87.8	17/32"x1/4"	1.51	1.21
	109	97.2	9/16"x1/4"	1.58	1.26
	112	113.8	5/8"x1/4"	1.75	1.40
95	92	50.7	11/32"x1/4"	1.15	.93
	93	55.9	3/8"x1/4" ‡	1.24	1.00
	96	62.8	13/32"x1/4"	1.31	1.05
	99	69.7	7/16"x1/4"	1.37	1.10
	101	77.3	15/32"x1/4"	1.46	1.17
	104	83.4	1/2"x1/4"	1.49	1.19
	107	90.6	17/32"x1/4"	1.52	1.22
	110	100.2	9/16"x1/4"	1.59	1.28
	114	117.5	5/8"x1/4"	1.74	1.40
100	93	52.3	11/32"x1/4"	1.16	.93
	94	57.6	3/8"x1/4" ‡	1.26	1.01
	97	64.8	13/32"x1/4"	1.33	1.06
	100	71.8	7/16"x1/4"	1.38	1.11
	102	79.7	15/32"x1/4"	1.48	1.18
	105	85.9	1/2"x1/4"	1.50	1.20
	108	93.4	17/32"x1/4"	1.54	1.24
	111	103.2	9/16"x1/4"	1.61	1.29
	115	121.2	5/8"x1/4"	1.77	1.42

Non-shaded areas in performance charts are recommended for optimum distribution.

‡ Standard Nozzle Size recommended.

630 SERIES
ROTARY SPRINKLERS

IRRIGATION DIVISION

MODEL 634

GEAR DRIVEN FULL CIRCLE 360°	MODEL NO.	MODEL NO.	MODEL NO.	MODEL NO.	DESCRIPTION
	634-01-31	634-01-32	634-01-33	634-01-34	Full circle, hydraulic valve-in-head (normally open).
	634-11-31	634-11-32	634-11-33	634-11-34	Rubber covered version of above sprinkler.
	634-02-31	634-02-32	634-02-33	634-02-34	Full circle, Checkomatic.
	634-12-31	634-12-32	634-12-33	634-12-34	Rubber covered version of above sprinkler.
	634-06-31	634-06-32	634-06-33	634-06-34	Full circle, electric valve-in-head.
	634-16-31	634-16-32	634-16-33	634-16-34	Rubber covered version of above sprinkler.

SPECIFICATIONS

INLET — 1" I.P.S. thread.
HEIGHT — 10".
ARC — Full circle.
DRIVE MECHANISM — Gear driven with grease packed gear assembly isolated from water stream.
SPRING RETRACTION — Positive spring retraction to pull cap and nozzles down when watering is finished.
NOZZLES — Two nozzles with a double orifice inner nozzle

to provide efficient distribution of water.
POP-UP — Nozzles and cap pop-up one inch when head is in operation.
SCREENING — Six square inches of screen keep nozzles from being plugged with debris.
ACCESSIBILITY — All internal parts of the sprinkler are accessible through the top of the sprinkler.
MAXIMUM WORKING PRESSURE — 150 PSI.

PERFORMANCE CHART

BASE PRESSURE	NOZZLE SET -31 SIZE 3/16"		NOZZLE SET -32 SIZE 7/32"		NOZZLE SET -33 SIZE 1/4"		NOZZLE SET -34 SIZE 5/16"	
PSI	RADIUS	G.P.M.	RADIUS	G.P.M.	RADIUS	G.P.M.	RADIUS	G.P.M.
40	49'	11.0	54'	13.0				
50	51'	11.7	55'	14.0	60'	16.1		
60	53'	12.7	57'	15.2	62'	17.8	63'	23.8
70					65'	19.5	67'	25.5
80	56'	15.6	60'	18.6	66'	20.5	68'	27.0
90							69'	28.6
100							72'	30.0

Red Numbers — Where pressure regulation begins on the electric valve-in-head models.

SPACING OF SPRINKLERS

Square Spacing		
No wind	—55% of diameter	
4 m.p.h. wind	—50% of diameter	
8 m.p.h. wind	—45% of diameter	
Triangular Spacing		
No wind	—60% of diameter	
4 m.p.h. wind	—55% of diameter	
8 m.p.h. wind	—50% of diameter	
Single Row Spacing		
No wind	—50% of diameter	
4 m.p.h. wind	—50% of diameter	
8 m.p.h. wind	—45% of diameter	

CONVERSION INFORMATION

- All gallons per minute shown are U.S.
- To convert to Imperial gallons per minute, multiply by .833.
- To convert to litres per minute, multiply by 3.78.
- To convert pounds per square inch (PSI) to atmospheres, divide by 14.7.
- To convert pounds per square inch (PSI) to kilograms per square centimeter, divide by 14.22.
- To convert feet to meters, divide by 3.28.

670 SERIES
ROTARY SPRINKLERS

MODEL 674

	MODEL NO.	MODEL NO.	MODEL NO.	MODEL NO.	MODEL NO.	DESCRIPTION
GEAR DRIVEN FULL CIRCLE **360°**	674-01-70	674-01-71	674-01-72	674-01-73	674-01-74	Full circle, hydraulic valve-in-head (normally open).
	674-11-70	674-11-71	674-11-72	674-11-73	674-11-74	Rubber covered version of above sprinkler.
	674-02-70	674-02-71	674-02-72	674-02-73	674-02-74	Full circle, Checkomatic.
	674-12-70	674-12-71	674-12-72	674-12-73	674-12-74	Rubber covered version of above sprinkler.
	674-05-70	674-05-71	674-05-72	674-05-73	674-05-74	Full circle, electric valve-in-head (using 3-way 24 V.A.C. solenoid).
	674-15-70	674-15-71	674-15-72	674-15-73	674-15-74	Rubber covered version of above sprinkler.
	674-06-70	674-06-71	674-06-72	674-06-73	674-06-74	Full circle, electric valve-in-head (pressure regulated, manual on-off-auto).
	674-16-70	674-16-71	674-16-72	674-16-73	674-16-74	Rubber covered version of above sprinkler.

SPECIFICATIONS

INLET — 1½" I.P.S. thread.
HEIGHT — 11".
ARC — Full circle.
DRIVE MECHANISM — Planetary gear driven with grease packed gear assembly isolated from water stream.
SPRING RETRACTION — Positive spring retraction to pull cap and nozzles down when watering is finished.
NOZZLES — Three nozzles with the main nozzle on the opposite side of the inner and intermediate nozzles.

CAP — Free turning to prevent damage.
POP-UP — Nozzle and cap pop-up 1⅜ of an inch when head is in operation.
SCREENING — Stator-screen prevents debris from plugging nozzles.
ACCESSIBILITY — All internal parts of the sprinkler are accessible through the top of the sprinkler.
MAXIMUM WORKING PRESSURE — 150 PSI.

PERFORMANCE CHART

BASE PRESSURE PSI	NOZZLE SET -70 SIZE 5/16" RADIUS	G.P.M.	NOZZLE SET -71 SIZE 11/32" RADIUS	G.P.M.	NOZZLE SET -72 SIZE 3/8" RADIUS	G.P.M.	NOZZLE SET -73 SIZE 13/32" RADIUS	G.P.M.	NOZZLE SET -74 SIZE 7/16" RADIUS	G.P.M.
60	76'	35.5	78'	39.5						
70	80'	38.4	82'	42.7	85'	47.9	86'	52.6		
80	84'	41.2	85'	45.6	89'	51.0	92'	56.3	94'	59.6
90	86'	43.8	87'	48.5	92'	54.5	95'	59.8	99'	63.4
100	88'	46.2	90'	51.2	95'	57.3	98'	62.8	102'	66.8

Red Numbers — Where pressure regulation begins on the electric valve-in-head models.

SPACING OF SPRINKLERS

Square Spacing	
No wind	—55% of diameter
4 m.p.h. wind	—50% of diameter
8 m.p.h. wind	—45% of diameter
Triangular Spacing	
No wind	—60% of diameter
4 m.p.h. wind	—55% of diameter
8 m.p.h. wind	—50% of diameter
Single Row Spacing	
No wind	—50% of diameter
4 m.p.h. wind	—50% of diameter
8 m.p.h. wind	—45% of diameter

CONVERSION INFORMATION

- All gallons per minute shown are U.S.
- To convert to Imperial gallons per minute, multiply by .833.
- To convert to litres per minute, multiply by 3.78.
- To convert pounds per square inch (PSI) to atmospheres, divide by 14.7.
- To convert pounds per square inch (PSI) to kilograms per square centimeter, divide by 14.22.
- To convert feet to meters, divide by 3.28.

MODEL 651

QUARTER CIRCLE 90°	MODEL NO.	MODEL NO.	MODEL NO.	MODEL NO.	MODEL NO.	DESCRIPTION
	651-01-54	651-01-55	651-01-56	651-01-57	651-01-58	90° quarter circle, hydraulic valve-in-head (normally open).
	651-11-54	651-11-55	651-11-56	651-11-57	651-11-58	Rubber covered version of above sprinkler.
	651-02-54	651-02-55	651-02-56	651-02-57	651-02-58	90° quarter circle, Checkomatic.
	651-12-54	651-12-55	651-12-56	651-12-57	651-12-58	Rubber covered version of above sprinkler.
	651-06-54	651-06-55	651-06-56	651-06-57	651-06-58	90° quarter circle, electric valve-in-head.
	651-16-54	651-16-55	651-16-56	651-16-57	651-16-58	Rubber covered version of above sprinkler.

MODEL 652

HALF CIRCLE 180°	MODEL NO.	MODEL NO.	MODEL NO.	MODEL NO.	MODEL NO.	DESCRIPTION
	652-01-54	652-01-55	652-01-56	652-01-57	652-01-58	180° half circle, hydraulic valve-in-head (normally open).
	652-11-54	652-11-55	652-11-56	652-11-57	652-11-58	Rubber covered version of above sprinkler.
	652-02-54	652-02-55	652-02-56	652-02-57	652-02-58	180° half circle, Checkomatic.
	652-12-54	652-12-55	652-12-56	652-12-57	652-12-58	Rubber covered version of above sprinkler.
	652-06-54	652-06-55	652-06-56	652-06-57	652-06-58	180° half circle, electric valve-in-head.
	652-16-54	652-16-55	652-16-56	652-16-57	652-16-58	Rubber covered version of above sprinkler.

MODEL 655

ADJUSTABLE PART CIRCLE 45° MIN. 315° MAX.	MODEL NO.	MODEL NO.	MODEL NO.	MODEL NO.	MODEL NO.	DESCRIPTION
	655-01-54	655-01-55	655-01-56	655-01-57	655-01-58	Adjustable part circle, hydraulic valve-in-head (normally open).
	655-11-54	655-11-55	655-11-56	655-11-57	655-11-58	Rubber covered version of above sprinkler.
	655-02-54	655-02-55	655-02-56	655-02-57	655-02-58	Adjustable part circle, Checkomatic.
	655-12-54	655-12-55	655-12-56	655-12-57	655-12-58	Rubber covered version of above sprinkler.
	655-06-54	655-06-55	655-06-56	655-06-57	655-06-58	Adjustable part circle, electric valve-in-head.
	655-16-54	655-16-55	655-16-56	655-16-57	655-16-58	Rubber covered version of above sprinkler.

MODEL 654

GEAR DRIVEN FULL CIRCLE 360°	MODEL NO.	MODEL NO.	MODEL NO.	MODEL NO.	MODEL NO.	DESCRIPTION
	654-01-54	654-01-55	654-01-56	654-01-57	654-01-58	Full circle, hydraulic valve-in-head (normally open).
	654-11-54	654-11-55	654-11-56	654-11-57	654-11-58	Rubber covered version of above sprinkler.
	654-02-54	654-02-55	654-02-56	654-02-57	654-02-58	Full circle, Checkomatic.
	654-12-54	654-12-55	654-12-56	654-12-57	654-12-58	Rubber covered version of above sprinkler.
	654-06-54	654-06-55	654-06-56	654-06-57	654-06-58	Full circle, electric valve-in-head.
	654-16-54	654-16-55	654-16-56	654-16-57	654-16-58	Rubber covered version of above sprinkler.

MODEL 656

TWO SPEED FULL CIRCLE IN-LINE SPACING (SINGLE ROW)	MODEL NO.	MODEL NO.	MODEL NO.	MODEL NO.	MODEL NO.	DESCRIPTION
	656-01-54	656-01-55	656-01-56	656-01-57	656-01-58	2-speed in-line full circle, hydraulic valve-in-head (normally open).
	656-11-54	656-11-55	656-11-56	656-11-57	656-11-58	Rubber covered version of above sprinkler.
	656-02-54	656-02-55	656-02-56	656-02-57	656-02-58	2-speed in-line full circle, Checkomatic.
	656-12-54	656-12-55	656-12-56	656-12-57	656-12-58	Rubber covered version of above sprinkler.
	656-06-54	656-06-55	656-06-56	656-06-57	656-06-58	2-speed in-line full circle, electric valve-in-head.
	656-16-54	656-16-55	656-16-56	656-16-57	656-16-58	Rubber covered version of above sprinkler.

MODEL 658

TWO SPEED FULL CIRCLE 180° REGULAR SPEED 180° HALF SPEED	MODEL NO.	MODEL NO.	MODEL NO.	MODEL NO.	MODEL NO.	DESCRIPTION
	658-01-54	658-01-55	658-01-56	658-01-57	658-01-58	180° 2-speed full circle, hydraulic valve-in-head (normally open).
	658-11-54	658-11-55	658-11-56	658-11-57	658-11-58	Rubber covered version of above sprinkler.
	658-02-54	658-02-55	658-02-56	658-02-57	658-02-58	180° 2-speed full circle, Checkomatic.
	658-12-54	658-12-55	658-12-56	658-12-57	658-12-58	Rubber covered version of above sprinkler.
	658-06-54	658-06-55	658-06-56	658-06-57	658-06-58	180° 2-speed full circle, electric valve-in-head.
	658-16-54	658-16-55	658-16-56	658-16-57	658-16-58	Rubber covered version of above sprinkler.

IRRIGATION DIVISION

PERFORMANCE CHART

BASE PRESSURE	NOZZLE SET -54 SIZE 13/64"		NOZZLE SET -55 SIZE 15/64"		NOZZLE SET -56 SIZE 17/64"		NOZZLE SET -57 SIZE 5/16"		NOZZLE SET -58 SIZE 3/8"	
PSI	RADIUS	G.P.M.	RADIUS	G.P.M.	RADIUS	G.P.M.	RADIUS	G.P.M.	RADIUS	G.P.M.
40	45'	14.1								
50			58'	18.7						
60	50'	17.0	61'	20.1	65'	21.5				
70			64'	21.5	67'	24.0	70'	31.5		
80	52'	19.6	65'	22.9	68'	25.4	72'	32.9	77'	37.2
90							75'	34.7	80'	39.8
100							76'	36.5	82'	41.9

Red Numbers—Where pressure regulation begins on the electric valve-in-head models.

PERFORMANCE CHART

BASE PRESSURE	NOZZLE SET -90 SIZE 3/8"		NOZZLE SET -91 SIZE 7/16"		NOZZLE SET -92 SIZE 1/2"	
PSI	RADIUS	G.P.M.	RADIUS	G.P.M.	RADIUS	G.P.M.
40						
50						
60	78'	45.1	87'	53.7		
70	82'	48.6	91'	57.2	96'	67.5
80	87'	51.0	96'	61.2	100'	74.0
90					105'	78.0
100	90'	57.1	100'	73.4	108'	82.2

Red Numbers—Where pressure regulation begins on the electric valve-in-head models.

MODEL 691

QUARTER CIRCLE 90°	MODEL NO.	MODEL NO.	MODEL NO.	DESCRIPTION
	691-01-90	691-01-91	691-01-92	Quarter circle, hydraulic valve-in-head (normally open).
	691-11-90	691-11-91	691-11-92	Rubber covered version of above sprinkler.
	691-02-90	691-02-91	691-02-92	Quarter circle, Checkomatic.
	691-12-90	691-12-91	691-12-92	Rubber covered version of above sprinkler.
	691-06-90	691-06-91	691-06-92	Quarter circle, electric valve-in-head.
	691-16-90	691-16-91	691-16-92	Rubber covered version of above sprinkler.

MODEL 692

GEAR DRIVEN HALF CIRCLE 180°	MODEL NO.	MODEL NO.	MODEL NO.	DESCRIPTION
	692-01-90	692-01-91	692-01-92	Half circle, hydraulic valve-in-head (normally open).
	692-11-90	692-11-91	692-11-92	Rubber covered version of above sprinkler.
	692-02-90	692-02-91	692-02-92	Half circle, Checkomatic.
	692-12-90	692-12-91	692-12-92	Rubber covered version of above sprinkler.
	692-06-90	692-06-91	692-06-92	Half circle, electric valve-in-head.
	692-16-90	692-16-91	692-16-92	Rubber covered version of above sprinkler.

MODEL 694

FULL CIRCLE 360°	MODEL NO.	MODEL NO.	MODEL NO.	DESCRIPTION
	694-01-90	694-01-91	694-01-92	Full circle, hydraulic valve-in-head (normally open).
	694-11-90	694-11-91	694-11-92	Rubber covered version of above sprinkler.
	694-02-90	694-02-91	694-02-92	Full circle, Checkomatic.
	694-12-90	694-12-91	694-12-92	Rubber covered version of above sprinkler.
	694-06-90	694-06-91	694-06-92	Full circle, electric valve-in-head.
	694-16-90	694-16-91	694-16-92	Rubber covered version of above sprinkler.

MODEL 696

TWO SPEED FULL CIRCLE IN-LINE SPACING (SINGLE ROW)	MODEL NO.	MODEL NO.	MODEL NO.	DESCRIPTION
	696-01-90	696-01-91	696-01-92	2-speed in-line full circle, hydraulic valve-in-head (normally open).
	696-11-90	696-11-91	696-11-92	Rubber covered version of above sprinkler.
	696-02-90	696-02-91	696-02-92	2-speed in-line full circle, Checkomatic.
	696-12-90	696-12-91	696-12-92	Rubber covered version of above sprinkler.
	696-06-90	696-06-91	696-06-92	2-speed in-line full circle, electric valve-in-head.
	696-16-90	696-16-91	696-16-92	Rubber covered version of above sprinkler.

MODEL 698

TWO SPEED FULL CIRCLE 180° REGULAR SPEED 180° HALF SPEED	MODEL NO.	MODEL NO.	MODEL NO.	DESCRIPTION
	698-01-90	698-01-91	698-01-92	180° 2-speed full circle, hydraulic valve-in-head (normally open).
	698-11-90	698-11-91	698-11-92	Rubber covered version of above sprinkler.
	698-02-90	698-02-91	698-02-92	180° 2-speed full circle, Checkomatic.
	698-12-90	698-12-91	698-12-92	Rubber covered version of above sprinkler.
	698-06-90	698-06-91	698-06-92	180° 2-speed full circle, electric valve-in-head.
	698-16-90	698-16-91	698-16-92	Rubber covered version of above sprinkler.

TORO SERIES 500— SHRUB BUBBLERS

ADJUSTABLE STREAM BUBBLER

MODEL NUMBER	STREAM OPENINGS	1 P.S.I. RADIUS	1 P.S.I. G.P.M.	2 P.S.I. RADIUS	2 P.S.I. G.P.M.	5 P.S.I. RADIUS	5 P.S.I. G.P.M.	10 P.S.I. RADIUS	10 P.S.I. G.P.M.	PATTERN
511-30	2	2½′	.29	3′	.31	3½′	.42	4½′	.50	60°
512-30	4	2½′	.58	3′	.62	3½′	.84	4½′	1.00	
514-30	6	2½′	.87	3′	.93	3½′	1.25	4½′	1.50	
516-30	2	2½′	.29	3′	.31	3½′	.42	4½′	.50	

ADJUSTABLE FLOOD BUBBLER—514-20

MODEL NUMBER	G.P.M. AT 15 P.S.I.	G.P.M. AT 20 P.S.I.	G.P.M. AT 25 P.S.I.	G.P.M. AT 30 P.S.I.	G.P.M. AT 35 P.S.I.	G.P.M. AT 40 P.S.I.	PATTERN
514-20	1.7	2.0	2.2	2.4	2.5	2.7	360°

TORO SERIES 550—STREAM SPRAY SHRUB HEAD

PERFORMANCE CHART

MODEL NUMBER	TRAJECTORY	PRESSURE (P.S.I.) AT BASE OF SPRINKLER 15 P.S.I. RADIUS*	15 P.S.I. G.P.M.	20 P.S.I. RADIUS*	20 P.S.I. G.P.M.	25 P.S.I. RADIUS*	25 P.S.I. G.P.M.	30 P.S.I. RADIUS*	30 P.S.I. G.P.M.	PATTERN
550-12-04	10°	13′	.5	14′	.6	15′	.7	16′	.8	90°
550-12-08	10°	13′	.9	14′	1.0	15′	1.1	16′	1.2	180°
550-12-16	10°	13′	1.5	14′	1.7	15′	1.9	16′	2.1	360°

SERIES 570—NOZZLES

SPEC. NO.	PSI	GPM	RADIUS	PATTERN
STANDARD GALLONAGE				
540P- 570S- 570P- 570HP- 570SR- } 15′-Q	20	.8	12	90°
	30	1.0	15	
540P- 570S- 570P- 570HP- 570SR- } 15′-120°	20	1.2	12	120°
	30	1.4	15	
540P- 570S- 570P- 570HP- 570SR- } 15′-H	20	1.7	12	180°
	30	2.0	15	
540P- 570S- 570P- 570HP- 570SR- } 15′-240°	20	2.2	12	240°
	30	2.6	15	
540P- 570S- 570P- 570HP- 570SR- } 15′-270°	20	2.5	12	270°
	30	3.0	15	
540P- 570S- 570P- 570HP- 570SR- } 15′-F	20	3.4	12	360°
	30	4.0	15	

SPECIAL PATTERNS				
540P- 570S- 570P- 570HP- 570SR- } 4′-EST	20	.5	3 x 12	END STRIP
	30	.6	4 x 15	
540P- 570S- 570P- 570HP- 570SR- } 4′-CST	20	1.0	3 x 24	CTR STRIP
	30	1.2	4 x 30	
540P- 570S- 570P- 570HP- 570SR- } 9′-SST	20	1.0	9 x 18	SIDE STRIP
	30	1.2	9 x 18	
540P- 570S- 570P- 570HP- 570SR- } 4′-SST	20	1.05	4 x 24	SIDE STRIP
	30	1.45	4 x 30	

TORO SERIES 640 — GEAR DRIVEN ROTARY STANDARD ARCS

◤ QUARTER CIRCLE

MODEL NUMBER		NOZZLE SIZE	P.S.I.	G.P.M.	RADIUS	PRECIP RATE
VALVE-IN-HEAD	CHECKOMATIC					
641-01-40	641-02-40	5/32	40 50 60	6.0 6.7 7.3	47' 50' 52'	.84
641-01-41	641-02-41	3/16	40 50 60	9.5 11.0 12.5	48' 53' 55'	1.76
641-01-42	641-02-42	7/32	40 50 60	12.0 13.5 15.0	52' 55' 57'	1.96
641-01-43	641-02-43	1/4	50 60 70	16.0 17.5 19.0	56' 59' 61'	2.24
641-01-44	641-02-44	5/16	60 75 90	22.5 25.0 27.5	60' 63' 65'	2.80

◗ HALF CIRCLE

MODEL NUMBER		NOZZLE SIZE	P.S.I.	G.P.M.	RADIUS	PRECIP RATE
VALVE-IN-HEAD	CHECKOMATIC					
642-01-40	642-02-40	5/32	40 50 60	6.0 6.7 7.3	47' 50' 52'	.42
642-01-41	642-02-41	3/16	40 50 60	9.5 11.0 12.5	48' 53' 55'	.88
642-01-42	642-02-42	7/32	40 50 60	12.0 13.5 15.0	52' 55' 57'	.98
642-01-43	642-02-43	1/4	50 60 70	16.0 17.5 19.0	56' 59' 61'	1.12
642-01-44	642-02-44	5/16	60 75 90	22.5 25.0 27.5	60' 63' 65'	1.40

◔ THREE QUARTER CIRCLE

MODEL NUMBER		NOZZLE SIZE	P.S.I.	G.P.M.	RADIUS	PRECIP. RATE
VALVE-IN-HEAD	CHECKOMATIC					
643-01-40	643-02-40	5/32	40 50 60	6.0 6.7 7.3	47' 50' 52'	.32
643-01-41	643-02-41	3/16	40 50 60	9.5 11.0 12.5	48' 53' 55'	.66
643-01-42	643-02-42	7/32	40 50 60	12.0 13.5 15.0	52' 55' 57'	.73
643-01-43	643-02-43	1/4	50 60 70	16.0 17.5 19.0	56' 59' 61'	.84
643-01-44	643-02-44	5/16	60 75 90	22.5 25.0 27.5	60' 63' 65'	1.05

● FULL CIRCLE

MODEL NUMBER		NOZZLE SIZE	P.S.I.	G.P.M.	DIAMETER	PRECIP. RATE
VALVE-IN-HEAD	CHECKOMATIC					
644-01-40	644-02-40	5/32	40 50 60	6.0 6.7 7.3	99' 100' 104'	.21
644-01-41	644-02-41	3/16	40 50 60	9.5 11.0 12.5	96' 106' 110'	.44
644-01-42	644-02-42	7/32	40 50 60	12.0 13.5 15.0	104' 110' 114'	.49
644-01-43	644-02-43	1/4	50 60 70	16.0 17.5 19.0	112' 118' 122'	.56
644-01-44	644-02-44	5/16	60 75 90	22.5 25.0 27.5	120' 126' 130'	.70

TORO SERIES 320 — RAIN PRO® STANDARD ARCS

90° COVERAGE

MODEL NUMBERS	PSI	GPM	RADIUS	PRECIP. RATE*
324-00-05 } 324-10-05	35	1.3	41'	.23
	40	1.4	44'	.22
	50	1.6	45'	.25
	60	1.8	47'	.25
324-00-06 } 324-10-06	40	2.0	44'	.32
	50	2.3	45'	.34
	60	2.4	47'	.34

180° COVERAGE

MODEL NUMBERS	PSI	GPM	RADIUS	PRECIP. RATE*
328-00-05 } 328-10-05	35	2.6	41'	.23
	40	2.8	44'	.22
	50	3.3	45'	.25
	60	3.6	47'	.25
328-00-06 } 328-10-06	40	4.0	44'	.32
	50	4.5	45'	.34
	60	4.9	47'	.34

360° COVERAGE

MODEL NUMBERS	PSI	GPM	RADIUS	PRECIP. RATE*
336-00-05 } 336-10-05	35	5.1	41'	.23
	40	5.6	44'	.22
	50	6.5	45'	.25
	60	7.1	47'	.25
336-00-06 } 336-10-06	40	7.9	44'	.32
	50	9.0	45'	.34
	60	9.7	47'	.34

TORO SERIES 320 — RAIN PRO ODD ARCS

115° COVERAGE
ARC DISC #9-8909

MODEL NUMBERS	PSI	GPM	RADIUS	PRECIP. RATE*
320-00-05-115° } 320-10-05-115°	35	1.6	41'	.23
	40	1.8	44'	.22
	50	2.1	45'	.25
	60	2.3	47'	.25
320-00-06-115° } 320-10-06-115°	40	2.5	44'	.32
	50	2.9	45'	.34
	60	3.1	47'	.34

140° COVERAGE
ARC DISC #9-8910

MODEL NUMBERS	PSI	GPM	RADIUS	PRECIP. RATE*
320-00-05-140° } 320-10-05-140°	35	2.0	41'	.23
	40	2.2	44'	.22
	50	2.5	45'	.25
	60	2.8	47'	.25
320-00-06-140° } 320-10-06-140°	40	3.1	44'	.32
	50	3.5	45'	.34
	60	3.8	47'	.34

165° COVERAGE
ARC DISC #9-6593

MODEL NUMBERS	PSI	GPM	RADIUS	PRECIP. RATE*
320-00-05-165° } 320-10-05-165°	35	2.4	41'	.23
	40	2.6	44'	.22
	50	3.0	45'	.25
	60	3.3	47'	.25
320-00-06-165° } 320-10-06-165°	40	3.6	44'	.32
	50	4.1	45'	.34
	60	4.5	47'	.34

195° COVERAGE
ARC DISC #9-6595

MODEL NUMBERS	PSI	GPM	RADIUS	PRECIP. RATE*
320-00-05-195° } 320-10-05-195°	35	2.8	41'	.23
	40	3.0	44'	.22
	50	3.5	45'	.25
	60	3.8	47'	.25
320-00-06-195° } 320-10-06-195°	40	4.3	44'	.32
	50	4.9	45'	.34
	60	5.2	47'	.34

210° COVERAGE
ARC DISC #9-8911

MODEL NUMBERS	PSI	GPM	RADIUS	PRECIP. RATE*
320-00-05-210° } 320-10-05-210°	35	3.0	41'	.23
	40	3.3	44'	.22
	50	3.8	45'	.25
	60	4.1	47'	.25
320-00-06-210° } 320-10-06-210°	40	4.6	44'	.32
	50	5.2	45'	.34
	60	5.6	47'	.34

225° COVERAGE
ARC DISC #9-8912

MODEL NUMBERS	PSI	GPM	RADIUS	PRECIP. RATE*
320-00-05-225° } 320-10-05-225°	35	3.2	41'	.23
	40	3.5	44'	.22
	50	4.1	45'	.25
	60	4.5	47'	.25
320-00-06-225° } 320-10-06-225°	40	5.0	44'	.32
	50	5.7	45'	.34
	60	6.1	47'	.34

250° COVERAGE
ARC DISC #9-8913

MODEL NUMBERS	PSI	GPM	RADIUS	PRECIP. RATE*
320-00-05-250° } 320-10-05-250°	35	3.5	41'	.23
	40	3.9	44'	.22
	50	4.5	45'	.25
	60	4.9	47'	.25
320-00-06-250° } 320-10-06-250°	40	5.5	44'	.32
	50	6.2	45'	.34
	60	6.7	47'	.34

270° COVERAGE
ARC DISC #9-6596

MODEL NUMBERS	PSI	GPM	RADIUS	PRECIP. RATE*
320-00-05-270° } 320-10-05-270°	35	3.8	41'	.23
	40	4.2	44'	.22
	50	4.9	45'	.25
	60	5.3	47'	.25
320-00-06-270° } 320-10-06-270°	40	5.9	44'	.32
	50	6.8	45'	.34
	60	7.3	47'	.34

TORO SERIES 300 PERFORMANCE CHARTS

STANDARD ARCS

90° COVERAGE

MODEL NUMBERS	PSI	GPM	RADIUS	PRECIP. RATE*
304-00-01 / 304-10-01 / 304-12-01	35 / 50	.57 / .72	16 / 18	.69 / .69
304-00-02 / 304-10-02 / 304-12-02	35 / 50	.70 / .89	21 / 24	.49 / .48
304-00-03 / 304-10-03 / 304-12-03	35 / 50	1.34 / 1.52	28 / 30	.53 / .52
304-00-63 / 304-10-63 / 304-12-63	35 / 50	.67 / .76	28 / 30	.26 / .26
304-00-93 / 304-10-93 / 304-12-93	35 / 50	1.00 / 1.14	28 / 30	.39 / .39

180° COVERAGE

MODEL NUMBERS	PSI	GPM	RADIUS	PRECIP. RATE*
308-00-01 / 308-10-01 / 308-12-01	35 / 50	1.14 / 1.44	16 / 18	.69 / .69
308-00-02 / 308-10-02 / 308-12-02	35 / 50	1.38 / 1.67	21 / 24	.48 / .45
308-00-03 / 308-10-03 / 308-12-03	35 / 50	2.77 / 3.31	28 / 30	.55 / .57
308-00-63 / 308-10-63 / 308-12-63	35 / 50	1.39 / 1.66	28 / 30	.27 / .28
308-00-93 / 308-10-93 / 308-12-93	35 / 50	2.08 / 2.48	28 / 30	.41 / .43

360° COVERAGE

MODEL NUMBERS	PSI	GPM	RADIUS	PRECIP. RATE*
316-00-01 / 316-10-01 / 316-12-01	35 / 50	2.28 / 2.88	16 / 18	.69 / .69
316-00-02 / 316-10-02 / 316-12-02	35 / 50	2.86 / 3.41	21 / 24	.50 / .46
316-00-03 / 316-10-03 / 316-12-03	35 / 50	5.43 / 6.45	28 / 30	.53 / .55
316-00-63 / 316-10-63 / 316-12-63	35 / 50	2.72 / 3.23	28 / 30	.27 / .28
316-00-93 / 316-10-93 / 316-12-93	35 / 50	4.07 / 4.84	28 / 30	.40 / .42

ODD ARCS

112½° COVERAGE — ARC DISC #9-3131

MODEL NUMBERS	PSI	GPM	RADIUS	PRECIP. RATE*
305-00-01 / 305-10-01 / 305-12-01	35 / 50	.71 / .89	16 / 18	.69 / .68
305-00-02 / 305-10-02 / 305-12-02	35 / 50	.87 / 1.08	21 / 24	.49 / .46
305-00-03 / 305-10-03 / 305-12-03	35 / 50	1.73 / 1.96	28 / 30	.55 / .54
305-00-63 / 305-10-63 / 305-12-63	35 / 50	.87 / .98	28 / 30	.27 / .27
305-00-93 / 305-10-93 / 305-12-93	35 / 50	1.30 / 1.47	28 / 30	.41 / .40

135° COVERAGE — ARC DISC #9-3132

MODEL NUMBERS	PSI	GPM	RADIUS	PRECIP. RATE*
306-00-01 / 306-10-01 / 306-12-01	35 / 50	.84 / 1.06	16 / 18	.68 / .67
306-00-02 / 306-10-02 / 306-12-02	35 / 50	1.04 / 1.27	21 / 24	.49 / .45
306-00-03 / 306-10-03 / 306-12-03	35 / 50	2.11 / 2.41	28 / 30	.55 / .55
306-00-63 / 306-10-63 / 306-12-63	35 / 50	1.06 / 1.21	28 / 30	.28 / .28
306-00-93 / 306-10-93 / 306-12-93	35 / 50	1.58 / 1.81	28 / 30	.42 / .41

157½° COVERAGE — ARC DISC #9-3133

MODEL NUMBERS	PSI	GPM	RADIUS	PRECIP. RATE*
307-00-01 / 307-10-01 / 307-12-01	35 / 50	.99 / 1.25	16 / 18	.68 / .68
307-00-02 / 307-10-02 / 307-12-02	35 / 50	1.21 / 1.47	21 / 24	.48 / .45
307-00-03 / 307-10-03 / 307-12-03	35 / 50	2.49 / 2.86	28 / 30	.56 / .56
307-00-63 / 307-10-63 / 307-12-63	35 / 50	1.25 / 1.43	28 / 30	.28 / .28
307-00-93 / 307-10-93 / 307-12-93	35 / 50	1.87 / 2.15	28 / 30	.42 / .42

202½° COVERAGE — ARC DISC #9-3134

MODEL NUMBERS	PSI	GPM	RADIUS	PRECIP. RATE*
309-00-01 / 309-10-01 / 309-12-01	35 / 50	1.28 / 1.61	16 / 18	.69 / .68
309-00-02 / 309-10-02 / 309-12-02	35 / 50	1.55 / 1.85	21 / 24	.48 / .44
309-00-03 / 309-10-03 / 309-12-03	35 / 50	3.11 / 3.74	28 / 30	.54 / .57
309-00-63 / 309-10-63 / 309-12-63	35 / 50	1.56 / 1.87	28 / 30	.27 / .29
309-00-93 / 309-10-93 / 309-12-93	35 / 50	2.33 / 2.81	28 / 30	.41 / .43

225° COVERAGE — ARC DISC #9-3135

MODEL NUMBERS	PSI	GPM	RADIUS	PRECIP. RATE*
310-00-01 / 310-10-01 / 310-12-01	35 / 50	1.43 / 1.79	16 / 18	.69 / .68
310-00-02 / 310-10-02 / 310-12-02	35 / 50	1.69 / 2.03	21 / 24	.47 / .44
310-00-03 / 310-10-03 / 310-12-03	35 / 50	3.45 / 4.17	28 / 30	.54 / .57
310-00-63 / 310-10-63 / 310-12-63	35 / 50	1.73 / 2.09	28 / 30	.27 / .29
310-00-93 / 310-10-93 / 310-12-93	35 / 50	2.59 / 3.13	28 / 30	.41 / .43

270° COVERAGE — ARC DISC #9-2663

MODEL NUMBERS	PSI	GPM	RADIUS	PRECIP. RATE*
312-00-01 / 312-10-01 / 312-12-01	35 / 50	1.71 / 2.16	16 / 18	.69 / .78
312-00-02 / 312-10-02 / 312-12-02	35 / 50	1.91 / 2.22	21 / 24	.45 / .40
312-00-03 / 312-10-03 / 312-12-03	35 / 50	3.80 / 4.61	28 / 30	.43 / .53
312-00-63 / 312-10-63 / 312-12-63	35 / 50	1.90 / 2.31	28 / 30	.25 / .26
312-00-93 / 312-10-93 / 312-12-93	50 / 50	2.85 / 3.46	28 / 30	.37 / .40

Royal Coach Sprinklers, Inc.

4381 N. Brawley Avenue · Fresno, California 93711 · (209) 442-0330

Model 10090
Full Circle

Single nozzle, adjustable break-up (Chart D)
or straight bore (Chart E), stream straightener.
Heavy duty bronze body and lid. Ideal for parks,
condominiums, golf courses, industrial and
recreational areas where heavy duty
equipment is required.

Recommended spacings: 45' to 75'.
1" female NPT inlet.
Options: Rubber cover and vandal
resistant screws.

10090

Chart D — Model 10090 — 1" Female NPT

Code	−09		−10		−11		−12	
PSI Nozzle Pressure	Nozzle 9/64"		*Nozzle 5/32"		Nozzle 11/64"		Nozzle 3/16"	
	Dia.	GPM	Dia.	GPM	Dia.	GPM	Dia.	GPM
40	84'	3.5	84'	4.4	86'	5.3	88'	6.4
45	84'	3.7	86'	4.7	87'	5.6	90'	6.7
50	85'	3.9	87'	4.9	88'	5.9	92'	7.1
55	86'	4.1	88'	5.2	89'	6.2	93'	7.5
60	86'	4.3	89'	5.4	90'	6.5	94'	7.8
65	87'	4.4	90'	5.6	91'	6.7	95'	8.1
70	88'	4.6	90'	5.8	92'	7.0	96'	8.4
75	88'	4.8	91'	6.0	93'	7.2	97'	8.7
80	89'	4.9	92'	6.2	94'	7.5	98'	9.0

Chart E — Model 10090 — 1" Female NPT

Code	−13		−14		−15		−16	
PSI Nozzle Pressure	Nozzle 13/64"		*Nozzle 7/32"		Nozzle 15/64"		Nozzle 1/4"	
	Dia.	GPM	Dia.	GPM	Dia.	GPM	Dia.	GPM
40	92'	7.5	94'	8.7	96'	10.4	98'	11.4
45	94'	8.0	96'	9.1	98'	10.9	100'	12.0
50	95'	8.4	98'	9.6	100'	11.4	102'	12.6
55	96'	8.8	100'	10.2	102'	11.9	104'	13.2
60	97'	9.2	102'	10.6	104'	12.5	106'	13.8
65	98'	9.6	104'	11.1	106'	13.1	108'	14.4
70	99'	10.0	106'	11.6	108'	13.7	110'	15.0
75	100'	10.3	108'	12.1	110'	14.2	112'	15.5
80	101'	10.7	110'	12.5	111'	14.7	113'	16.2

Model 10092
Full Circle

Two nozzles. Inner nozzle is
spreader type. Stream straightener
in range nozzle. Bronze body and
lid. Recommended spacings: 55' to
100' depending on range nozzle
selection. (Chart for G) A high performance sprinkler for wide coverage
with reasonable water pressure. Ideal
for parks, golf courses and large
industrial plants where heavy duty
equipment is required. 1" female
NPT inlet.
Options: Rubber cover and vandal
resistant screws.

10092

Chart F 1" Female NPT — Model 10092

Code	−11−11		−12−11		−13−11		−14−11		−14−12	
PSI Nozzle Pressure	Nozzle 11/64" x 11/64"		Nozzle 3/16" x 11/64"		Nozzle 13/64" x 11/64"		*Nozzle 7/32" x 11/64"		Nozzle 7/32" x 3/16"	
	Dia.	GPM	Dia.	GPM	Dia.	GPM	Dia.	GPM	Dia.	GPM
45	102'	11.5	105'	12.5	108'	13.6	113'	14.7	113'	16.0
50	104'	12.2	107'	13.2	110'	14.4	115'	15.5	115'	16.8
55	105'	12.7	108'	13.8	112'	15.1	117'	16.4	117'	17.6
60	106'	13.3	110'	14.4	114'	15.8	119'	17.1	119'	18.3
65	107'	13.9	111'	15.0	116'	16.4	121'	17.8	121'	19.1
70	108'	14.4	112'	15.6	117'	16.9	123'	18.4	123'	19.9
75	109'	14.9	113'	16.1	118'	17.6	124'	19.1	124'	20.6
80	110'	15.4	114'	16.7	120'	18.2	125'	19.6	125'	21.2
85	111'	15.9	115'	17.2	120'	18.8	126'	20.2	126'	21.8

Chart G 1" Female NPT — Model 10092

Code	−16−11		−16−12		−18−12		−20−12		−22−13		−24−14		−26−15	
PSI Nozzle Pressure	Nozzle 1/4" x 11/64"		Nozzle 1/4" x 3/16"		Nozzle 9/32" x 3/16"		*Nozzle 5/16" x 3/16"		Nozzle 11/32" x 13/64"		Nozzle 3/8" x 7/32"		Nozzle 13/32" x 15/64"	
	Dia.	GPM	Dia.	GPM	Dia.	GPM	Dia.	GPM	Dia.	GPM	Dia.	GPM	Dia.	GPM
45	116'	17.1	116'	18.4	119'	20.5	—	—	—	—	—	—	—	—
50	118'	18.1	118'	19.3	122'	21.8	126'	25.1	130'	29.7	—	—	—	—
55	121'	19.0	121'	20.2	124'	22.9	128'	26.3	131'	31.1	134'	35.1	—	—
60	123'	19.8	123'	21.1	126'	23.9	130'	27.5	134'	32.6	137'	36.6	139'	41.6
65	125'	20.6	125'	22.0	128'	25.1	133'	28.8	137'	34.1	142'	38.1	143'	43.2
70	127'	21.4	127'	22.9	130'	26.0	135'	29.9	141'	35.4	145'	39.5	146'	44.8
75	129'	22.2	129'	23.8	132'	27.0	138'	30.9	144'	36.7	149'	41.0	151'	46.5
80	131'	23.0	131'	24.6	134'	27.9	140'	32.0	147'	37.9	153'	42.4	155'	48.1
85	132'	23.8	132'	25.4	136'	28.8	142'	33.0	150'	39.2	156'	43.9	159'	49.8
90	133'	24.6	133'	26.1	137'	29.6	144'	34.0	152'	40.3	158'	45.1	163'	51.3
95	134'	25.4	134'	26.8	138'	30.4	145'	35.0	153'	41.4	161'	46.4	164'	52.8
100	135'	26.2	135'	27.6	140'	31.2	147'	36.0	156'	42.6	163'	47.8	168'	54.2

*Standard nozzle size.
Shaded area NOT recommended for
best distribution.
Water pressure is at bottom of sprinkler.

Model 10100
Full Circle

Two nozzles. Inner nozzle is adjustable break-up. Stream straightener in both nozzles. Heavy duty bronze body and lid. Use on golf courses, parks and in open areas where greater economy can be acquired from larger spacings. Recommended spacings: 75' to 110'. 1 1/4" female NPT inlet.

Options: Rubber cover and vandal resistant screws.

10100   10101

Royal Coach Sprinklers, Inc.

4381 N. Brawley Avenue · Fresno, California 93711 · (209) 442-0330

TWX 910 362 1167

Models 10100 and 10101   **1 1/4" Female NPT**

Code	−20−13		−22−13		−24−13		−26−13		−28−13		−32−13	
	Nozzle 5/16" x 13/64"		Nozzle 11/32" x 13/64"		Nozzle 3/8" x 13/64"		*Nozzle 13/32" x 13/64"		Nozzle 7/16" x 13/64"		Nozzle 1/2" x 13/64"	
PSI Nozzle Pressure	Dia.	GPM	Dia.	GPM	Dia.	GPM	Dia.	GPM	Dia.	GPM	Dia.	GPM
60	140'	27.9	146'	32.5	152'	37.6	160'	43.5	168'	49.2	176'	61.8
70	144'	30.2	150'	35.1	157'	40.6	166'	46.4	174'	52.6	182'	66.4
80	149'	32.2	156'	37.5	163'	43.3	172'	49.6	180'	56.3	188'	71.0
90	153'	34.3	161'	39.8	169'	46.1	177'	52.5	186'	59.9	194'	75.2

*Standard nozzle size.

Model 10110
Full Circle

Two nozzles with stream straighteners. Inner nozzle is adjustable break-up. Baked enamel coated cast iron body and aluminum lid. Recommended spacings: 75' to 130' depending on range nozzle selection. Break-up inner nozzle provides excellent coverage close to the sprinkler. Use on golf courses, parks, sport fields and open areas for wide coverage where large spacing can be utilized. 1 1/2" female NPT inlet.

Options: Rubber cover and vandal resistant screws.

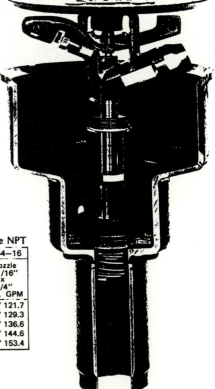

Model 10110   **1 1/2" Female NPT**

Code	−24−14		−28−14		−32−16		−34−16		−36−16		−40−16		−44−16	
	Nozzle 3/8" x 7/32"		Nozzle 7/16" x 7/32"		Nozzle 1/2" x 1/4"		*Nozzle 17/32" x 1/4"		Nozzle 9/16" x 1/4"		Nozzle 5/8" x 1/4"		Nozzle 11/16" x 1/4"	
PSI Nozzle Pressure	Dia.	GPM	Dia.	GPM	Dia.	GPM	Dia.	GPM	Dia.	GPM	Dia.	GPM	Dia.	GPM
60	167'	41.6	178'	52.7	191'	70.3	197'	73.7	204'	85.0	213'	102.8	224'	121.7
70	173'	45.0	184'	57.0	197'	74.3	203'	78.8	210'	90.4	220'	109.2	232'	129.3
80	178'	47.9	190'	60.9	203'	79.4	209'	84.1	216'	96.5	227'	115.4	240'	136.6
90	183'	50.9	196'	64.7	211'	84.1	215'	89.2	223'	102.3	234'	121.8	248'	144.6
100	188'	54.1	201'	67.9	218'	88.3	221'	94.0	229'	106.5	240'	128.7	256'	153.4

*Standard nozzle size.

WEATHER-TEC / SKINNER

- Full circle [Part cirlce: adjustable 20° to 340° arc of coverage]
- Single adjustable nozzle - 26° trajectory
- Vinyl coated cast iron case with 1" female N.P.T. inlet [1]
- Free rotating green die-cast aluminum cover [2]
- Entire internal assembly removable from top. Positive closure pop-up mechanism of high impact resistant plastic
- Cast bronze head with cored water passage and double bridge construction
- Cast bronze lever with I-beam construction and wide impact area
- 'K' type bearing for dependable sand / silt resistant seal and uniform speed of rotation
- Stainless steel spindle, fulcrum [and trip] pins, lever, bearing, retract [and trip] springs [trips and trip collars] [3]
- [Stainless steel part circle only trips are standard]
- Designed as a single nozzle sprinkler for all medium to heavy turf applications. Ideal for major landscaping, commerical and industrial use, parks, golf courses and all other medium to large turf areas.

Model 30-20   Pop-Up Full Circle Impact

Highest point of stream above nozzle is 7' *

PSI	Nozzle 7/64" Dia	GPM	Nozzle 1/8" Dia	GPM	Nozzle 9/64" Dia	GPM	Nozzle 5/32" ** Dia	GPM	Nozzle 11/64" Dia	GPM	Nozzle 3/16" Dia	GPM
20	66	1.54	68	2.08	71	2.53	74	3.05	76	3.63	78	4.26
25	69	1.73	71	2.33	74	2.84	77	3.41	79	4.07	82	4.77
30	72	1.89	75	2.55	78	3.12	81	3.75	83	4.46	85	5.22
35	73	2.04	76	2.76	79	3.37	82	4.05	84	4.82	86	5.64
40	74	2.18	77	2.95	80	3.61	83	4.34	85	5.16	87	6.04
45	75	2.32	78	3.13	81	3.83	84	4.60	86	5.48	88	6.40
50	76	2.45	79	3.30	82	4.04	85	4.86	87	5.78	89	6.75
55	77	2.56	80	3.46	83	4.24	86	5.10	88	6.06	90	7.08
60	78	2.68	81	3.61	84	4.43	87	5.33	89	6.34	91	7.40
65	79	2.79	82	3.76	85	4.61	88	5.55	90	6.60	92	7.70
70	80	2.89	83	3.90	86	4.79	89	5.76	91	6.85	93	7.99

Model 30-81   Pop-Up Full Circle Impact

Nominal stream height 11' above nozzle @ normal pressure *

PSI	Nozzle 11/64" Dia	GPM	Nozzle 3/16" ** Dia	GPM	Nozzle 13/64" Dia	GPM	Nozzle 7/32" Dia	GPM
45	93	5.57	98	6.54	103	7.43	106	8.41
50	94	5.87	100	6.90	104	7.83	108	8.87
55	95	6.16	101	7.25	105	8.22	109	9.31
60	96	6.48	102	7.59	106	8.58	110	9.73
65	97	6.70	103	7.91	107	8.94	111	10.13
70	98	6.95	104	8.22	108	9.28	112	10.51
75	99	7.19	105	8.52	109	9.61	113	10.88
80	100	7.49	106	8.82	110	9.93	114	11.24

* Standard nozzle at mid-point of pressure range
** Indicates standard nozzle size furnished unless otherwise specified
Data in unshaded chart area is recommended for best performance

Model 30-83   Pop-Up Full Circle Impact

Highest point of stream above nozzle is 17' *

PSI	Nozzle 11/64"x11/64" Dia	GPM	Nozzle 3/16"x11/64" Dia	GPM	Nozzle 13/16"x11/64" Dia	GPM	Nozzle 7/32"x11/64" Dia	GPM	Nozzle 1/4"x11/64" ** Dia	GPM	Nozzle 9/32"x11/64" Dia	GPM	Nozzle 5/16"x11/64" Dia	GPM	Nozzle 11/32"x11/64" Dia	GPM	Nozzle 3/8"x11/64" Dia	GPM	Nozzle 13/32"x11/64" Dia	GPM
50	95	11.57	100	12.63	104	14.01	108	15.28	116	17.91	124	21.75	132	24.47	138	29.82	144	35.10	150	39.34
55	96	12.13	100	13.23	105	14.67	110	16.00	118	18.75	126	22.76	134	25.60	140	31.21	148	36.76	154	41.17
60	97	12.66	101	13.81	106	15.29	112	16.68	120	19.55	128	23.72	136	26.67	142	32.54	150	38.35	156	42.92
65	98	13.16	102	14.36	107	15.89	113	17.33	121	20.32	130	24.63	138	27.70	146	33.81	152	39.87	160	44.59
70	99	13.65	103	14.89	108	16.47	114	17.96	122	21.06	132	25.52	140	28.69	148	35.04	156	41.34	164	46.19
75	99	14.12	104	15.40	109	17.02	115	18.56	124	21.77	134	26.36	142	29.64	150	36.22	158	42.75	166	47.74
80	100	14.58	105	15.90	110	17.55	116	19.15	126	22.45	136	27.19	144	30.55	154	37.35	162	44.11	170	49.24
85	101	15.01	106	16.38	112	18.07	117	19.71	128	23.12	138	27.98	146	31.44	156	38.46	164	45.43	172	50.68
90	102	15.44	107	16.84	114	18.57	118	20.26	130	23.76	140	28.75	148	32.29	158	39.52	166	46.71	176	52.09
95	103	15.86	108	17.29	115	19.06	120	20.79	131	24.39	142	29.49	152	33.13	160	42.56	170	47.95	178	53.45
100	104	16.26	109	17.74	116	19.54	122	21.31	132	25.80	144	30.22	154	33.95	164	43.57	172	49.16	182	54.77

WEATHER-TEC / SKINNER

- Full circle [Part cirlce: adjustable 20° to 340° arc of coverage]
- Dual offset over/under nozzles, adjustable - 23° range trajectory
- Vinyl coated cast iron case with 1 1/4" female N.P.T. inlet [1]
- Free rotating green die-cast aluminum cover [2]
- Entire internal assembly removable from top. Positive closure pop-up mechanism of high impact resistant plastic
- Cast bronze head with cored water passage and double bridge construction
- Cast bronze lever with I-beam construction and wide impact area
- 'K' type bearing for dependable sand/silt resistant seal and uniform speed of rotation
- Stainless steel spindle, fulcrum [and trip] pins, lever, bearing, retract [and trip] springs [trips and trip collars] [3]
- [Stainless steel part circle only trips are standard]
- Designed as a dual nozzle, high flow, large diameter sprinkler for all heavy turf applications. Ideal for parks, golf courses, athletic fields and all heavy turf, large area usage.

Model 30-84   Pop-Up Full Circle Impact

Highest point of stream above nozzle is 17.5' *

PSI	Nozzle 11/32"x11/64" Dia	GPM	Nozzle 3/8"x11/64" ** Dia	GPM	Nozzle 13/32"x11/64" Dia	GPM	Nozzle 7/16"x11/64" Dia	GPM	Nozzle 1/2"x11/64" Dia	GPM
50	138	29.82	144	35.10	150	39.34	156	45.73	168	57.26
55	140	31.21	148	36.76	154	41.17	160	48.05	172	60.23
60	142	32.54	150	38.35	156	42.92	162	50.28	174	63.08
65	146	33.81	152	39.87	160	44.59	166	52.41	180	65.83
70	148	35.04	156	41.34	164	46.19	170	54.47	184	68.47
75	150	36.22	158	42.75	166	47.74	174	56.46	190	71.03
80	154	37.35	162	44.11	170	49.24	178	58.39	192	73.51
85	156	38.46	164	45.43	172	50.68	182	60.26	196	75.91
90	158	39.52	166	46.71	176	52.09	184	62.08	200	78.25
95	160	42.56	170	47.95	178	53.45	186	63.85	204	80.54
100	164	43.57	172	49.16	182	54.77	190	65.58	208	82.76

* Standard nozzle at mid-point of pressure range
** Indicates standard nozzle size furnished unless otherwise specified
Data in unshaded chart area is recommended for best performance

Appendix B
PIPE PERFORMANCE DATA

Data presented on tables B–1 through B–7 are taken with permission from Rain Bird, 1976. Figure B–1 is taken with permission from Wolfe, 1950.

Table B–1 FRICTION LOSS CHARACTERISTICS
PVC CLASS 160 IPS PLASTIC PIPE
(1120, 1220) SDR 26 C = 150
PSI LOSS PER 100 FEET OF PIPE (PSI/100 FT)

Sizes 1″ thru 5″. Flow GPM 1 thru 1250.

SIZE	1.00	1.25	1.50	2.00	2.50	3.00	3.50	4.00	5.00	SIZE
OD	1.315	1.660	1.900	2.375	2.875	3.500	4.000	4.500	5.563	OD
ID	1.195	1.532	1.754	2.193	2.655	3.230	3.692	4.154	5.133	ID
WALL THK	0.060	0.064	0.073	0.091	0.110	0.135	0.154	0.173	0.214	WALL THK

Flow G.P.M.	Velocity F.P.S.	P.S.I. Loss	Velocity F.P.S.	P.S.I. Loss	Velocity F.P.S.	P.S.I. Loss	Velocity F.P.S.	P.S.I. Loss	Velocity F.P.S.	P.S.I. Loss	Velocity F.P.S.	P.S.I. Loss	Velocity F.P.S.	P.S.I. Loss	Velocity F.P.S.	P.S.I. Loss	Velocity F.P.S.	P.S.I. Loss	Flow G.P.M.
1	0.28	0.02	0.17	0.01	0.13	0.00													1
2	0.57	0.06	0.34	0.02	0.26	0.01	0.16	0.00											2
3	0.85	0.14	0.52	0.04	0.39	0.02	0.25	0.01											3
4	1.14	0.23	0.69	0.07	0.53	0.04	0.33	0.01	0.23	0.00									4
5	1.42	0.35	0.86	0.11	0.66	0.05	0.42	0.02	0.28	0.01									5
6	1.71	0.49	1.04	0.15	0.79	0.08	0.50	0.03	0.34	0.01	0.23	0.00							6
7	1.99	0.66	1.21	0.20	0.92	0.10	0.59	0.03	0.40	0.01	0.27	0.01							7
8	2.28	0.84	1.39	0.25	1.06	0.13	0.67	0.04	0.46	0.02	0.31	0.01							8
9	2.57	1.05	1.56	0.31	1.19	0.16	0.76	0.05	0.52	0.02	0.35	0.01	0.26	0.00					9
10	2.85	1.27	1.73	0.38	1.32	0.20	0.84	0.07	0.57	0.03	0.39	0.01	0.29	0.01					10
11	3.14	1.52	1.91	0.45	1.45	0.23	0.93	0.08	0.63	0.03	0.43	0.01	0.32	0.01					11
12	3.42	1.78	2.08	0.53	1.59	0.28	1.01	0.09	0.69	0.04	0.46	0.01	0.35	0.01	0.28	0.00			12
14	3.99	2.37	2.43	0.71	1.85	0.37	1.18	0.12	0.81	0.05	0.54	0.02	0.41	0.01	0.33	0.01			14
16	4.57	3.04	2.78	0.91	2.12	0.47	1.35	0.16	0.92	0.06	0.62	0.02	0.47	0.01	0.37	0.01			16
18	5.14	3.78	3.12	1.13	2.38	0.58	1.52	0.20	1.04	0.08	0.70	0.03	0.53	0.02	0.42	0.01			18
20	5.71	4.59	3.47	1.37	2.65	0.71	1.69	0.24	1.15	0.09	0.78	0.04	0.59	0.02	0.47	0.01			20
22	6.28	5.48	3.82	1.64	2.91	0.85	1.86	0.29	1.27	0.11	0.86	0.04	0.65	0.02	0.52	0.01	0.34	0.00	22
24	6.85	6.44	4.17	1.92	3.18	1.00	2.03	0.34	1.38	0.13	0.93	0.05	0.71	0.03	0.56	0.02	0.37	0.01	24
26	7.42	7.47	4.51	2.23	3.44	1.15	2.20	0.39	1.50	0.15	1.01	0.06	0.77	0.03	0.61	0.02	0.40	0.01	26
28	7.99	8.57	4.86	2.56	3.71	1.32	2.37	0.45	1.62	0.18	1.09	0.07	0.83	0.04	0.66	0.02	0.43	0.01	28
30	8.57	9.74	5.21	2.91	3.97	1.50	2.54	0.51	1.73	0.20	1.17	0.08	0.89	0.04	0.70	0.02	0.46	0.01	30
35	9.99	12.95	6.08	3.87	4.64	2.00	2.96	0.68	2.02	0.27	1.36	0.10	1.04	0.05	0.82	0.03	0.54	0.01	35
40	11.42	16.59	6.95	4.95	5.30	2.56	3.39	0.87	2.31	0.34	1.56	0.13	1.19	0.07	0.94	0.04	0.61	0.01	40
45	12.85	20.63	7.82	6.16	5.96	3.19	3.81	1.08	2.60	0.42	1.75	0.16	1.34	0.09	1.06	0.05	0.69	0.02	45
50	14.28	25.07	8.69	7.49	6.63	3.88	4.24	1.31	2.89	0.52	1.95	0.20	1.49	0.10	1.18	0.06	0.77	0.02	50
55	15.71	29.91	9.56	8.93	7.29	4.62	4.66	1.56	3.18	0.62	2.15	0.24	1.64	0.12	1.30	0.07	0.85	0.02	55
60	17.14	35.14	10.43	10.49	7.95	5.43	5.09	1.83	3.47	0.72	2.34	0.28	1.79	0.15	1.41	0.08	0.92	0.03	60
65	18.57	40.76	11.29	12.17	8.62	6.30	5.51	2.12	3.76	0.84	2.54	0.32	1.94	0.17	1.53	0.09	1.00	0.03	65
70	19.99	46.76	12.16	13.96	9.28	7.23	5.93	2.44	4.05	0.96	2.73	0.37	2.09	0.19	1.65	0.11	1.08	0.04	70
75			13.03	15.86	9.94	8.21	6.36	2.77	4.34	1.09	2.93	0.42	2.24	0.22	1.77	0.12	1.16	0.04	75
80			13.90	17.88	10.60	9.25	6.78	3.12	4.63	1.23	3.12	0.47	2.39	0.25	1.89	0.14	1.23	0.05	80
85			14.77	20.00	11.27	10.35	7.21	3.49	4.91	1.38	3.32	0.53	2.54	0.28	2.00	0.16	1.31	0.06	85
90			15.64	22.23	11.93	11.51	7.63	3.88	5.20	1.53	3.51	0.59	2.69	0.31	2.12	0.17	1.39	0.06	90
95			16.51	24.58	12.59	12.72	8.05	4.29	5.49	1.69	3.71	0.65	2.84	0.34	2.24	0.19	1.47	0.07	95
100			17.38	27.03	13.26	13.99	8.48	4.72	5.78	1.86	3.91	0.72	2.99	0.37	2.36	0.21	1.54	0.08	100
110			19.12	32.24	14.58	16.69	9.33	5.63	6.36	2.22	4.30	0.86	3.29	0.45	2.60	0.25	1.70	0.09	110
120					15.91	19.61	10.18	6.61	6.94	2.61	4.69	1.01	3.59	0.52	2.83	0.30	1.85	0.11	120
130					17.24	22.74	11.02	7.67	7.52	3.03	5.08	1.17	3.89	0.61	3.07	0.34	2.01	0.12	130
140					18.56	26.09	11.87	8.80	8.10	3.47	5.47	1.34	4.19	0.70	3.31	0.39	2.16	0.14	140
150					19.89	29.64	12.72	10.00	8.68	3.94	5.86	1.52	4.48	0.79	3.54	0.45	2.32	0.16	150
160							13.57	11.27	9.26	4.45	6.25	1.71	4.78	0.89	3.78	0.50	2.47	0.18	160
170							14.42	12.61	9.83	4.97	6.64	1.92	5.08	1.00	4.01	0.56	2.63	0.20	170
180							15.27	14.02	10.41	5.53	7.03	2.13	5.38	1.11	4.25	0.63	2.78	0.22	180
190							16.11	15.49	10.99	6.11	7.43	2.35	5.68	1.23	4.49	0.69	2.94	0.25	190
200							16.96	17.03	11.57	6.72	7.82	2.59	5.98	1.35	4.72	0.76	3.09	0.27	200
225							19.08	21.19	13.02	8.36	8.79	3.22	6.73	1.68	5.31	0.95	3.48	0.34	225
250									14.47	10.16	9.77	3.91	7.48	2.04	5.91	1.15	3.87	0.41	250
275									15.91	12.12	10.75	4.67	8.23	2.44	6.50	1.37	4.25	0.49	275
300									17.36	14.24	11.73	5.49	8.97	2.86	7.09	1.61	4.64	0.58	300
325									18.81	16.51	12.70	6.36	9.72	3.32	7.68	1.87	5.03	0.67	325
350											13.68	7.30	10.47	3.81	8.27	2.15	5.41	0.77	350
375											14.66	8.29	11.22	4.33	8.86	2.44	5.80	0.87	375
400											15.64	9.35	11.97	4.88	9.45	2.75	6.19	0.98	400
425											16.62	10.46	12.72	5.46	10.04	3.07	6.58	1.10	425
450											17.59	11.62	13.46	6.07	10.63	3.42	6.96	1.22	450
475											18.57	12.85	14.21	6.70	11.23	3.78	7.35	1.35	475
500											19.55	14.13	14.96	7.37	11.82	4.15	7.74	1.48	500
550													16.46	8.80	13.00	4.96	8.51	1.77	550
600													17.95	10.33	14.18	5.82	9.29	2.08	600
650													19.45	11.99	15.36	6.75	10.06	2.41	650
700															16.55	7.75	10.83	2.77	700
750															17.73	8.80	11.61	3.14	750
800															18.91	9.92	12.38	3.54	800
850																	13.16	3.96	850
900																	13.93	4.41	900
950																	14.71	4.87	950
1000																	15.48	5.36	1000
1050																	16.25	5.86	1050
1100																	17.03	6.39	1100
1150																	17.80	6.94	1150
1200																	18.58	7.51	1200
1250																	19.35	8.10	1250

Note: Shaded areas of chart indicate velocities over 5′ per second. **Use with Caution.**

(Continued)

Table B–1 (con't) FRICTION LOSS CHARACTERISTICS
PVC CLASS 160 IPS PLASTIC PIPE
(1120, 1220) SDR 26 C = 150
PSI LOSS PER 100 FEET OF PIPE (PSI/100 FT)
Sizes 6" thru 12"
Flow GPM 1 thru 5000

SIZE	6.00	8.00	10.00	12.00
OD	6.625	8.625	10.750	12.750
ID	6.115	7.961	9.924	11.770
WALL THK	0.225	0.332	0.413	0.490

Flow G.P.M.	6.00 Velocity F.P.S.	6.00 P.S.I. Loss	8.00 Velocity F.P.S.	8.00 P.S.I. Loss	10.00 Velocity F.P.S.	10.00 P.S.I. Loss	12.00 Velocity F.P.S.	12.00 P.S.I. Loss
1								
2								
3								
4								
5								
6								
7								
8								
9								
10								
11								
12								
14								
16								
18								
20								
22								
24								
26								
28								
30								
35	0.38	0.00						
40	0.43	0.01						
45	0.49	0.01						
50	0.54	0.01						
55	0.60	0.01						
60	0.65	0.01						
65	0.70	0.01						
70	0.76	0.02	0.45	0.00				
75	0.81	0.02	0.48	0.01				
80	0.87	0.02	0.51	0.01				
85	0.92	0.02	0.54	0.01				
90	0.98	0.03	0.57	0.01				
95	1.03	0.03	0.61	0.01				
100	1.09	0.03	0.64	0.01				
110	1.20	0.04	0.70	0.01				
120	1.30	0.05	0.77	0.01				
130	1.41	0.05	0.83	0.01	0.53	0.00		
140	1.52	0.06	0.90	0.02	0.57	0.01		
150	1.63	0.07	0.96	0.02	0.62	0.01		
160	1.74	0.08	1.02	0.02	0.66	0.01		
170	1.85	0.09	1.09	0.02	0.70	0.01		
180	1.96	0.10	1.15	0.03	0.74	0.01		
190	2.07	0.11	1.22	0.03	0.78	0.01		
200	2.18	0.12	1.28	0.03	0.82	0.01	0.58	0.00
225	2.45	0.14	1.44	0.04	0.93	0.01	0.66	0.01
250	2.72	0.18	1.60	0.05	1.03	0.02	0.73	0.01
275	3.00	0.21	1.77	0.06	1.13	0.02	0.80	0.01
300	3.27	0.25	1.93	0.07	1.24	0.02	0.88	0.01
325	3.54	0.29	2.09	0.08	1.34	0.03	0.95	0.01
350	3.81	0.33	2.25	0.09	1.44	0.03	1.03	0.01
375	4.09	0.37	2.41	0.10	1.55	0.04	1.10	0.02
400	4.36	0.42	2.57	0.12	1.65	0.04	1.17	0.02
425	4.63	0.47	2.73	0.13	1.76	0.04	1.25	0.02
450	4.90	0.52	2.89	0.14	1.86	0.05	1.32	0.02
475	5.18	0.58	3.05	0.16	1.96	0.05	1.39	0.02
500	5.45	0.63	3.21	0.18	2.07	0.06	1.47	0.03
550	6.00	0.76	3.54	0.21	2.27	0.07	1.61	0.03
600	6.54	0.89	3.86	0.25	2.48	0.08	1.76	0.04

Flow G.P.M.	6.00 Velocity F.P.S.	6.00 P.S.I. Loss	8.00 Velocity F.P.S.	8.00 P.S.I. Loss	10.00 Velocity F.P.S.	10.00 P.S.I. Loss	12.00 Velocity F.P.S.	12.00 P.S.I. Loss
650	7.09	1.03	4.18	0.29	2.69	0.10	1.91	0.04
700	7.63	1.18	4.50	0.33	2.89	0.11	2.06	0.05
750	8.18	1.34	4.82	0.37	3.10	0.13	2.20	0.06
800	8.72	1.51	5.15	0.42	3.31	0.14	2.35	0.06
850	9.27	1.69	5.47	0.47	3.52	0.16	2.50	0.07
900	9.81	1.88	5.79	0.52	3.72	0.18	2.65	0.08
950	10.36	2.08	6.11	0.58	3.93	0.20	2.79	0.09
1000	10.91	2.29	6.43	0.63	4.14	0.22	2.94	0.09
1050	11.45	2.50	6.75	0.69	4.34	0.24	3.09	0.10
1100	12.00	2.73	7.08	0.76	4.55	0.26	3.23	0.11
1150	12.54	2.96	7.40	0.82	4.76	0.28	3.38	0.12
1200	13.09	3.20	7.72	0.89	4.97	0.30	3.53	0.13
1250	13.63	3.45	8.04	0.96	5.17	0.33	3.68	0.14
1300	14.18	3.72	8.36	1.03	5.38	0.35	3.82	0.15
1350	14.72	3.98	8.69	1.10	5.59	0.38	3.97	0.16
1400	15.27	4.26	9.01	1.18	5.79	0.40	4.12	0.18
1450	15.82	4.55	9.33	1.26	6.00	0.43	4.27	0.19
1500	16.36	4.84	9.65	1.34	6.21	0.46	4.41	0.20
1550	16.91	5.15	9.97	1.43	6.42	0.49	4.56	0.21
1600	17.45	5.46	10.30	1.51	6.62	0.52	4.71	0.23
1650	18.00	5.78	10.62	1.60	6.83	0.55	4.85	0.24
1700	18.54	6.11	10.94	1.69	7.04	0.58	5.00	0.25
1750	19.09	6.44	11.26	1.78	7.24	0.61	5.15	0.27
1800	19.63	6.79	11.58	1.88	7.45	0.64	5.30	0.28
1850			11.90	1.98	7.66	0.68	5.44	0.30
1900			12.23	2.08	7.87	0.71	5.59	0.31
1950			12.55	2.18	8.07	0.75	5.74	0.33
2000			12.87	2.29	8.28	0.78	5.89	0.34
2100			13.51	2.50	8.69	0.86	6.18	0.37
2200			14.16	2.73	9.11	0.93	6.47	0.41
2300			14.80	2.96	9.52	1.01	6.77	0.44
2400			15.45	3.20	9.94	1.10	7.06	0.48
2500			16.09	3.46	10.35	1.18	7.36	0.52
2600			16.73	3.72	10.77	1.27	7.65	0.55
2700			17.38	3.98	11.18	1.36	7.95	0.59
2800			18.02	4.26	11.59	1.46	8.24	0.64
2900			18.66	4.55	12.01	1.56	8.54	0.68
3000			19.31	4.84	12.42	1.66	8.83	0.72
3100			19.95	5.15	12.84	1.76	9.12	0.77
3200					13.25	1.87	9.42	0.81
3300					13.67	1.98	9.71	0.86
3400					14.08	2.09	10.01	0.91
3500					14.49	2.20	10.30	0.96
3600					14.91	2.32	10.60	1.01
3700					15.32	2.44	10.89	1.07
3800					15.74	2.57	11.19	1.12
3900					16.15	2.69	11.48	1.17
4000					16.57	2.82	11.78	1.23
4100					16.98	2.96	12.07	1.29
4200					17.39	3.09	12.36	1.35
4300					17.81	3.23	12.66	1.41
4400					18.22	3.37	12.95	1.47
4500					18.64	3.51	13.25	1.53
4600					19.05	3.66	13.54	1.59
4700					19.47	3.81	13.84	1.66
4800					19.88	3.96	14.13	1.73
4900							14.43	1.79
5000							14.72	1.86

(Continued)

Note: Shaded areas of chart indicate velocities over 5' per second. Use with Caution.

Table B–2 FRICTION LOSS CHARACTERISTICS
PVC CLASS 200 IPS PLASTIC PIPE
(1120, 1220) SDR 21 C = 150
PSI LOSS PER 100 FEET OF PIPE (PSI/100)

Sizes 1″ thru 5″
Flow GPM 1 thru 1200

	1.00	1.25	1.50	2.00	2.50	3.00	3.50	4.00	5.00	
SIZE	1.00	1.25	1.50	2.00	2.50	3.00	3.50	4.00	5.00	SIZE
OD	1.315	1.660	1.900	2.375	2.875	3.500	4.000	4.500	5.563	OD
ID	1.189	1.502	1.720	2.149	2.601	3.166	3.620	4.072	5.033	ID
WALL THK	0.063	0.079	0.090	0.113	0.137	0.167	0.190	0.214	0.265	WALL THK

Flow G.P.M.	Velocity F.P.S.	P.S.I. Loss	Velocity F.P.S.	P.S.I. Loss	Velocity F.P.S.	P.S.I. Loss	Velocity F.P.S.	P.S.I. Loss	Velocity F.P.S.	P.S.I. Loss	Velocity F.P.S.	P.S.I. Loss	Velocity F.P.S.	P.S.I. Loss	Velocity F.P.S.	P.S.I. Loss	Velocity F.P.S.	P.S.I. Loss	Flow G.P.M.
1	0.28	0.02	0.18	0.01	0.13	0.00													1
2	0.57	0.07	0.36	0.02	0.27	0.01	0.17	0.00											2
3	0.86	0.14	0.54	0.04	0.41	0.02	0.26	0.01	0.18	0.00									3
4	1.15	0.24	0.72	0.08	0.55	0.04	0.35	0.01	0.24	0.01									4
5	1.44	0.36	0.90	0.12	0.68	0.06	0.44	0.02	0.30	0.01									5
6	1.73	0.51	1.08	0.16	0.82	0.08	0.53	0.03	0.36	0.01	0.24	0.00							6
7	2.02	0.67	1.26	0.22	0.96	0.11	0.61	0.04	0.42	0.01	0.28	0.01							7
8	2.30	0.86	1.44	0.28	1.10	0.14	0.70	0.05	0.48	0.02	0.32	0.01							8
9	2.59	1.07	1.62	0.34	1.24	0.18	0.79	0.06	0.54	0.02	0.36	0.01	0.28	0.00					9
10	2.88	1.30	1.80	0.42	1.37	0.22	0.88	0.07	0.60	0.03	0.40	0.01	0.31	0.01					10
11	3.17	1.56	1.98	0.50	1.51	0.26	0.97	0.09	0.66	0.03	0.44	0.01	0.34	0.01					11
12	3.46	1.83	2.17	0.59	1.65	0.30	1.06	0.10	0.72	0.04	0.48	0.02	0.37	0.01	0.29	0.00			12
14	4.04	2.43	2.53	0.78	1.93	0.40	1.23	0.14	0.84	0.05	0.56	0.02	0.43	0.01	0.34	0.01			14
16	4.61	3.11	2.89	1.00	2.20	0.52	1.41	0.17	0.96	0.07	0.65	0.03	0.49	0.01	0.39	0.01			16
18	5.19	3.87	3.25	1.24	2.48	0.64	1.59	0.22	1.08	0.09	0.73	0.03	0.56	0.02	0.44	0.01			18
20	5.77	4.71	3.61	1.51	2.75	0.78	1.76	0.26	1.20	0.10	0.81	0.04	0.62	0.02	0.49	0.01	0.32	0.00	20
22	6.34	5.62	3.97	1.80	3.03	0.93	1.94	0.32	1.32	0.12	0.89	0.05	0.68	0.02	0.54	0.01	0.35	0.01	22
24	6.92	6.60	4.34	2.12	3.30	1.09	2.12	0.37	1.44	0.15	0.97	0.06	0.74	0.03	0.59	0.02	0.38	0.01	24
26	7.50	7.65	4.70	2.46	3.58	1.27	2.29	0.43	1.56	0.17	1.05	0.07	0.80	0.03	0.63	0.02	0.41	0.01	26
28	8.08	8.78	5.06	2.82	3.86	1.46	2.47	0.49	1.68	0.19	1.13	0.07	0.87	0.04	0.68	0.02	0.45	0.01	28
30	8.65	9.98	5.42	3.20	4.13	1.66	2.65	0.56	1.80	0.22	1.22	0.09	0.93	0.04	0.73	0.02	0.48	0.01	30
35	10.10	13.27	6.32	4.26	4.82	2.20	3.09	0.75	2.11	0.29	1.42	0.11	1.08	0.06	0.86	0.03	0.56	0.01	35
40	11.54	17.00	7.23	5.45	5.51	2.82	3.53	0.95	2.41	0.38	1.62	0.14	1.24	0.08	0.98	0.04	0.64	0.02	40
45	12.98	21.14	8.13	6.78	6.20	3.51	3.97	1.19	2.71	0.47	1.83	0.18	1.40	0.09	1.10	0.05	0.72	0.02	45
50	14.42	25.70	9.04	8.24	6.89	4.26	4.41	1.44	3.01	0.57	2.03	0.22	1.55	0.11	1.23	0.06	0.80	0.02	50
55	15.87	30.66	9.94	9.83	7.58	5.09	4.85	1.72	3.31	0.68	2.23	0.26	1.71	0.14	1.35	0.08	0.88	0.03	55
60	17.31	36.02	10.85	11.55	8.27	5.97	5.30	2.02	3.61	0.80	2.44	0.31	1.86	0.16	1.47	0.09	0.96	0.03	60
65	18.75	41.77	11.75	13.40	8.96	6.93	5.74	2.35	3.92	0.93	2.64	0.36	2.02	0.19	1.59	0.10	1.04	0.04	65
70			12.65	15.37	9.65	7.95	6.18	2.69	4.22	1.06	2.84	0.41	2.17	0.21	1.72	0.12	1.12	0.04	70
75			13.56	17.47	10.34	9.03	6.62	3.06	4.52	1.21	3.05	0.46	2.33	0.24	1.84	0.14	1.20	0.05	75
80			14.46	19.68	11.03	10.18	7.06	3.44	4.82	1.36	3.25	0.52	2.49	0.27	1.96	0.15	1.28	0.05	80
85			15.37	22.02	11.72	11.39	7.50	3.85	5.12	1.52	3.45	0.59	2.64	0.30	2.09	0.17	1.36	0.06	85
90			16.27	24.48	12.41	12.66	7.95	4.28	5.42	1.69	3.66	0.66	2.80	0.34	2.21	0.19	1.44	0.07	90
95			17.18	27.06	13.10	13.99	8.39	4.74	5.72	1.87	3.86	0.72	2.95	0.37	2.33	0.21	1.53	0.07	95
100			18.08	29.76	13.79	15.39	8.83	5.21	6.03	2.06	4.07	0.79	3.11	0.41	2.46	0.23	1.61	0.08	100
110			19.89	35.50	15.17	18.36	9.71	6.21	6.63	2.45	4.47	0.94	3.42	0.49	2.70	0.28	1.77	0.10	110
120					16.54	21.57	10.60	7.30	7.23	2.88	4.88	1.11	3.73	0.58	2.95	0.33	1.93	0.12	120
130					17.92	25.02	11.48	8.47	7.84	3.34	5.29	1.29	4.04	0.67	3.19	0.38	2.09	0.13	130
140					19.30	28.70	12.36	9.71	8.44	3.84	5.69	1.47	4.35	0.77	3.44	0.43	2.25	0.15	140
150							13.25	11.04	9.04	4.36	6.10	1.68	4.67	0.87	3.69	0.49	2.41	0.18	150
160							14.13	12.44	9.64	4.91	6.51	1.89	4.98	0.98	3.93	0.55	2.57	0.20	160
170							15.01	13.91	10.25	5.50	6.91	2.11	5.29	1.10	4.18	0.62	2.73	0.22	170
180							15.90	15.47	10.85	6.11	7.32	2.35	5.60	1.22	4.42	0.69	2.89	0.25	180
190							16.78	17.10	11.45	6.75	7.73	2.60	5.91	1.35	4.67	0.76	3.06	0.27	190
200							17.66	18.80	12.06	7.43	8.14	2.85	6.22	1.49	4.92	0.84	3.22	0.30	200
225							19.87	23.38	13.56	9.24	9.15	3.55	7.00	1.85	5.53	1.04	3.62	0.37	225
250									15.07	11.23	10.17	4.31	7.78	2.25	6.15	1.27	4.02	0.45	250
275									16.58	13.39	11.19	5.15	8.56	2.68	6.76	1.51	4.42	0.54	275
300									18.09	15.74	12.21	6.05	9.34	3.15	7.38	1.78	4.83	0.63	300
325									19.60	18.25	13.22	7.01	10.11	3.65	7.99	2.06	5.23	0.74	325
350											14.24	8.05	10.89	4.19	8.61	2.36	5.63	0.84	350
375											15.26	9.14	11.67	4.76	9.22	2.69	6.03	0.96	375
400											16.28	10.30	12.45	5.37	9.84	3.03	6.44	1.08	400
425											17.29	11.53	13.23	6.01	10.45	3.39	6.84	1.21	425
450											18.31	12.81	14.01	6.68	11.07	3.77	7.24	1.34	450
475											19.33	14.16	14.78	7.38	11.68	4.16	7.65	1.48	475
500													15.56	8.11	12.30	4.58	8.05	1.63	500
550													17.12	9.68	13.53	5.46	8.85	1.95	550
600													18.68	11.37	14.76	6.42	9.66	2.29	600
650															15.99	7.44	10.46	2.65	650
700															17.22	8.54	11.27	3.04	700
750															18.45	9.70	12.07	3.46	750
800															19.68	10.93	12.88	3.90	800
850																	13.69	4.36	850
900																	14.49	4.85	900
950																	15.30	5.36	950
1000																	16.10	5.89	1000
1050																	16.91	6.45	1050
1100																	17.71	7.03	1100
1150																	18.52	7.64	1150
1200																	19.32	8.26	1200

Note: Shaded areas of chart indicate velocities over 5′ per second. **Use with Caution.**

(Continued)

Table B–2 (con't) FRICTION LOSS CHARACTERISTICS
PVC CLASS 200 IPS PLASTIC PIPE
(1120, 1220) SDR 21 C = 150
PSI LOSS PER 100 FEET OF PIPE (PSI/100)
Sizes 6″ thru 12″
Flow GPM 1 thru 5000

SIZE	6.00	8.00	10.00	12.00
OD	6.625	8.625	10.750	12.750
ID	5.993	7.805	9.728	11.538
WALL THK	0.316	0.410	0.511	0.606

Flow G.P.M.	Velocity F.P.S.	P.S.I. Loss	Velocity F.P.S.	P.S.I. Loss	Velocity F.P.S.	P.S.I. Loss	Velocity F.P.S.	P.S.I. Loss
1								
2								
3								
4								
5								
6								
7								
8								
9								
10								
11								
12								
14								
16								
18								
20								
22								
24								
26								
28								
30	0.34	0.00						
35	0.39	0.01						
40	0.45	0.01						
45	0.51	0.01						
50	0.56	0.01						
55	0.62	0.01						
60	0.68	0.01						
65	0.73	0.02	0.43	0.00				
70	0.79	0.02	0.46	0.01				
75	0.85	0.02	0.50	0.01				
80	0.90	0.02	0.53	0.01				
85	0.96	0.03	0.56	0.01				
90	1.02	0.03	0.60	0.01				
95	1.07	0.03	0.63	0.01				
100	1.13	0.04	0.66	0.01				
110	1.24	0.04	0.73	0.01				
120	1.36	0.05	0.80	0.01	0.51	0.00		
130	1.47	0.06	0.87	0.02	0.56	0.01		
140	1.59	0.07	0.93	0.02	0.60	0.01		
150	1.70	0.08	1.00	0.02	0.64	0.01		
160	1.81	0.08	1.07	0.02	0.68	0.01		
170	1.93	0.09	1.13	0.03	0.73	0.01		
180	2.04	0.11	1.20	0.03	0.77	0.01		
190	2.15	0.12	1.27	0.03	0.81	0.01	0.58	0.00
200	2.27	0.13	1.33	0.04	0.86	0.01	0.61	0.01
225	2.55	0.16	1.50	0.04	0.97	0.02	0.68	0.01
250	2.83	0.19	1.67	0.05	1.07	0.02	0.76	0.01
275	3.12	0.23	1.84	0.06	1.18	0.02	0.84	0.01
300	3.40	0.27	2.00	0.07	1.29	0.03	0.91	0.01
325	3.69	0.31	2.17	0.09	1.40	0.03	0.99	0.01
350	3.97	0.36	2.34	0.10	1.50	0.03	1.07	0.01
375	4.25	0.41	2.51	0.11	1.61	0.04	1.14	0.02
400	4.54	0.46	2.67	0.13	1.72	0.04	1.22	0.02
425	4.82	0.52	2.84	0.14	1.83	0.05	1.30	0.02
450	5.11	0.57	3.01	0.16	1.94	0.05	1.37	0.02
475	5.39	0.63	3.18	0.18	2.04	0.06	1.45	0.03
500	5.67	0.70	3.34	0.19	2.15	0.07	1.53	0.03
550	6.24	0.83	3.68	0.23	2.37	0.08	1.68	0.03
600	6.81	0.98	4.01	0.27	2.58	0.09	1.83	0.04

Flow G.P.M.	Velocity F.P.S.	P.S.I. Loss	Velocity F.P.S.	P.S.I. Loss	Velocity F.P.S.	P.S.I. Loss	Velocity F.P.S.	P.S.I. Loss
650	7.38	1.14	4.35	0.31	2.80	0.11	1.99	0.05
700	7.95	1.30	4.68	0.36	3.01	0.12	2.14	0.05
750	8.51	1.48	5.02	0.41	3.23	0.14	2.29	0.06
800	9.08	1.67	5.35	0.46	3.44	0.16	2.45	0.07
850	9.65	1.87	5.69	0.52	3.66	0.18	2.60	0.08
900	10.22	2.07	6.02	0.57	3.88	0.20	2.75	0.09
950	10.79	2.29	6.36	0.63	4.09	0.22	2.91	0.09
1000	11.35	2.52	6.69	0.70	4.31	0.24	3.06	0.10
1050	11.92	2.76	7.03	0.76	4.52	0.26	3.21	0.11
1100	12.49	3.01	7.36	0.83	4.74	0.28	3.37	0.12
1150	13.06	3.27	7.70	0.90	4.95	0.31	3.52	0.13
1200	13.63	3.53	8.03	0.98	5.17	0.33	3.67	0.15
1250	14.19	3.81	8.37	1.05	5.38	0.36	3.83	0.16
1300	14.76	4.10	8.70	1.13	5.60	0.39	3.98	0.17
1350	15.33	4.39	9.04	1.22	5.82	0.42	4.13	0.18
1400	15.90	4.70	9.37	1.30	6.03	0.45	4.29	0.19
1450	16.47	5.02	9.71	1.39	6.25	0.48	4.44	0.21
1500	17.03	5.34	10.04	1.48	6.46	0.51	4.59	0.22
1550	17.60	5.68	10.38	1.57	6.68	0.54	4.75	0.23
1600	18.17	6.02	10.71	1.66	6.89	0.57	4.90	0.25
1650	18.74	6.37	11.05	1.76	7.11	0.60	5.05	0.26
1700	19.31	6.73	11.38	1.86	7.32	0.64	5.21	0.28
1750	19.87	7.11	11.72	1.97	7.54	0.67	5.36	0.29
1800			12.05	2.07	7.76	0.71	5.51	0.31
1850			12.39	2.18	7.97	0.75	5.66	0.33
1900			12.72	2.29	8.19	0.78	5.82	0.34
1950			13.06	2.40	8.40	0.82	5.97	0.36
2000			13.39	2.52	8.62	0.86	6.12	0.38
2100			14.06	2.75	9.05	0.94	6.43	0.41
2200			14.73	3.00	9.48	1.03	6.74	0.45
2300			15.40	3.26	9.91	1.12	7.04	0.49
2400			16.07	3.53	10.34	1.21	7.35	0.53
2500			16.74	3.80	10.77	1.30	7.66	0.57
2600			17.41	4.09	11.20	1.40	7.96	0.61
2700			18.08	4.39	11.64	1.50	8.27	0.66
2800			18.75	4.69	12.07	1.61	8.58	0.70
2900			19.42	5.01	12.50	1.72	8.88	0.75
3000					12.93	1.83	9.19	0.80
3100					13.36	1.94	9.50	0.85
3200					13.79	2.06	9.80	0.90
3300					14.22	2.18	10.11	0.95
3400					14.65	2.30	10.42	1.00
3500					15.08	2.43	10.72	1.06
3600					15.52	2.56	11.03	1.12
3700					15.95	2.69	11.33	1.17
3800					16.38	2.83	11.64	1.23
3900					16.81	2.97	11.95	1.29
4000					17.24	3.11	12.25	1.36
4100					17.67	3.26	12.56	1.42
4200					18.10	3.41	12.87	1.48
4300					18.53	3.56	13.17	1.55
4400					18.96	3.71	13.48	1.62
4500					19.40	3.87	13.79	1.69
4600					19.83	4.03	14.09	1.76
4700							14.40	1.83
4800							14.71	1.90
4900							15.01	1.98
5000							15.32	2.05

(Continued)

Note: Shaded areas of chart indicate velocities over 5′ per second. Use with Caution.

Table B–3 FRICTION LOSS CHARACTERISTICS
PVC CLASS 315 IPS PLASTIC PIPE
(1120, 1220) SDR 13.5 C = 150
PSI LOSS PER 100 FEET OF PIPE (PSI/100 FT)

Sizes ½'' thru 3½''
Flow GPM 1 thru 600

SIZE	0.50	0.75	1.00	1.25	1.50	2.00	2.50	3.00	3.50	SIZE
OD	0.840	1.050	1.315	1.660	1.900	2.375	2.875	3.500	4.000	OD
ID	0.716	0.894	1.121	1.414	1.618	2.023	2.449	2.982	3.408	ID
WALL THK	0.062	0.078	0.097	0.123	0.141	0.176	0.213	0.259	0.296	WALL THK

Flow G.P.M.	Velocity F.P.S.	P.S.I. Loss	Velocity F.P.S.	P.S.I. Loss	Velocity F.P.S.	P.S.I. Loss	Velocity F.P.S.	P.S.I. Loss	Velocity F.P.S.	P.S.I. Loss	Velocity F.P.S.	P.S.I. Loss	Velocity F.P.S.	P.S.I. Loss	Velocity F.P.S.	P.S.I. Loss	Velocity F.P.S.	P.S.I. Loss	Flow G.P.M.
1	0.79	0.22	0.51	0.07	0.32	0.02	0.20	0.01	0.15	0.00									1
2	1.59	0.78	1.02	0.27	0.64	0.09	0.40	0.03	0.31	0.01	0.19	0.00							2
3	2.38	1.65	1.53	0.56	0.97	0.19	0.61	0.06	0.46	0.03	0.29	0.01	0.20	0.00					3
4	3.18	2.82	2.04	0.96	1.29	0.32	0.81	0.10	0.62	0.05	0.39	0.02	0.27	0.01					4
5	3.97	4.26	2.55	1.45	1.62	0.48	1.02	0.16	0.77	0.08	0.49	0.03	0.34	0.01	0.22	0.00			5
6	4.77	5.97	3.06	2.03	1.94	0.67	1.22	0.22	0.93	0.11	0.59	0.04	0.40	0.02	0.27	0.01			6
7	5.57	7.95	3.57	2.70	2.27	0.90	1.42	0.29	1.09	0.15	0.69	0.05	0.47	0.02	0.32	0.01	0.24	0.00	7
8	6.36	10.18	4.08	3.45	2.59	1.15	1.63	0.37	1.24	0.19	0.79	0.06	0.54	0.03	0.36	0.01	0.28	0.01	8
9	7.16	12.66	4.59	4.30	2.92	1.43	1.83	0.46	1.40	0.24	0.89	0.08	0.61	0.03	0.41	0.01	0.31	0.01	9
10	7.95	15.38	5.10	5.22	3.24	1.74	2.04	0.56	1.55	0.29	0.99	0.10	0.68	0.04	0.45	0.01	0.35	0.01	10
11	8.75	18.35	5.61	6.23	3.57	2.07	2.24	0.67	1.71	0.35	1.09	0.12	0.74	0.05	0.50	0.02	0.38	0.01	11
12	9.55	21.56	6.12	7.32	3.89	2.43	2.44	0.79	1.87	0.41	1.19	0.14	0.81	0.05	0.55	0.02	0.42	0.01	12
14	11.14	28.69	7.14	9.74	4.54	3.24	2.85	1.05	2.18	0.53	1.39	0.18	0.95	0.07	0.64	0.03	0.49	0.01	14
16	12.73	36.74	8.16	12.47	5.19	4.15	3.26	1.34	2.49	0.70	1.59	0.23	1.08	0.09	0.73	0.04	0.56	0.02	16
18	14.32	45.69	9.18	15.51	5.84	5.16	3.67	1.67	2.80	0.87	1.79	0.29	1.22	0.12	0.82	0.04	0.63	0.02	18
20	15.91	55.54	10.20	18.86	6.49	6.27	4.08	2.03	3.11	1.05	1.99	0.35	1.36	0.14	0.91	0.05	0.70	0.03	20
22	17.50	66.26	11.23	22.50	7.14	7.48	4.48	2.42	3.42	1.25	2.19	0.42	1.49	0.17	1.00	0.06	0.77	0.03	22
24	19.10	77.84	12.25	26.43	7.79	8.79	4.89	2.84	3.74	1.47	2.39	0.50	1.63	0.20	1.10	0.08	0.84	0.04	24
26			13.27	30.65	8.44	10.19	5.30	3.29	4.05	1.71	2.59	0.58	1.76	0.23	1.19	0.09	0.91	0.05	26
28			14.29	35.16	9.09	11.69	5.71	3.78	4.36	1.96	2.79	0.66	1.90	0.26	1.28	0.10	0.98	0.05	28
30			15.31	39.95	9.74	13.29	6.12	4.29	4.67	2.23	2.99	0.75	2.04	0.30	1.37	0.11	1.05	0.06	30
35			17.86	53.15	11.36	17.68	7.14	5.71	5.45	2.96	3.48	1.00	2.38	0.39	1.60	0.15	1.22	0.08	35
40					12.98	22.64	8.16	7.31	6.23	3.80	3.98	1.28	2.72	0.51	1.83	0.19	1.40	0.10	40
45					14.61	28.15	9.18	9.10	7.01	4.72	4.48	1.59	3.06	0.63	2.06	0.24	1.58	0.12	45
50					16.23	34.22	10.20	11.06	7.79	5.74	4.98	1.94	3.40	0.76	2.29	0.29	1.75	0.15	50
55					17.85	40.83	11.22	13.19	8.57	6.85	5.48	2.31	3.74	0.91	2.52	0.35	1.93	0.18	55
60					19.48	47.97	12.24	15.50	9.35	8.04	5.98	2.71	4.08	1.07	2.75	0.41	2.10	0.21	60
65							13.26	17.97	10.13	9.33	6.48	3.15	4.42	1.24	2.98	0.48	2.28	0.25	65
70							14.28	20.62	10.90	10.70	6.97	3.61	4.76	1.42	3.21	0.55	2.45	0.29	70
75							15.30	23.43	11.68	12.16	7.47	4.10	5.10	1.62	3.44	0.62	2.63	0.32	75
80							16.32	26.40	12.46	13.71	7.97	4.62	5.44	1.82	3.67	0.70	2.81	0.37	80
85							17.34	29.54	13.24	15.33	8.47	5.17	5.78	2.04	3.89	0.78	2.98	0.41	85
90							18.36	32.84	14.02	17.05	8.97	5.75	6.12	2.27	4.12	0.87	3.16	0.45	90
95							19.38	36.30	14.80	18.84	9.47	6.35	6.46	2.51	4.35	0.96	3.33	0.50	95
100									15.58	20.72	9.96	6.99	6.80	2.76	4.58	1.06	3.51	0.55	100
110									17.14	24.72	10.96	8.34	7.48	3.29	5.04	1.26	3.86	0.66	110
120									18.70	29.04	11.96	9.79	8.16	3.87	5.50	1.48	4.21	0.77	120
130											12.96	11.36	8.84	4.48	5.96	1.72	4.56	0.90	130
140											13.95	13.03	9.52	5.14	6.42	1.97	4.91	1.03	140
150											14.95	14.81	10.20	5.84	6.88	2.24	5.26	1.17	150
160											15.95	16.69	10.88	6.59	7.34	2.53	5.62	1.32	160
170											16.94	18.67	11.56	7.37	7.79	2.83	5.97	1.48	170
180											17.94	20.75	12.24	8.19	8.25	3.14	6.32	1.64	180
190											18.94	22.94	12.92	9.05	8.71	3.47	6.67	1.81	190
200											19.93	25.23	13.60	9.95	9.17	3.82	7.02	1.99	200
225													15.30	12.38	10.32	4.75	7.90	2.49	225
250													17.00	15.05	11.47	5.77	8.78	3.01	250
275													18.70	17.95	12.61	6.89	9.66	3.60	275
300															13.76	8.09	10.53	4.23	300
325															14.91	9.39	11.41	4.90	325
350															16.05	10.77	12.29	5.62	350
375															17.20	12.23	13.17	6.39	375
400															18.35	13.79	14.05	7.20	400
425															19.49	15.42	14.92	8.05	425
450																	15.80	8.95	450
475																	16.68	9.90	475
500																	17.56	10.88	500
550																	19.32	12.98	550
600																			600

(Continued)

Note: Shaded areas of chart indicate velocities over 5' per second. **Use with Caution.**

Table B–3 (con't) FRICTION LOSS CHARACTERISTICS
PVC CLASS 315 IPS PLASTIC PIPE
(1120, 1220) SDR 13.5 C = 150
PSI LOSS PER 100 FEET OF PIPE (PSI/100 FT)
Sizes 4″ thru 6″
Flow GPM 1 thru 1750

SIZE	4.00	5.00	6.00
OD	4.500	5.563	6.625
ID	3.834	4.739	5.643
WALL THK	0.333	0.412	0.491

Flow G.P.M.	Velocity F.P.S.	P.S.I. Loss	Velocity F.P.S.	P.S.I. Loss	Velocity F.P.S.	P.S.I. Loss
1						
2						
3						
4						
5						
6						
7						
8						
9						
10	0.27	0.00				
11	0.30	0.01				
12	0.33	0.01				
14	0.38	0.01				
16	0.44	0.01				
18	0.49	0.01	0.32	0.00		
20	0.55	0.02	0.36	0.01		
22	0.61	0.02	0.39	0.01		
24	0.66	0.02	0.43	0.01		
26	0.72	0.03	0.47	0.01		
28	0.77	0.03	0.50	0.01	0.35	0.00
30	0.83	0.03	0.54	0.01	0.38	0.01
35	0.97	0.04	0.63	0.02	0.44	0.01
40	1.11	0.06	0.72	0.02	0.51	0.01
45	1.24	0.07	0.81	0.03	0.57	0.01
50	1.38	0.09	0.90	0.03	0.64	0.01
55	1.52	0.10	0.99	0.04	0.70	0.02
60	1.66	0.12	1.09	0.04	0.76	0.02
65	1.80	0.14	1.18	0.05	0.83	0.02
70	1.94	0.16	1.27	0.06	0.89	0.02
75	2.08	0.18	1.36	0.07	0.96	0.03
80	2.22	0.21	1.45	0.07	1.02	0.03
85	2.35	0.23	1.54	0.08	1.08	0.04
90	2.49	0.26	1.63	0.09	1.15	0.04
95	2.63	0.28	1.72	0.10	1.21	0.04
100	2.77	0.31	1.81	0.11	1.28	0.05
110	3.05	0.37	1.99	0.13	1.40	0.06
120	3.33	0.44	2.18	0.16	1.53	0.07
130	3.60	0.51	2.36	0.18	1.66	0.08
140	3.88	0.58	2.54	0.21	1.79	0.09
150	4.16	0.66	2.72	0.24	1.92	0.10
160	4.44	0.74	2.90	0.27	2.04	0.11
170	4.71	0.83	3.08	0.30	2.17	0.13
180	4.99	0.93	3.27	0.33	2.30	0.14
190	5.27	1.02	3.45	0.36	2.43	0.16
200	5.55	1.12	3.63	0.40	2.56	0.17
225	6.24	1.40	4.08	0.50	2.88	0.21
250	6.93	1.70	4.54	0.61	3.20	0.26
275	7.63	2.03	4.99	0.72	3.52	0.31
300	8.32	2.38	5.45	0.85	3.84	0.36
325	9.02	2.76	5.90	0.99	4.16	0.42
350	9.71	3.17	6.35	1.13	4.48	0.48
375	10.40	3.60	6.81	1.28	4.80	0.55
400	11.10	4.06	7.26	1.45	5.12	0.62
425	11.79	4.54	7.72	1.62	5.44	0.69
450	12.49	5.05	8.17	1.80	5.76	0.77
475	13.18	5.58	8.62	1.99	6.08	0.85
500	13.87	6.14	9.08	2.19	6.40	0.94
550	15.26	7.32	9.99	2.61	7.04	1.12
600	16.65	8.60	10.90	3.07	7.68	1.31

SIZE	4.00	5.00	6.00
OD	4.500	5.563	6.625
ID	3.834	4.739	5.643
WALL THK	0.333	0.412	0.491

Flow G.P.M.	Velocity F.P.S.	P.S.I. Loss	Velocity F.P.S.	P.S.I. Loss	Velocity F.P.S.	P.S.I. Loss
650	18.04	9.97	11.80	3.56	8.32	1.52
700	19.42	11.44	12.71	4.08	8.96	1.75
750			13.62	4.64	9.60	1.98
800			14.53	5.23	10.25	2.23
850			15.44	5.85	10.89	2.50
900			16.35	6.50	11.53	2.78
950			17.25	7.18	12.17	3.07
1000			18.16	7.90	12.81	3.38
1050			19.07	8.65	13.45	3.70
1100			19.98	9.42	14.09	4.03
1150					14.73	4.38
1200					15.37	4.74
1250					16.01	5.11
1300					16.65	5.49
1350					17.29	5.89
1400					17.93	6.30
1450					18.57	6.72
1500					19.21	7.16
1550					19.85	7.61
1600						
1650						
1700						
1750						

(Continued)

Note: Shaded areas of chart indicate velocities over 5' per second. Use with Caution.

Table B–4 FRICTION LOSS CHARACTERISTICS
PVC SCHEDULE 40 IPS PLASTIC PIPE
(1120, 1220) C = 150
PSI LOSS PER 100 FEET OF TUBE (PSI/100 FT)
Sizes ½" thru 3½"
Flow GPM 1 thru 600

SIZE	0.50	0.75	1.00	1.25	1.50	2.00	2.50	3.00	3.50	SIZE
OD	0.840	1.050	1.315	1.660	1.900	2.375	2.875	3.500	4.000	OD
ID	0.622	0.824	1.049	1.380	1.610	2.067	2.469	3.068	3.548	ID
WALL THK	0.109	0.113	0.133	0.140	0.145	0.154	0.203	0.216	0.226	WALL THK

Flow G.P.M.	Velocity F.P.S.	P.S.I. Loss	Velocity F.P.S.	P.S.I. Loss	Velocity F.P.S.	P.S.I. Loss	Velocity F.P.S.	P.S.I. Loss	Velocity F.P.S.	P.S.I. Loss	Velocity F.P.S.	P.S.I. Loss	Velocity F.P.S.	P.S.I. Loss	Velocity F.P.S.	P.S.I. Loss	Velocity F.P.S.	P.S.I. Loss	Flow G.P.M.
1	0.93	0.32	0.60	0.11	0.37	0.03	0.21	0.01	0.15	0.00									1
2	1.86	1.14	1.20	0.39	0.74	0.12	0.42	0.03	0.31	0.02	0.19	0.00							2
3	2.79	2.42	1.80	0.84	1.11	0.26	0.64	0.07	0.47	0.03	0.28	0.01	0.20	0.00					3
4	3.72	4.13	2.40	1.42	1.48	0.44	0.85	0.12	0.62	0.05	0.38	0.02	0.26	0.01					4
5	4.65	6.24	3.00	2.15	1.85	0.66	1.07	0.18	0.78	0.08	0.47	0.02	0.33	0.01	0.21	0.00			5
6	5.58	8.75	3.60	3.02	2.22	0.93	1.28	0.25	0.94	0.12	0.57	0.03	0.40	0.01	0.26	0.01			6
7	6.51	11.64	4.20	4.01	2.59	1.24	1.49	0.33	1.10	0.15	0.66	0.05	0.46	0.02	0.30	0.01			7
8	7.44	14.90	4.80	5.14	2.96	1.59	1.71	0.42	1.25	0.20	0.76	0.06	0.53	0.02	0.34	0.01	0.25	0.00	8
9	8.37	18.54	5.40	6.39	3.33	1.97	1.92	0.52	1.41	0.25	0.85	0.07	0.60	0.03	0.39	0.01	0.29	0.01	9
10	9.30	22.53	6.00	7.77	3.70	2.40	2.14	0.63	1.57	0.30	0.95	0.09	0.66	0.04	0.43	0.01	0.32	0.01	10
11	10.24	26.88	6.60	9.27	4.07	2.86	2.35	0.75	1.73	0.36	1.05	0.11	0.73	0.04	0.47	0.02	0.35	0.01	11
12	11.17	31.58	7.21	10.89	4.44	3.36	2.57	0.89	1.88	0.42	1.14	0.12	0.80	0.05	0.52	0.02	0.38	0.01	12
14	13.03	42.01	8.41	14.48	5.19	4.47	2.99	1.18	2.20	0.56	1.33	0.17	0.93	0.07	0.60	0.02	0.45	0.01	14
16	14.89	53.80	9.61	18.55	5.93	5.73	3.42	1.51	2.51	0.71	1.52	0.21	1.07	0.09	0.69	0.03	0.51	0.02	16
18	16.75	66.92	10.81	23.07	6.67	7.13	3.85	1.88	2.83	0.89	1.71	0.26	1.20	0.11	0.78	0.04	0.58	0.02	18
20	18.61	81.34	12.01	28.04	7.41	8.66	4.28	2.28	3.14	1.08	1.90	0.32	1.33	0.13	0.86	0.05	0.64	0.02	20
22			13.21	33.45	8.15	10.33	4.71	2.72	3.46	1.29	2.10	0.38	1.47	0.16	0.95	0.06	0.71	0.03	22
24			14.42	39.30	8.89	12.14	5.14	3.20	3.77	1.51	2.29	0.45	1.60	0.19	1.04	0.07	0.77	0.03	24
26			15.62	45.58	9.64	14.08	5.57	3.17	4.09	1.75	2.48	0.52	1.74	0.22	1.12	0.08	0.84	0.04	26
28			16.82	52.28	10.38	16.15	5.99	4.25	4.40	2.01	2.67	0.60	1.87	0.25	1.21	0.09	0.90	0.04	28
30			18.02	59.41	11.12	18.35	6.42	4.83	4.72	2.28	2.86	0.68	2.00	0.29	1.30	0.10	0.97	0.05	30
35					12.97	24.42	7.49	6.43	5.50	3.04	3.34	0.90	2.34	0.38	1.51	0.13	1.13	0.06	35
40					14.83	31.27	8.56	8.23	6.29	3.89	3.81	1.15	2.67	0.49	1.73	0.17	1.29	0.08	40
45					16.68	38.89	9.64	10.24	7.08	4.84	4.29	1.43	3.01	0.60	1.95	0.21	1.45	0.10	45
50					18.53	47.27	10.71	12.45	7.87	5.88	4.77	1.74	3.34	0.73	2.16	0.26	1.62	0.13	50
55							11.78	14.85	8.65	7.01	5.25	2.08	3.68	0.88	2.38	0.30	1.78	0.15	55
60							12.85	17.45	9.44	8.24	5.72	2.44	4.01	1.03	2.60	0.36	1.94	0.18	60
65							13.92	20.23	10.23	9.56	6.20	2.83	4.35	1.19	2.81	0.41	2.10	0.20	65
70							14.99	23.21	11.01	10.96	6.68	3.25	4.68	1.37	3.03	0.48	2.26	0.23	70
75							16.06	26.37	11.80	12.46	7.16	3.69	5.01	1.56	3.25	0.54	2.43	0.27	75
80							17.13	29.72	12.59	14.04	7.63	4.16	5.35	1.75	3.46	0.61	2.59	0.30	80
85							18.21	33.26	13.37	15.71	8.11	4.66	5.68	1.96	3.68	0.68	2.75	0.34	85
90							19.28	36.97	14.16	17.46	8.59	5.18	6.02	2.18	3.90	0.76	2.91	0.37	90
95									14.95	19.30	9.07	5.72	6.35	2.41	4.11	0.84	3.07	0.41	95
100									15.74	21.22	9.54	6.29	6.69	2.65	4.33	0.92	3.24	0.45	100
110									17.31	25.32	10.50	7.51	7.36	3.16	4.76	1.10	3.56	0.54	110
120									18.88	29.75	11.45	8.82	8.03	3.72	5.20	1.29	3.88	0.64	120
130											12.41	10.23	8.70	4.31	5.63	1.50	4.21	0.74	130
140											13.36	11.74	9.37	4.94	6.06	1.72	4.53	0.85	140
150											14.32	13.33	10.03	5.62	6.50	1.95	4.86	0.96	150
160											15.27	15.03	10.70	6.33	6.93	2.20	5.18	1.08	160
170											16.23	16.81	11.37	7.08	7.36	2.46	5.50	1.21	170
180											17.18	18.69	12.04	7.87	7.80	2.74	5.83	1.35	180
190											18.14	20.66	12.71	8.70	8.23	3.02	6.15	1.49	190
200											19.09	22.72	13.38	9.57	8.66	3.33	6.48	1.64	200
225													15.05	11.90	9.75	4.14	7.29	2.04	225
250													16.73	14.47	10.83	5.03	8.10	2.48	250
275													18.40	17.26	11.92	6.00	8.91	2.96	275
300															13.00	7.05	9.72	3.47	300
325															14.08	8.17	10.53	4.03	325
350															15.17	9.38	11.34	4.62	350
375															16.25	10.65	12.15	5.25	375
400															17.33	12.01	12.96	5.92	400
425															18.42	13.43	13.77	6.62	425
450															19.50	14.93	14.58	7.36	450
475																	15.39	8.14	475
500																	16.20	8.95	500
550																	17.82	10.67	550
600																	19.44	12.54	600

(Continued)

Note: Shaded areas of chart indicate velocities over 5' per second. **Use with Caution.**

Table B–4 (con't) FRICTION LOSS CHARACTERISTICS
PVC SCHEDULE 40 IPS PLASTIC PIPE
(1120, 1220) C = 150
PSI LOSS PER 100 FEET OF TUBE (PSI/100 FT)
Sizes 4'' thru 12''
Flow GPM 1 thru 600

SIZE	4.00		5.00		6.00		8.00		10.00		12.00		SIZE
OD	4.500		5.563		6.625		8.625		10.750		12.750		OD
ID	4.026		5.047		6.065		7.981		10.020		11.814		ID
WALL THK	0.237		0.258		0.280		0.322		0.365		0.406		WALL THK
Flow G.P.M.	Velocity F.P.S.	P.S.I. Loss	Velocity F.P.S.	P.S.I. Loss	Velocity F.P.S.	P.S.I. Loss	Velocity F.P.S.	P.S.I. Loss	Velocity F.P.S.	P.S.I. Loss	Velocity F.P.S.	P.S.I. Loss	Flow G.P.M.
1													1
2													2
3													3
4													4
5													5
6													6
7													7
8													8
9													9
10													10
11													11
12	0.30	0.00											12
14	0.35	0.01											14
16	0.40	0.01											16
18	0.45	0.01											18
20	0.50	0.01											20
22	0.55	0.01	0.35	0.00									22
24	0.60	0.02	0.38	0.01									24
26	0.65	0.02	0.41	0.01									26
28	0.70	0.02	0.44	0.01									28
30	0.75	0.03	0.48	0.01									30
35	0.88	0.04	0.56	0.01	0.38	0.00							35
40	1.00	0.04	0.64	0.01	0.44	0.01							40
45	1.13	0.06	0.72	0.02	0.49	0.01							45
50	1.25	0.07	0.80	0.02	0.55	0.01							50
55	1.38	0.08	0.88	0.03	0.61	0.01							55
60	1.51	0.10	0.96	0.03	0.66	0.01							60
65	1.63	0.11	1.04	0.04	0.72	0.02							65
70	1.76	0.13	1.12	0.04	0.77	0.02	0.44	0.00					70
75	1.88	0.14	1.20	0.05	0.83	0.02	0.48	0.01					75
80	2.01	0.16	1.28	0.05	0.88	0.02	0.51	0.01					80
85	2.13	0.18	1.36	0.06	0.94	0.02	0.54	0.01					85
90	2.26	0.20	1.44	0.07	0.99	0.03	0.57	0.01					90
95	2.39	0.22	1.52	0.07	1.05	0.03	0.60	0.01					95
100	2.51	0.25	1.60	0.08	1.10	0.03	0.64	0.01					100
110	2.76	0.29	1.76	0.10	1.22	0.04	0.70	0.01					110
120	3.02	0.34	1.92	0.11	1.33	0.05	0.76	0.01					120
130	3.27	0.40	2.08	0.13	1.44	0.05	0.83	0.01	0.52	0.00			130
140	3.52	0.46	2.24	0.15	1.55	0.06	0.89	0.02	0.56	0.01			140
150	3.77	0.52	2.40	0.17	1.66	0.07	0.96	0.02	0.60	0.01			150
160	4.02	0.59	2.56	0.20	1.77	0.08	1.02	0.02	0.65	0.01			160
170	4.27	0.66	2.72	0.22	1.88	0.09	1.09	0.02	0.69	0.01			170
180	4.53	0.73	2.88	0.24	1.99	0.10	1.15	0.03	0.73	0.01			180
190	4.78	0.81	3.04	0.27	2.10	0.11	1.21	0.03	0.77	0.01			190
200	5.03	0.89	3.20	0.30	2.21	0.12	1.28	0.03	0.81	0.01	0.58	0.00	200
225	5.66	1.10	3.60	0.37	2.49	0.15	1.44	0.04	0.91	0.01	0.65	0.01	225
250	6.29	1.34	4.00	0.45	2.77	0.18	1.60	0.05	1.01	0.02	0.73	0.01	250
275	6.92	1.60	4.40	0.53	3.05	0.22	1.76	0.06	1.11	0.02	0.80	0.01	275
300	7.55	1.88	4.80	0.63	3.32	0.26	1.92	0.07	1.21	0.02	0.87	0.01	300
325	8.18	2.18	5.20	0.73	3.60	0.30	2.08	0.08	1.32	0.03	0.95	0.01	325
350	8.81	2.50	5.60	0.83	3.88	0.34	2.24	0.09	1.42	0.03	1.02	0.01	350
375	9.43	2.84	6.00	0.95	4.15	0.39	2.40	0.10	1.52	0.03	1.09	0.02	375
400	10.06	3.20	6.40	1.07	4.43	0.44	2.56	0.11	1.62	0.04	1.16	0.02	400
425	10.69	3.58	6.80	1.19	4.71	0.49	2.72	0.13	1.72	0.04	1.24	0.02	425
450	11.32	3.98	7.20	1.33	4.99	0.54	2.88	0.14	1.82	0.05	1.31	0.02	450
475	11.95	4.40	7.60	1.46	5.26	0.60	3.04	0.16	1.93	0.05	1.38	0.02	475
500	12.58	4.84	8.00	1.61	5.54	0.66	3.20	0.17	2.03	0.06	1.46	0.03	500
550	13.84	5.77	8.80	1.92	6.10	0.79	3.52	0.21	2.23	0.07	1.60	0.03	550
600	15.10	6.78	9.61	2.26	6.65	0.92	3.84	0.24	2.43	0.08	1.75	0.04	600

(Continued)

Note: Shaded areas of chart indicate velocities over 5' per second. Use with Caution.

Table B–5 FRICTION LOSS CHARACTERISTICS
POLYETHYLENE (PE) SDR-PRESSURE RATED TUBE
(2306, 3206, 3306) SDR 7, 9, 11.5, 15 C = 140
PSI LOSS PER 100 FEET OF TUBE (PSI/100 FT)

Sizes 1/2" thru 6"
Flow GPM 1 thru 1800

	0.50	0.75	1.00	1.25	1.50	2.00	2.50	3.00	4.00	6.00	
SIZE	0.50	0.75	1.00	1.25	1.50	2.00	2.50	3.00	4.00	6.00	SIZE
OD	0.000	0.000	0.000	0.000	0.000	0.000	0.000	0.000	0.000	0.000	OD
ID	0.622	0.824	1.049	1.380	1.610	2.067	2.469	3.068	4.026	6.065	ID
WALL THK	0.000	0.000	0.000	0.000	0.000	0.000	0.000	0.000	0.000	0.000	WALL THK

Flow G.P.M.	0.50 Vel F.P.S.	0.50 P.S.I. Loss	0.75 Vel F.P.S.	0.75 P.S.I. Loss	1.00 Vel F.P.S.	1.00 P.S.I. Loss	1.25 Vel F.P.S.	1.25 P.S.I. Loss	1.50 Vel F.P.S.	1.50 P.S.I. Loss	2.00 Vel F.P.S.	2.00 P.S.I. Loss	2.50 Vel F.P.S.	2.50 P.S.I. Loss	3.00 Vel F.P.S.	3.00 P.S.I. Loss	4.00 Vel F.P.S.	4.00 P.S.I. Loss	6.00 Vel F.P.S.	6.00 P.S.I. Loss	Flow G.P.M.
1	1.05	0.49	0.60	0.12	0.37	0.04	0.21	0.01	0.15	0.00	0.09	0.00									1
2	2.10	1.76	1.20	0.45	0.74	0.14	0.42	0.04	0.31	0.02	0.19	0.01									2
3	3.16	3.73	1.80	0.95	1.11	0.29	0.64	0.08	0.47	0.04	0.28	0.01	0.20	0.00							3
4	4.21	6.35	2.40	1.62	1.48	0.50	0.85	0.13	0.62	0.06	0.38	0.02	0.26	0.01	0.21	0.00					4
5	5.27	9.60	3.00	2.44	1.85	0.76	1.07	0.20	0.78	0.09	0.47	0.03	0.33	0.01	0.21	0.00					5
6	6.32	13.46	3.60	3.43	2.22	1.06	1.28	0.28	0.94	0.13	0.57	0.04	0.40	0.02	0.26	0.01					6
7	7.38	17.91	4.20	4.56	2.59	1.41	1.49	0.37	1.10	0.18	0.66	0.05	0.46	0.02	0.30	0.01					7
8	8.43	22.93	4.80	5.84	2.96	1.80	1.71	0.47	1.25	0.22	0.76	0.07	0.53	0.03	0.34	0.01					8
9	9.49	28.52	5.40	7.26	3.33	2.24	1.92	0.59	1.41	0.28	0.85	0.08	0.60	0.03	0.39	0.01					9
10	10.54	34.67	6.00	8.82	3.70	2.73	2.14	0.72	1.57	0.34	0.95	0.10	0.66	0.04	0.43	0.01					10
11	11.60	41.36	6.00	10.53	4.07	3.25	2.35	0.86	1.73	0.40	1.05	0.12	0.73	0.05	0.47	0.02	0.27	0.00			11
12	12.65	48.60	7.21	12.37	4.44	3.82	2.57	1.01	1.88	0.48	1.14	0.14	0.80	0.06	0.52	0.02	0.30	0.01			12
14	14.76	64.65	8.41	16.46	5.19	5.08	2.99	1.34	2.20	0.63	1.33	0.19	0.93	0.08	0.60	0.03	0.35	0.01			14
16	16.87	82.79	9.61	21.07	5.93	6.51	3.42	1.71	2.51	0.81	1.52	0.24	1.07	0.10	0.69	0.04	0.40	0.01			16
18	18.98	02.97	10.81	26.21	6.67	8.10	3.85	2.13	2.83	1.01	1.71	0.30	1.20	0.13	0.78	0.04	0.45	0.01			18
20			12.01	31.86	7.41	9.84	4.28	2.59	3.14	1.22	1.90	0.36	1.33	0.15	0.86	0.05	0.50	0.01			20
22			13.21	38.01	8.15	11.74	4.71	3.09	3.46	1.46	2.10	0.43	1.47	0.18	0.95	0.06	0.55	0.02			22
24			14.42	44.65	8.89	13.79	5.14	3.63	3.77	1.72	2.29	0.51	1.60	0.21	1.04	0.07	0.60	0.02			24
26			15.62	51.79	9.64	16.00	5.57	4.21	4.09	1.99	2.48	0.59	1.74	0.25	1.12	0.09	0.65	0.02			26
28			16.82	59.41	10.38	18.35	5.99	4.83	4.40	2.28	2.67	0.68	1.87	0.29	1.21	0.10	0.70	0.03			28
30			18.02	67.50	11.12	20.85	6.42	5.49	4.72	2.59	2.86	0.77	2.00	0.32	1.30	0.11	0.75	0.03	0.33	0.00	30
35					12.97	27.74	7.49	7.31	5.50	3.45	3.34	1.02	2.34	0.43	1.51	0.15	0.88	0.04	0.38	0.01	35
40					14.83	35.53	8.56	9.36	6.29	4.42	3.81	1.31	2.67	0.55	1.73	0.19	1.00	0.05	0.44	0.01	40
45					16.68	44.19	9.64	11.64	7.08	5.50	4.29	1.63	3.01	0.69	1.95	0.24	1.13	0.06	0.49	0.01	45
50					18.53	53.71	10.71	14.14	7.87	6.68	4.77	1.98	3.34	0.83	2.16	0.29	1.25	0.08	0.55	0.01	50
55							11.78	16.87	8.65	7.97	5.25	2.36	3.68	1.00	2.38	0.35	1.38	0.09	0.61	0.01	55
60							12.85	19.82	9.44	9.36	5.72	2.78	4.01	1.17	2.60	0.41	1.51	0.11	0.66	0.01	60
65							13.92	22.99	10.23	10.86	6.20	3.22	4.35	1.36	2.81	0.47	1.63	0.13	0.72	0.02	65
70							14.99	26.37	11.01	12.46	6.68	3.69	4.68	1.56	3.03	0.54	1.76	0.16	0.77	0.02	70
75							16.06	29.97	11.80	14.16	7.16	4.20	5.01	1.77	3.25	0.61	1.88	0.16	0.83	0.02	75
80							17.13	33.77	12.59	15.95	7.63	4.73	5.35	1.99	3.46	0.69	2.01	0.18	0.88	0.03	80
85							18.21	37.79	13.37	17.85	8.11	5.29	5.68	2.23	3.68	0.77	2.13	0.21	0.94	0.03	85
90							19.28	42.01	14.16	19.84	8.59	5.88	6.02	2.48	3.90	0.86	2.26	0.23	0.99	0.03	90
95									14.95	21.93	9.07	6.50	6.35	2.74	4.11	0.95	2.39	0.28	1.05	0.03	95
100									15.74	24.12	9.54	7.15	6.69	3.01	4.33	1.05	2.51	0.28	1.10	0.04	100
110									17.31	28.77	10.50	8.53	7.36	3.59	4.76	1.25	2.76	0.33	1.22	0.05	110
120									18.88	33.80	11.45	10.02	8.03	4.22	5.20	1.47	3.02	0.39	1.33	0.05	120
130											12.41	11.62	8.70	4.90	5.63	1.70	3.27	0.45	1.44	0.06	130
140											13.36	13.33	9.37	5.62	6.06	1.95	3.52	0.52	1.55	0.07	140
150											14.32	15.15	10.03	6.38	6.50	2.22	3.77	0.59	1.66	0.08	150
160											15.27	17.08	10.70	7.19	6.93	2.50	4.02	0.67	1.77	0.09	160
170											16.23	19.11	11.37	8.05	7.36	2.80	4.27	0.75	1.88	0.10	170
180											17.18	21.24	12.04	8.95	7.80	3.11	4.53	0.83	1.99	0.11	180
190											18.14	23.48	12.71	9.89	8.23	3.44	4.78	0.92	2.10	0.12	190
200											19.09	25.81	13.38	10.87	8.66	3.78	5.03	1.01	2.21	0.14	200
225													15.05	13.52	9.75	4.70	5.66	1.25	2.49	0.17	225
250													16.73	16.44	10.83	5.71	6.29	1.52	2.77	0.21	250
275													18.40	19.61	11.92	6.82	6.92	1.82	3.05	0.25	275
300															13.00	8.01	7.55	2.13	3.32	0.29	300
325															14.08	9.29	8.18	2.48	3.60	0.34	325
350															15.17	10.65	8.81	2.84	3.88	0.39	350
375															16.25	12.10	9.43	3.23	4.15	0.44	375
400															17.33	13.64	10.06	3.64	4.43	0.50	400
425															18.42	15.26	10.69	4.07	4.71	0.55	425
450															19.50	16.97	11.32	4.52	4.99	0.62	450
475																	11.95	5.00	5.26	0.68	475
500																	12.58	5.50	5.54	0.75	500
550																	13.84	6.56	6.10	0.89	550
600																	15.10	7.70	6.65	1.05	600

Flow GPM 650 thru 1800

	4.00	6.00	
SIZE	4.00	6.00	
OD	0.000	0.000	
ID	4.026	6.065	
WALL THK	0.000	0.000	

Flow G.P.M.	4.00 Vel F.P.S.	4.00 P.S.I. Loss	6.00 Vel F.P.S.	6.00 P.S.I. Loss
650	16.36	8.94	7.20	1.22
700	17.62	10.25	7.76	1.40
750	18.87	11.65	8.31	1.59
800			8.87	1.79
850			9.42	2.00
900			9.98	2.22
950			10.53	2.46
1000			11.09	2.70
1050			11.64	2.96
1100			12.20	3.22
1150			12.75	3.50
1200			13.31	3.79
1250			13.86	4.09
1300			14.41	4.39
1350			14.97	4.71
1400			15.52	5.04
1450			16.08	5.38
1500			16.63	5.73
1550			17.19	6.09
1600			17.74	6.45
1650			18.30	6.83
1700			18.85	7.22
1750			19.41	7.62
1800			19.96	8.03

Note: Shaded areas of chart indicate velocities over 5' per second. **Use with Caution.**

Table B–6 FRICTION LOSS CHARACTERISTICS
TYPE L COPPER WATER TUBE C = 140
PSI LOSS PER 100 FEET OF TUBE (PSI/100)

Sizes ½" thru 3"
Flow GPM 1 thru 600

SIZE	0.50	0.63	0.75	1.00	1.25	1.50	2.00	2.50	3.00	SIZE
OD	0.625	0.750	0.875	1.125	1.375	1.625	2.125	2.625	3.125	OD
ID	0.542	0.666	0.785	1.025	1.265	1.505	1.985	2.465	2.945	ID
WALL THK	0.040	0.042	0.045	0.050	0.055	0.060	0.070	0.080	0.090	WALL THK

Flow G.P.M.	0.50 Velocity F.P.S.	0.50 P.S.I. Loss	0.63 Velocity F.P.S.	0.63 P.S.I. Loss	0.75 Velocity F.P.S.	0.75 P.S.I. Loss	1.00 Velocity F.P.S.	1.00 P.S.I. Loss	1.25 Velocity F.P.S.	1.25 P.S.I. Loss	1.50 Velocity F.P.S.	1.50 P.S.I. Loss	2.00 Velocity F.P.S.	2.00 P.S.I. Loss	2.50 Velocity F.P.S.	2.50 P.S.I. Loss	3.00 Velocity F.P.S.	3.00 P.S.I. Loss	Flow G.P.M.
1	1.38	0.95	0.91	0.35	0.66	0.16	0.38	0.04	0.25	0.02	0.18	0.01	0.10	0.00					1
2	2.77	3.44	1.83	1.26	1.32	0.57	0.77	0.15	0.50	0.06	0.36	0.02	0.20	0.01					2
3	4.16	7.29	2.75	2.67	1.98	1.20	1.16	0.33	0.76	0.12	0.54	0.05	0.31	0.01	0.20	0.00			3
4	5.55	12.41	3.67	4.56	2.64	2.05	1.55	0.56	1.01	0.20	0.72	0.09	0.41	0.02	0.26	0.01			4
5	6.94	18.77	4.59	6.89	3.31	3.09	1.94	0.85	1.27	0.30	0.90	0.13	0.51	0.03	0.33	0.01	0.23	0.00	5
6	8.33	26.30	5.51	9.65	3.97	4.34	2.33	1.18	1.52	0.43	1.08	0.18	0.62	0.05	0.40	0.02	0.28	0.01	6
7	9.72	34.99	6.43	12.84	4.63	5.77	2.71	1.58	1.78	0.57	1.26	0.24	0.72	0.06	0.47	0.02	0.32	0.01	7
8	11.11	44.81	7.35	16.45	5.29	7.39	3.10	2.02	2.03	0.73	1.44	0.31	0.82	0.08	0.53	0.03	0.37	0.01	8
9	12.49	55.74	8.27	20.45	5.95	9.19	3.49	2.51	2.29	0.90	1.62	0.39	0.93	0.10	0.60	0.04	0.42	0.01	9
10	13.88	67.74	9.19	24.86	6.62	11.17	3.88	3.05	2.54	1.10	1.80	0.47	1.03	0.12	0.67	0.04	0.47	0.02	10
11	15.27	80.82	10.11	29.66	7.28	13.33	4.27	3.64	2.80	1.31	1.98	0.56	1.13	0.15	0.73	0.05	0.51	0.02	11
12	16.66	94.95	11.03	34.85	7.94	15.66	4.66	4.28	3.05	1.54	2.16	0.66	1.24	0.17	0.80	0.06	0.56	0.03	12
14	19.44	26.33	12.87	46.36	9.26	20.83	5.43	5.69	3.56	2.04	2.52	0.88	1.44	0.23	0.94	0.08	0.65	0.03	14
16			14.71	59.37	10.59	26.68	6.21	7.29	4.07	2.62	2.88	1.12	1.65	0.29	1.07	0.10	0.75	0.04	16
18			16.55	73.84	11.91	33.18	6.99	9.06	4.58	3.26	3.24	1.40	1.86	0.36	1.20	0.13	0.84	0.05	18
20			18.39	89.75	13.24	40.33	7.76	11.01	5.09	3.96	3.60	1.70	2.07	0.44	1.34	0.15	0.94	0.06	20
22					14.56	48.12	8.54	13.14	5.60	4.72	3.96	2.03	2.27	0.53	1.47	0.18	1.03	0.08	22
24					15.89	56.53	9.32	15.44	6.11	5.55	4.32	2.38	2.48	0.62	1.61	0.22	1.12	0.09	24
26					17.21	65.57	10.09	17.91	6.62	6.43	4.68	2.76	2.69	0.72	1.74	0.25	1.22	0.11	26
28					18.53	75.21	10.87	20.54	7.13	7.38	5.04	3.17	2.89	0.82	1.88	0.29	1.31	0.12	28
30					19.86	85.46	11.65	23.34	7.64	8.39	5.40	3.60	3.10	0.94	2.01	0.33	1.41	0.14	30
35							13.59	31.05	8.92	11.16	6.30	4.79	3.62	1.25	2.35	0.43	1.64	0.18	35
40							15.53	39.76	10.19	14.29	7.20	6.14	4.14	1.60	2.68	0.56	1.88	0.23	40
45							17.47	49.46	11.47	17.77	8.10	7.63	4.65	1.98	3.02	0.69	2.11	0.29	45
50							19.41	60.11	12.74	21.60	9.00	9.28	5.17	2.41	3.35	0.84	2.35	0.35	50
55									14.02	25.77	9.90	11.07	5.69	2.88	3.69	1.00	2.58	0.42	55
60									15.29	30.27	10.80	13.00	6.21	3.38	4.02	1.18	2.82	0.50	60
65									16.57	35.11	11.70	15.08	6.73	3.92	4.36	1.37	3.05	0.58	65
70									17.84	40.28	12.60	17.30	7.24	4.50	4.70	1.57	3.29	0.66	70
75									19.12	45.77	13.50	19.65	7.76	5.11	5.03	1.78	3.52	0.75	75
80											14.41	22.15	8.28	5.76	5.37	2.01	3.76	0.84	80
85											15.31	24.78	8.80	6.44	5.70	2.25	3.99	0.95	85
90											16.21	27.55	9.31	7.16	6.04	2.50	4.23	1.05	90
95											17.11	30.45	9.83	7.92	6.37	2.76	4.46	1.16	95
100											18.01	33.48	10.35	8.71	6.71	3.04	4.70	1.28	100
110											19.81	39.95	11.39	10.39	7.38	3.62	5.17	1.52	110
120													12.42	12.20	8.05	4.26	5.64	1.79	120
130													13.46	14.16	8.72	4.93	6.11	2.08	130
140													14.49	16.24	9.40	5.66	6.58	2.38	140
150													15.53	18.45	10.07	6.43	7.05	2.71	150
160													16.56	20.79	10.74	7.25	7.52	3.05	160
170													17.60	23.26	11.41	8.11	7.99	3.41	170
180													18.63	25.86	12.08	9.02	8.46	3.79	180
190													19.67	28.59	12.75	9.97	8.93	4.19	190
200															13.42	10.96	9.40	4.61	200
225															15.10	13.63	10.58	5.74	225
250															16.78	16.57	11.76	6.97	250
275															18.46	19.77	12.93	8.32	275
300																	14.11	9.77	300
325																	15.28	11.33	325
350																	16.46	13.00	350
375																	17.64	14.77	375
400																	18.81	16.65	400
425																	19.99	18.62	425
450																			450
475																			475
500																			500
550																			550
600																			600

(Continued)

Note: Shaded areas of chart indicate velocities over 5' per second. **Use with Caution.**

Table B–6 (con't) FRICTION LOSS CHARACTERISTICS
TYPE L COPPER WATER TUBE C = 140
PSI LOSS PER 100 FEET OF TUBE (PSI/100)

Sizes 3½" thru 12"
Flow GPM 1 thru 600

	SIZE 3.50		SIZE 4.00		SIZE 5.00		SIZE 6.00		SIZE 8.00		SIZE 10.00		SIZE 12.00	
OD	3.625		4.125		5.125		6.125		8.125		10.125		12.125	
ID	3.425		3.905		4.875		5.845		7.725		9.625		11.565	
WALL THK	0.100		0.110		0.125		0.140		0.200		0.250		0.280	

Flow G.P.M.	Velocity F.P.S.	P.S.I. Loss	Velocity F.P.S.	P.S.I. Loss	Velocity F.P.S.	P.S.I. Loss	Velocity F.P.S.	P.S.I. Loss	Velocity F.P.S.	P.S.I. Loss	Velocity F.P.S.	P.S.I. Loss	Velocity F.P.S.	P.S.I. Loss	Flow G.P.M.
1															1
2															2
3															3
4															4
5															5
6															6
7	0.24	0.00													7
8	0.27	0.01													8
9	0.31	0.01													9
10	0.34	0.01	0.26	0.00											10
11	0.38	0.01	0.29	0.01											11
12	0.41	0.01	0.32	0.01											12
14	0.48	0.02	0.37	0.01											14
16	0.55	0.02	0.42	0.01											16
18	0.62	0.03	0.48	0.01	0.30	0.00									18
20	0.69	0.03	0.53	0.02	0.34	0.01									20
22	0.76	0.04	0.58	0.02	0.37	0.01									22
24	0.83	0.04	0.64	0.02	0.41	0.01									24
26	0.90	0.05	0.69	0.03	0.44	0.01									26
28	0.97	0.06	0.74	0.03	0.48	0.01									28
30	1.04	0.07	0.80	0.03	0.51	0.01	0.35	0.00							30
35	1.21	0.09	0.93	0.05	0.60	0.02	0.41	0.01							35
40	1.39	0.11	1.07	0.06	0.68	0.02	0.47	0.01							40
45	1.56	0.14	1.20	0.07	0.77	0.03	0.53	0.01							45
50	1.73	0.17	1.33	0.09	0.85	0.03	0.59	0.01							50
55	1.91	0.20	1.47	0.11	0.94	0.04	0.65	0.02							55
60	2.08	0.24	1.60	0.13	1.03	0.04	0.71	0.02	0.41	0.00					60
65	2.26	0.28	1.73	0.15	1.11	0.05	0.77	0.02	0.44	0.01					65
70	2.43	0.32	1.87	0.17	1.20	0.06	0.83	0.02	0.47	0.01					70
75	2.60	0.36	2.00	0.19	1.28	0.06	0.89	0.03	0.51	0.01					75
80	2.78	0.41	2.14	0.21	1.37	0.07	0.95	0.03	0.54	0.01					80
85	2.95	0.45	2.27	0.24	1.45	0.08	1.01	0.03	0.58	0.01					85
90	3.13	0.50	2.40	0.27	1.54	0.09	1.07	0.04	0.61	0.01					90
95	3.30	0.56	2.54	0.29	1.63	0.10	1.13	0.04	0.64	0.01					95
100	3.47	0.61	2.67	0.32	1.71	0.11	1.19	0.05	0.68	0.01					100
110	3.82	0.73	2.94	0.39	1.88	0.13	1.31	0.05	0.75	0.01	0.48	0.00			110
120	4.17	0.86	3.21	0.45	2.06	0.15	1.43	0.06	0.82	0.02	0.52	0.01			120
130	4.52	1.00	3.47	0.53	2.23	0.18	1.55	0.07	0.88	0.02	0.57	0.01			130
140	4.86	1.14	3.74	0.60	2.40	0.21	1.67	0.08	0.95	0.02	0.61	0.01			140
150	5.21	1.30	4.01	0.69	2.57	0.23	1.79	0.08	1.02	0.02	0.66	0.01			150
160	5.56	1.46	4.28	0.77	2.74	0.26	1.91	0.11	1.09	0.03	0.70	0.01			160
170	5.91	1.64	4.54	0.86	2.91	0.29	2.03	0.12	1.16	0.03	0.74	0.01			170
180	6.26	1.82	4.81	0.96	3.09	0.33	2.14	0.14	1.23	0.03	0.79	0.01	0.54	0.00	180
190	6.60	2.01	5.08	1.06	3.26	0.36	2.26	0.15	1.29	0.04	0.83	0.01	0.57	0.01	190
200	6.95	2.21	5.35	1.17	3.43	0.40	2.38	0.16	1.36	0.04	0.88	0.01	0.61	0.01	200
225	7.82	2.75	6.02	1.45	3.86	0.49	2.68	0.20	1.53	0.05	0.99	0.02	0.68	0.01	225
250	8.69	3.34	6.68	1.77	4.29	0.60	2.98	0.25	1.70	0.06	1.10	0.02	0.76	0.01	250
275	9.56	3.99	7.35	2.11	4.72	0.72	3.28	0.30	1.88	0.08	1.21	0.03	0.83	0.01	275
300	10.43	4.69	8.02	2.48	5.15	0.84	3.58	0.35	2.05	0.09	1.32	0.03	0.91	0.01	300
325	11.30	5.44	8.69	2.87	5.57	0.98	3.88	0.40	2.22	0.10	1.43	0.04	0.99	0.01	325
350	12.17	6.24	9.36	3.29	6.00	1.12	4.17	0.46	2.39	0.12	1.54	0.04	1.06	0.02	350
375	13.04	7.09	10.03	3.74	6.43	1.27	4.47	0.53	2.56	0.14	1.65	0.05	1.14	0.02	375
400	13.91	7.98	10.70	4.22	6.86	1.43	4.77	0.59	2.73	0.15	1.76	0.05	1.22	0.02	400
425	14.78	8.93	11.37	4.72	7.29	1.60	5.07	0.66	2.90	0.17	1.87	0.06	1.29	0.02	425
450	15.65	9.93	12.04	5.25	7.72	1.78	5.37	0.74	3.07	0.19	1.98	0.07	1.37	0.03	450
475	16.52	10.98	12.70	5.80	8.15	1.97	5.67	0.81	3.24	0.21	2.09	0.07	1.44	0.03	475
500	17.39	12.07	13.37	6.38	8.58	2.17	5.97	0.90	3.41	0.23	2.20	0.08	1.52	0.03	500
550	19.12	14.40	14.71	7.61	9.44	2.58	6.56	1.07	3.76	0.28	2.42	0.09	1.67	0.04	550
600			16.05	8.94	10.30	3.04	7.16	1.26	4.10	0.32	2.64	0.11	1.83	0.05	600

(Continued)

Note: Shaded areas of chart indicate velocities over 5' per second. Use with Caution.

Table B-7 FRICTION LOSS CHARACTERISTICS
SCHEDULE 40 STANDARD STEEL PIPE C = 100
PSI LOSS PER 100 FEET OF PIPE (PSI/100 FT)
Sizes ½'' thru 3½''
Flow GPM 1 thru 600

SIZE	0.50	0.75	1.00	1.25	1.50	2.00	2.50	3.00	3.50	SIZE
OD	0.840	1.050	1.315	1.660	1.900	2.375	2.875	3.500	4.000	OD
ID	0.622	0.824	1.049	1.380	1.610	2.067	2.469	3.068	3.548	ID
WALL THK	0.109	0.113	0.133	0.140	0.145	0.154	0.203	0.216	0.226	WALL THK

Flow G.P.M.	Velocity F.P.S.	P.S.I. Loss	Velocity F.P.S.	P.S.I. Loss	Velocity F.P.S.	P.S.I. Loss	Velocity F.P.S.	P.S.I. Loss	Velocity F.P.S.	P.S.I. Loss	Velocity F.P.S.	P.S.I. Loss	Velocity F.P.S.	P.S.I. Loss	Velocity F.P.S.	P.S.I. Loss	Velocity F.P.S.	P.S.I. Loss	Flow G.P.M.
1	1.05	0.91	0.60	0.23	0.37	0.07	0.21	0.02	0.15	0.01	0.09	0.00							1
2	2.10	3.28	1.20	0.84	0.74	0.26	0.42	0.07	0.31	0.03	0.19	0.01	0.13	0.00			0.13	0.00	2
3	3.16	6.95	1.80	1.77	1.11	0.55	0.64	0.14	0.47	0.07	0.28	0.02	0.20	0.01	0.13	0.00			3
4	4.21	11.85	2.40	3.02	1.48	0.93	0.85	0.25	0.62	0.12	0.38	0.03	0.26	0.01	0.17	0.01			4
5	5.27	17.91	3.00	4.56	1.85	1.41	1.07	0.37	0.78	0.18	0.47	0.05	0.33	0.02	0.21	0.01	0.16	0.00	5
6	6.32	25.10	3.60	6.39	2.22	1.97	1.28	0.52	0.94	0.25	0.57	0.07	0.40	0.03	0.26	0.01	0.19	0.01	6
7	7.38	33.40	4.20	8.50	2.59	2.63	1.49	0.69	1.10	0.33	0.66	0.10	0.46	0.04	0.30	0.01	0.22	0.01	7
8	8.43	42.77	4.80	10.89	2.96	3.36	1.71	0.89	1.25	0.42	0.76	0.12	0.53	0.05	0.34	0.02	0.25	0.01	8
9	9.49	53.19	5.40	13.54	3.33	4.18	1.92	1.10	1.41	0.52	0.85	0.15	0.60	0.06	0.39	0.02	0.29	0.01	9
10	10.54	64.65	6.00	16.46	3.70	5.08	2.14	1.34	1.57	0.63	0.95	0.19	0.66	0.08	0.43	0.03	0.32	0.01	10
11	11.60	77.13	6.60	19.63	4.07	6.07	2.35	1.60	1.73	0.75	1.05	0.22	0.73	0.09	0.47	0.03	0.35	0.02	11
12	12.65	90.62	7.21	23.07	4.44	7.13	2.57	1.88	1.88	0.89	1.14	0.26	0.80	0.11	0.52	0.04	0.38	0.02	12
14	14.76	20.56	8.41	30.69	5.19	9.48	2.99	2.50	2.20	1.18	1.33	0.35	0.93	0.15	0.60	0.05	0.45	0.03	14
16	16.87	54.39	9.61	39.30	5.93	12.14	3.42	3.20	2.51	1.51	1.52	0.45	1.07	0.19	0.69	0.07	0.51	0.03	16
18	18.98	92.02	10.81	48.88	6.67	15.10	3.85	3.98	2.83	1.88	1.71	0.56	1.20	0.23	0.78	0.08	0.58	0.04	18
20			12.01	59.41	7.41	18.35	4.28	4.83	3.14	2.28	1.90	0.68	1.33	0.29	0.86	0.10	0.64	0.05	20
22			13.21	70.88	8.15	21.90	4.71	5.77	3.46	2.72	2.10	0.81	1.47	0.34	0.95	0.12	0.71	0.06	22
24			14.42	83.27	8.89	25.72	5.14	6.77	3.77	3.20	2.29	0.95	1.60	0.40	1.04	0.14	0.77	0.07	24
26			15.62	96.57	9.64	29.83	5.57	7.86	4.09	3.71	2.48	1.10	1.74	0.46	1.12	0.16	0.84	0.08	26
28			16.82	10.78	10.38	34.22	5.99	9.01	4.40	4.26	2.67	1.26	1.87	0.53	1.21	0.18	0.90	0.09	28
30			18.02	25.88	11.12	38.89	6.42	10.24	4.72	4.84	2.86	1.43	2.00	0.60	1.30	0.21	0.97	0.10	30
35					12.97	51.74	7.49	13.62	5.50	6.44	3.34	1.91	2.34	0.80	1.51	0.28	1.13	0.14	35
40					14.83	66.25	8.56	17.45	6.29	8.24	3.81	2.44	2.67	1.03	1.73	0.36	1.29	0.18	40
45					16.68	82.40	9.64	21.70	7.08	10.25	4.29	3.04	3.01	1.28	1.95	0.44	1.45	0.22	45
50					18.53	00.16	10.71	26.37	7.87	12.46	4.77	3.69	3.34	1.56	2.16	0.54	1.62	0.27	50
55							11.78	31.47	8.65	14.86	5.25	4.41	3.68	1.86	2.38	0.65	1.78	0.32	55
60							12.85	36.97	9.44	17.46	5.72	5.18	4.01	2.18	2.60	0.76	1.94	0.37	60
65							13.92	42.88	10.23	20.25	6.20	6.00	4.35	2.53	2.81	0.88	2.10	0.43	65
70							14.99	49.18	11.01	23.23	6.68	6.89	4.68	2.90	3.03	1.01	2.26	0.50	70
75							16.06	55.89	11.80	26.40	7.16	7.83	5.01	3.30	3.25	1.15	2.43	0.56	75
80							17.13	62.98	12.59	29.75	7.63	8.82	5.35	3.72	3.46	1.29	2.59	0.64	80
85							18.21	70.47	13.37	33.29	8.11	9.87	5.68	4.16	3.68	1.44	2.75	0.71	85
90							19.28	78.33	14.16	37.00	8.59	10.97	6.02	4.62	3.90	1.61	2.91	0.79	90
95									14.95	40.90	9.07	12.13	6.35	5.11	4.11	1.78	3.07	0.88	95
100									15.74	44.97	9.54	13.33	6.69	5.62	4.33	1.95	3.24	0.96	100
110									17.31	53.66	10.50	15.91	7.36	6.70	4.76	2.33	3.56	1.15	110
120									18.88	63.04	11.45	18.69	8.03	7.87	5.20	2.74	3.88	1.35	120
130											12.41	21.68	8.70	9.13	5.63	3.17	4.21	1.56	130
140											13.36	24.87	9.37	10.47	6.06	3.64	4.53	1.79	140
150											14.32	28.26	10.03	11.90	6.50	4.14	4.86	2.04	150
160											15.27	31.84	10.70	13.41	6.93	4.66	5.18	2.30	160
170											16.23	35.63	11.37	15.01	7.36	5.22	5.50	2.57	170
180											17.18	39.61	12.04	16.68	7.80	5.80	5.83	2.86	180
190											18.14	43.78	12.71	18.44	8.23	6.41	6.15	3.16	190
200											19.09	48.14	13.38	20.28	8.66	7.05	6.48	3.47	200
225													15.08	25.22	9.75	8.76	7.29	4.32	225
250													16.73	30.65	10.83	10.65	8.10	5.25	250
275													18.40	36.57	11.92	12.71	8.91	6.27	275
300															13.00	14.93	9.72	7.36	300
325															14.08	17.32	10.53	8.54	325
350															15.17	19.87	11.34	9.79	350
375															16.25	22.57	12.15	11.13	375
400															17.33	25.44	12.96	12.54	400
425															18.42	28.46	13.77	14.03	425
450															19.50	31.64	14.58	15.60	450
475																	15.39	17.24	475
500																	16.20	18.96	500
550																	17.82	22.62	550
600																	19.44	26.57	600

(Continued)

Note: Shaded areas of chart indicate velocities over 5' per second. **Use with Caution.**

Table B-7 (con't) FRICTION LOSS CHARACTERISTICS
SCHEDULE 40 STANDARD STEEL PIPE C = 100
PSI LOSS PER 100 FEET OF PIPE (PSI/100 FT)

Sizes 4" thru 6"
Flow GPM 1 thru 600

SIZE	4.00	5.00	6.00	8.00	10.00	12.00	14.00	16.00	18.00	SIZE
OD	4.500	5.563	6.625	8.625	10.750	12.750	14.000	16.000	18.000	OD
ID	4.026	5.047	6.065	7.981	10.020	11.938	13.126	15.000	16.876	ID
WALL THK	0.237	0.258	0.280	0.322	0.365	0.406	0.438	0.500	0.562	WALL THK

Flow G.P.M.	4" Vel FPS	4" PSI Loss	5" Vel FPS	5" PSI Loss	6" Vel FPS	6" PSI Loss	8" Vel FPS	8" PSI Loss	10" Vel FPS	10" PSI Loss	12" Vel FPS	12" PSI Loss	14" Vel FPS	14" PSI Loss	16" Vel FPS	16" PSI Loss	18" Vel FPS	18" PSI Loss	Flow G.P.M.
1																			1
2																			2
3																			3
4																			4
5																			5
6																			6
7																			7
8	0.20	0.00																	8
9	0.22	0.01																	9
10	0.25	0.01																	10
11	0.27	0.01																	11
12	0.30	0.01																	12
14	0.35	0.01	0.22	0.00															14
16	0.40	0.02	0.25	0.01															16
18	0.45	0.02	0.28	0.01															18
20	0.50	0.03	0.32	0.01															20
22	0.55	0.03	0.35	0.01	0.24	0.00													22
24	0.60	0.04	0.38	0.01	0.26	0.01													24
26	0.65	0.04	0.41	0.01	0.28	0.01													26
28	0.70	0.05	0.44	0.02	0.31	0.01													28
30	0.75	0.06	0.48	0.02	0.33	0.01													30
35	0.88	0.07	0.56	0.02	0.38	0.01													35
40	1.00	0.10	0.64	0.03	0.44	0.01													40
45	1.13	0.12	0.72	0.04	0.49	0.02	0.28	0.00											45
50	1.25	0.14	0.80	0.05	0.55	0.02	0.32	0.01											50
55	1.38	0.17	0.88	0.06	0.61	0.02	0.35	0.01											55
60	1.51	0.20	0.96	0.07	0.66	0.03	0.38	0.01											60
65	1.63	0.23	1.04	0.08	0.72	0.03	0.41	0.01											65
70	1.76	0.27	1.12	0.09	0.77	0.04	0.44	0.01											70
75	1.88	0.31	1.20	0.10	0.83	0.04	0.48	0.01											75
80	2.01	0.34	1.28	0.11	0.88	0.05	0.51	0.00											80
85	2.13	0.39	1.36	0.13	0.94	0.05	0.54	0.01	0.34	0.00									85
90	2.26	0.43	1.44	0.14	0.99	0.06	0.57	0.02	0.36	0.01									90
95	2.39	0.47	1.52	0.16	1.05	0.06	0.60	0.02	0.38	0.01									95
100	2.51	0.52	1.60	0.17	1.10	0.07	0.64	0.02	0.40	0.01									100
110	2.76	0.62	1.76	0.21	1.22	0.08	0.70	0.02	0.44	0.01									110
120	3.02	0.73	1.92	0.24	1.33	0.10	0.76	0.03	0.48	0.01									120
130	3.27	0.85	2.08	0.28	1.44	0.12	0.83	0.03	0.52	0.01									130
140	3.52	0.97	2.24	0.32	1.55	0.13	0.89	0.03	0.56	0.01	0.40	0.00							140
150	3.77	1.10	2.40	0.37	1.66	0.15	0.96	0.04	0.60	0.01	0.42	0.01							150
160	4.02	1.24	2.56	0.41	1.77	0.17	1.02	0.04	0.65	0.01	0.45	0.01							160
170	4.27	1.39	2.72	0.46	1.88	0.19	1.08	0.05	0.69	0.02	0.48	0.01							170
180	4.53	1.55	2.88	0.51	1.99	0.21	1.15	0.06	0.73	0.02	0.51	0.01	0.42	0.00					180
190	4.78	1.71	3.04	0.57	2.10	0.23	1.21	0.06	0.77	0.02	0.54	0.01	0.44	0.01					190
200	5.03	1.88	3.20	0.63	2.21	0.26	1.28	0.07	0.81	0.02	0.57	0.01	0.47	0.01					200
225	5.66	2.34	3.60	0.78	2.49	0.32	1.44	0.08	0.91	0.03	0.64	0.01	0.53	0.01					225
250	6.29	2.84	4.00	0.95	2.77	0.39	1.60	0.10	1.01	0.03	0.71	0.01	0.59	0.01	0.45	0.00			250
275	6.92	3.39	4.40	1.13	3.05	0.46	1.76	0.12	1.11	0.04	0.78	0.02	0.65	0.01	0.49	0.01			275
300	7.55	3.98	4.80	1.33	3.32	0.54	1.92	0.14	1.21	0.05	0.85	0.02	0.71	0.01	0.54	0.01			300
325	8.18	4.62	5.20	1.54	3.60	0.63	2.08	0.17	1.32	0.05	0.93	0.02	0.76	0.01	0.58	0.01			325
350	8.81	5.30	5.60	1.76	3.88	0.72	2.24	0.19	1.42	0.06	1.00	0.03	0.82	0.02	0.63	0.01	0.50	0.00	350
375	9.43	6.02	6.00	2.00	4.15	0.82	2.40	0.22	1.52	0.07	1.07	0.03	0.88	0.02	0.67	0.01	0.53	0.01	375
400	10.06	6.78	6.40	2.26	4.43	0.92	2.56	0.24	1.62	0.08	1.14	0.03	0.94	0.02	0.72	0.01	0.57	0.01	400
425	10.69	7.59	6.80	2.53	4.71	1.03	2.72	0.27	1.72	0.09	1.21	0.04	1.00	0.02	0.77	0.01	0.60	0.01	425
450	11.32	8.43	7.20	2.81	4.99	1.15	2.88	0.30	1.82	0.10	1.28	0.04	1.06	0.03	0.81	0.01	0.64	0.01	450
475	11.95	9.32	7.60	3.10	5.26	1.27	3.04	0.33	1.93	0.11	1.35	0.05	1.12	0.03	0.86	0.02	0.68	0.01	475
500	12.58	10.25	8.00	3.41	5.54	1.40	3.20	0.37	2.03	0.12	1.43	0.05	1.18	0.03	0.90	0.02	0.71	0.01	500
550	13.84	12.23	8.80	4.07	6.10	1.67	3.52	0.44	2.23	0.14	1.57	0.06	1.30	0.04	0.99	0.02	0.78	0.01	550
600	15.10	14.37	9.61	4.78	6.65	1.96	3.84	0.51	2.43	0.17	1.71	0.07	1.42	0.05	1.08	0.02	0.85	0.01	600

(Continued)

Note: Shaded areas of chart indicate velocities over 5' per second. **Use with Caution.**

Table B–7 (con't) FRICTION LOSS CHARACTERISTICS
SCHEDULE 40 STANDARD STEEL PIPE C = 100
PSI LOSS PER 100 FEET OF PIPE (PSI/100 FT)
Sizes 4″ thru 18″
Flow GPM 650 thru 5000

SIZE	4.00	5.00	6.00	8.00	10.00	12.00	14.00	16.00	18.00	SIZE
OD	4.500	5.563	6.625	8.625	10.750	12.750	14.000	16.000	18.000	OD
ID	4.026	5.047	6.065	7.981	10.020	11.938	13.126	15.000	16.876	ID
WALL THK	0.237	0.258	0.280	0.322	0.365	0.406	0.438	0.500	0.562	WALL THK

Flow G.P.M.	Velocity F.P.S.	P.S.I. Loss	Velocity F.P.S.	P.S.I. Loss	Velocity F.P.S.	P.S.I. Loss	Velocity F.P.S.	P.S.I. Loss	Velocity F.P.S.	P.S.I. Loss	Velocity F.P.S.	P.S.I. Loss	Velocity F.P.S.	P.S.I. Loss	Velocity F.P.S.	P.S.I. Loss	Velocity F.P.S.	P.S.I. Loss	Flow G.P.M.
650	16.36	16.66	10.41	5.55	7.20	2.27	4.16	0.60	2.64	0.20	1.86	0.08	1.53	0.05	1.17	0.03	0.93	0.02	650
700	17.62	19.12	11.21	6.36	7.76	2.60	4.48	0.68	2.84	0.23	2.00	0.10	1.65	0.06	1.26	0.03	1.00	0.02	700
750	18.87	21.72	12.01	7.23	8.31	2.96	4.80	0.78	3.04	0.26	2.14	0.11	1.77	0.07	1.35	0.04	1.07	0.02	750
800			12.81	8.15	8.87	3.33	5.12	0.88	3.25	0.29	2.29	0.12	1.89	0.08	1.45	0.04	1.14	0.02	800
850			13.61	9.12	9.42	3.73	5.44	0.98	3.45	0.32	2.43	0.14	2.01	0.09	1.54	0.05	1.21	0.03	850
900			14.41	10.14	9.98	4.15	5.76	1.09	3.65	0.36	2.57	0.15	2.13	0.10	1.63	0.05	1.28	0.03	900
950			15.21	11.21	10.53	4.58	6.08	1.21	3.86	0.40	2.71	0.17	2.24	0.11	1.72	0.06	1.36	0.03	950
1000			16.01	12.32	11.09	5.04	6.40	1.33	4.06	0.44	2.86	0.19	2.36	0.12	1.81	0.06	1.43	0.03	1000
1050			16.81	13.49	11.64	5.52	6.72	1.45	4.26	0.48	3.00	0.20	2.48	0.13	1.90	0.07	1.50	0.04	1050
1100			17.61	14.70	12.20	6.01	7.04	1.58	4.47	0.52	3.14	0.22	2.60	0.14	1.99	0.07	1.57	0.04	1100
1150			18.42	15.96	12.75	6.53	7.36	1.72	4.67	0.57	3.29	0.24	2.72	0.15	2.08	0.08	1.64	0.04	1150
1200			19.22	17.27	13.31	7.06	7.68	1.86	4.87	0.61	3.43	0.26	2.84	0.17	2.17	0.09	1.71	0.05	1200
1250					13.86	7.62	8.00	2.00	5.07	0.66	3.57	0.28	2.96	0.18	2.26	0.09	1.79	0.05	1250
1300					14.41	8.19	8.32	2.15	5.28	0.71	3.72	0.30	3.07	0.19	2.35	0.10	1.86	0.06	1300
1350					14.97	8.79	8.64	2.31	5.48	0.76	3.86	0.33	3.19	0.21	2.44	0.11	1.93	0.06	1350
1400					15.52	9.40	8.96	2.47	5.68	0.82	4.00	0.35	3.31	0.22	2.53	0.11	2.00	0.06	1400
1450					16.08	10.03	9.28	2.64	5.89	0.87	4.15	0.37	3.43	0.23	2.62	0.12	2.07	0.07	1450
1500					16.63	10.68	9.60	2.81	6.09	0.93	4.29	0.40	3.55	0.25	2.71	0.13	2.14	0.07	1500
1550					17.19	11.35	9.92	2.98	6.29	0.99	4.43	0.42	3.67	0.27	2.81	0.14	2.22	0.08	1550
1600					17.74	12.03	10.24	3.16	6.50	1.05	4.58	0.45	3.78	0.28	2.90	0.15	2.29	0.08	1600
1650					18.30	12.74	10.56	3.35	6.70	1.11	4.72	0.47	3.90	0.30	2.99	0.16	2.36	0.09	1650
1700					18.85	13.45	10.88	3.54	6.90	1.17	4.86	0.50	4.02	0.31	3.08	0.16	2.43	0.09	1700
1750					19.41	14.21	11.20	3.74	7.11	1.23	5.00	0.53	4.14	0.33	3.17	0.17	2.50	0.10	1750
1800					19.96	14.97	11.52	3.94	7.31	1.30	5.15	0.55	4.26	0.35	3.26	0.18	2.57	0.10	1800
1850							11.84	4.14	7.51	1.37	5.29	0.58	4.38	0.37	3.35	0.19	2.65	0.11	1850
1900							12.17	4.35	7.72	1.44	5.43	0.61	4.49	0.39	3.44	0.20	2.72	0.11	1900
1950							12.49	4.57	7.92	1.51	5.58	0.64	4.61	0.41	3.53	0.21	2.79	0.12	1950
2000							12.81	4.78	8.12	1.58	5.72	0.67	4.73	0.43	3.62	0.22	2.86	0.13	2000
2100							13.45	5.24	8.53	1.73	6.01	0.74	4.97	0.47	3.80	0.24	3.00	0.14	2100
2200							14.09	5.71	8.94	1.89	6.29	0.80	5.20	0.51	3.98	0.26	3.15	0.15	2200
2300							14.73	6.20	9.34	2.05	6.58	0.87	5.44	0.55	4.17	0.29	3.29	0.16	2300
2400							15.37	6.71	9.75	2.22	6.87	0.95	5.68	0.60	4.35	0.31	3.43	0.18	2400
2500							16.01	7.23	10.15	2.39	7.15	1.02	5.92	0.64	4.53	0.34	3.58	0.19	2500
2600							16.65	7.78	10.56	2.57	7.44	1.10	6.15	0.69	4.71	0.36	3.72	0.20	2600
2700							17.29	8.34	10.97	2.76	7.72	1.18	6.39	0.74	4.89	0.39	3.86	0.22	2700
2800							17.93	8.92	11.37	2.95	8.01	1.26	6.63	0.79	5.07	0.41	4.01	0.23	2800
2900							18.57	9.52	11.78	3.15	8.30	1.34	6.86	0.85	5.25	0.44	4.15	0.25	2900
3000							19.21	10.14	12.19	3.35	8.58	1.43	7.10	0.90	5.43	0.47	4.29	0.27	3000
3100							19.85	10.77	12.59	3.56	8.87	1.52	7.34	0.96	5.62	0.50	4.44	0.28	3100
3200									13.00	3.78	9.16	1.61	7.57	1.02	5.80	0.53	4.58	0.30	3200
3300									13.41	4.00	9.44	1.71	7.81	1.07	5.98	0.56	4.72	0.32	3300
3400									13.81	4.23	9.73	1.80	8.05	1.14	6.16	0.59	4.87	0.33	3400
3500									14.22	4.46	10.01	1.90	8.28	1.20	6.34	0.63	5.01	0.35	3500
3600									14.62	4.70	10.30	2.00	8.52	1.26	6.52	0.66	5.15	0.37	3600
3700									15.03	4.94	10.59	2.11	8.76	1.33	6.70	0.69	5.30	0.39	3700
3800									15.44	5.19	10.87	2.21	8.99	1.40	6.89	0.73	5.44	0.41	3800
3900									15.84	5.45	11.16	2.32	9.23	1.46	7.07	0.76	5.58	0.43	3900
4000									16.25	5.71	11.45	2.43	9.47	1.53	7.25	0.80	5.73	0.45	4000
4100									16.66	5.98	11.73	2.55	9.70	1.61	7.43	0.84	5.87	0.47	4100
4200									17.06	6.25	12.02	2.67	9.94	1.68	7.61	0.88	6.01	0.49	4200
4300									17.47	6.53	12.31	2.78	10.18	1.75	7.79	0.92	6.16	0.52	4300
4400									17.88	6.81	12.59	2.90	10.41	1.83	7.97	0.96	6.30	0.54	4400
4500									18.28	7.10	12.88	3.03	10.65	1.91	8.16	1.00	6.44	0.56	4500
4600									18.69	7.40	13.16	3.15	10.89	1.99	8.34	1.04	6.58	0.59	4600
4700									19.09	7.70	13.45	3.28	11.12	2.07	8.52	1.08	6.73	0.61	4700
4800									19.50	8.00	13.74	3.41	11.36	2.15	8.70	1.12	6.87	0.63	4800
4900									19.91	8.31	14.02	3.55	11.60	2.23	8.88	1.17	7.01	0.66	4900
5000											14.31	3.68	11.84	2.32	9.06	1.21	7.16	0.68	5000

(Continued)

Note: Shaded areas of chart indicate velocities over 5′ per second. **Use with Caution.**

Table B–7 (con't) FRICTION LOSS CHARACTERISTICS
SCHEDULE 40 STANDARD STEEL PIPE C = 100
PSI LOSS PER 100 FEET OF PIPE (PSI/100 FT)
Sizes 20" thru 24"
Flow GPM 450 thru 5000

SIZE	20.00		24.00		SIZE
OD	20.000		24.000		OD
ID	18.814		22.626		ID
WALL THK	0.593		0.687		WALL THK

Flow G.P.M.	Velocity F.P.S.	P.S.I. Loss	Velocity F.P.S.	P.S.I. Loss	Flow G.P.M.
450	0.51	0.00			450
475	0.54	0.01			475
500	0.57	0.01			500
550	0.63	0.01			550
600	0.69	0.01			600
650	0.74	0.01			650
700	0.80	0.01			700
750	0.86	0.01	0.59	0.00	750
800	0.92	0.01	0.63	0.01	800
850	0.97	0.02	0.67	0.01	850
900	1.03	0.02	0.71	0.01	900
950	1.09	0.02	0.75	0.01	950
1000	1.15	0.02	0.79	0.01	1000
1050	1.21	0.02	0.83	0.01	1050
1100	1.26	0.02	0.87	0.01	1100
1150	1.32	0.03	0.91	0.01	1150
1200	1.38	0.03	0.95	0.01	1200
1250	1.44	0.03	0.99	0.01	1250
1300	1.49	0.03	1.03	0.01	1300
1350	1.55	0.04	1.07	0.01	1350
1400	1.61	0.04	1.11	0.02	1400
1450	1.67	0.04	1.15	0.02	1450
1500	1.72	0.04	1.19	0.02	1500
1550	1.78	0.05	1.23	0.02	1550
1600	1.84	0.05	1.27	0.02	1600
1650	1.90	0.05	1.31	0.02	1650
1700	1.95	0.05	1.35	0.02	1700
1750	2.01	0.06	1.39	0.02	1750
1800	2.07	0.06	1.43	0.02	1800
1850	2.13	0.06	1.47	0.03	1850
1900	2.19	0.07	1.51	0.03	1900
1950	2.24	0.07	1.55	0.03	1950
2000	2.30	0.07	1.59	0.03	2000
2100	2.42	0.08	1.67	0.03	2100
2200	2.53	0.09	1.75	0.04	2200
2300	2.65	0.10	1.83	0.04	2300
2400	2.76	0.10	1.91	0.04	2400
2500	2.88	0.11	1.99	0.05	2500
2600	2.99	0.12	2.07	0.05	2600
2700	3.11	0.13	2.15	0.05	2700
2800	3.22	0.14	2.23	0.06	2800
2900	3.34	0.15	2.31	0.06	2900
3000	3.45	0.16	2.39	0.06	3000
3100	3.57	0.17	2.47	0.07	3100
3200	3.68	0.18	2.55	0.07	3200
3300	3.80	0.19	2.63	0.08	3300
3400	3.91	0.20	2.70	0.08	3400
3500	4.03	0.21	2.78	0.08	3500
3600	4.14	0.22	2.86	0.09	3600
3700	4.26	0.23	2.94	0.09	3700
3800	4.38	0.24	3.02	0.10	3800
3900	4.49	0.25	3.10	0.10	3900
4000	4.61	0.27	3.18	0.11	4000
4100	4.72	0.28	3.26	0.11	4100
4200	4.84	0.29	3.34	0.12	4200
4300	4.95	0.30	3.42	0.12	4300
4400	5.07	0.32	3.50	0.13	4400
4500	5.18	0.33	3.58	0.13	4500
4600	5.30	0.34	3.66	0.14	4600
4700	5.41	0.36	3.74	0.15	4700
4800	5.53	0.37	3.82	0.15	4800
4900	5.64	0.39	3.90	0.16	4900
5000	5.76	0.40	3.98	0.16	5000

Note: Shaded areas of chart indicate velocities over 5' per second. Use with Caution.

Table B-8 Friction Loss Characteristics
Asbestos – Cement

C = 140
Vel = velocity (ft/sec)
Loss = Head Loss (ft/100 ft)

Flow G.P.M.	3" Vel.	3" Loss	3 1/2" Vel.	3 1/2" Loss	4" Vel.	4" Loss	4 1/2" Vel.	4 1/2" Loss	5" Vel.	5" Loss	6" Vel.	6" Loss	7" Vel.	7" Loss	8" Vel.	8" Loss	10" Vel.	10" Loss
20	0.93	0.14	0.68	0.07														
25	1.15	0.20	0.80	0.09														
30	1.45	0.29	1.00	0.13	0.79	0.07												
40	1.90	0.50	1.40	0.23	1.05	0.12	0.82	0.07										
50	2.30	0.75	1.75	0.35	1.35	0.18	1.00	0.10	0.82	0.06								
60	2.70	1.04	2.00	0.50	1.70	0.25	1.30	0.14	1.00	0.09								
70	3.20	1.40	2.35	0.64	1.85	0.35	1.55	0.20	1.20	0.11	0.80	0.05						
80	3.70	1.80	2.75	0.84	2.05	0.44	1.70	0.25	1.40	0.16	0.91	0.06						
90	4.20	2.30	3.00	1.05	2.35	0.54	1.85	0.32	1.65	0.19	1.00	0.07						
100	4.70	2.80	3.40	1.30	2.70	0.66	2.05	0.38	1.80	0.23	1.20	0.09	0.88	0.05				
150	6.90	5.80	5.00	2.60	3.90	1.40	3.10	0.80	2.50	0.48	1.75	0.19	1.30	0.09	0.98	0.05		
200	9.00	9.80	6.70	4.60	5.00	2.30	4.00	1.35	3.30	0.82	2.40	0.33	1.70	0.16	1.30	0.08		
300			9.99	9.80	7.80	5.00	6.10	2.90	5.00	1.70	3.40	0.70	2.60	0.35	1.95	0.18	1.30	0.06
400					9.95	8.40	8.10	4.90	6.70	3.00	4.60	1.20	3.40	0.58	2.75	0.30	1.75	0.10
500							9.95	7.20	8.20	4.40	5.85	1.80	4.25	0.88	3.20	0.44	2.10	0.15
600									9.90	6.40	6.90	2.50	5.00	1.20	3.85	0.62	2.45	0.21
700											8.00	3.30	6.00	1.70	4.50	0.84	2.90	0.29
800											9.10	4.40	6.85	2.10	5.00	1.05	3.30	0.36
900											9.95	5.40	7.60	2.60	5.75	1.30	3.75	0.44
1000													8.40	3.10	6.40	1.60	4.15	0.54
1500															9.70	3.40	6.00	1.10
2000																	8.10	1.90

Table B–9 Friction Loss Characteristics
Aluminum Pipe with Couplers
C = 130

Vel = velocity (ft/sec)
Loss = Head Loss (ft/100 ft)

Flow G.P.M.	2" Vel.	2" Loss	3" Vel.	3" Loss	4" Vel.	4" Loss	5" Vel.	5" Loss	6" Vel.	6" Loss	7" Vel.	7" Loss	8" Vel.	8" Loss
5	0.51	0.07												
10	1.02	0.32	0.45	0.04										
20	2.04	1.20	0.91	0.15	0.51	0.04								
30	3.06	2.58	1.36	0.32	0.77	0.08								
40	4.08	4.49	1.81	0.56	1.02	0.13	0.65	0.04						
50	5.10	6.85	2.27	0.85	1.28	0.20	0.82	0.07	0.57	0.03				
60	6.12	9.67	2.72	1.21	1.53	0.28	0.98	0.09	0.68	0.04				
70	7.14	12.95	3.17	1.61	1.79	0.38	1.14	0.12	0.79	0.05				
80	8.16	16.70	3.63	2.06	2.04	0.49	1.31	0.16	0.91	0.06	0.67	0.03		
90	9.18	20.80	4.08	2.58	2.30	0.60	1.47	0.20	1.02	0.08	0.75	0.04		
100	10.20	25.40	4.53	3.18	2.55	0.74	1.63	0.24	1.13	0.10	0.83	0.05	0.64	0.03
120			5.44	4.51	3.06	1.06	1.96	0.34	1.36	0.14	1.00	0.07	0.77	0.04
140			6.35	6.00	3.57	1.41	2.28	0.46	1.59	0.19	1.17	0.09	0.89	0.05
160			7.25	7.76	4.08	1.82	2.61	0.59	1.81	0.25	1.33	0.11	1.02	0.06
180			8.16	9.67	4.59	2.27	2.94	0.73	2.04	0.30	1.50	0.14	1.15	0.07
200			9.07	11.83	5.10	2.78	3.26	0.89	2.27	0.36	1.67	0.17	1.28	0.09
220			9.97	14.12	5.61	3.31	3.59	1.07	2.49	0.44	1.83	0.20	1.40	0.11
240			10.88	16.72	6.12	3.91	3.92	1.27	2.72	0.52	2.00	0.24	1.53	0.13
260			11.79	19.42	6.63	4.56	4.24	1.47	2.95	0.60	2.16	0.28	1.66	0.15
280			12.69	22.40	7.14	5.26	4.57	1.71	3.17	0.69	2.33	0.33	1.79	0.17
300			13.60	25.45	7.65	5.98	4.90	1.93	3.40	0.79	2.50	0.37	1.91	0.19
350					8.93	8.03	5.71	2.59	3.97	1.05	2.91	0.50	2.23	0.26
400					10.20	10.36	6.53	3.33	4.53	1.35	3.33	0.64	2.55	0.33
450					11.48	12.90	7.34	4.15	5.10	1.69	3.75	0.80	2.87	0.41
500					12.75	15.73	8.16	5.07	5.67	2.06	4.16	0.97	3.19	0.50
550					14.03	19.12	8.98	6.16	6.23	2.50	4.58	1.18	3.51	0.62
600					15.30	22.46	9.79	7.24	6.80	2.94	5.00	1.38	3.83	0.72
650					16.58	26.10	10.61	8.42	7.37	3.41	5.41	1.62	4.14	0.84
700							11.42	9.68	7.93	3.92	5.83	1.82	4.46	0.97

Table B-10 FRICTION LOSS IN ORDINARY RUBBER HOSE
Pounds Per Square Inch (P.S.I.) per 100 Feet of Pipe

HOSE SIZE

Flow G.P.M.	½"	⅝"	¾"	1"	1¼"	1½"	2"	Flow G.P.M.
0.5	0.4							0.5
1.5	3.02	1.01	0.42					1.5
2.5	7.75	2.58	1.08					2.5
5	27.80	9.37	3.86	0.95	0.32	0.13		5
10	99.50	33.20	13.80	3.38	1.14	0.47	0.12	10
15		71.00	29.60	7.25	2.45	1.01	0.25	15
20		121.00	50.30	12.40	4.15	1.71	0.42	20
25			76.50	18.70	6.34	2.60	0.64	25
30			108.00	26.50	8.96	3.68	0.90	30
35			142.00	34.80	11.80	4.83	1.18	35
40				44.70	15.10	6.20	1.52	40
45				55.00	18.60	7.65	1.87	45
50				67.50	22.80	9.35	2.28	50
60				94.30	31.80	13.10	3.19	60
70				126.00	42.50	17.50	4.25	70
80					54.60	22.50	5.48	80
90					67.50	27.80	6.80	90
100					81.50	33.50	8.19	100
125					124.00	50.60	12.40	125
150						72.10	17.60	150
175						94.50	23.10	175
200						122.00	29.60	200
225							36.80	225
250							44.60	250
275							53.30	275
300							62.50	300
325							72.50	325
350							83.20	350
375							94.50	375
400							107.00	400

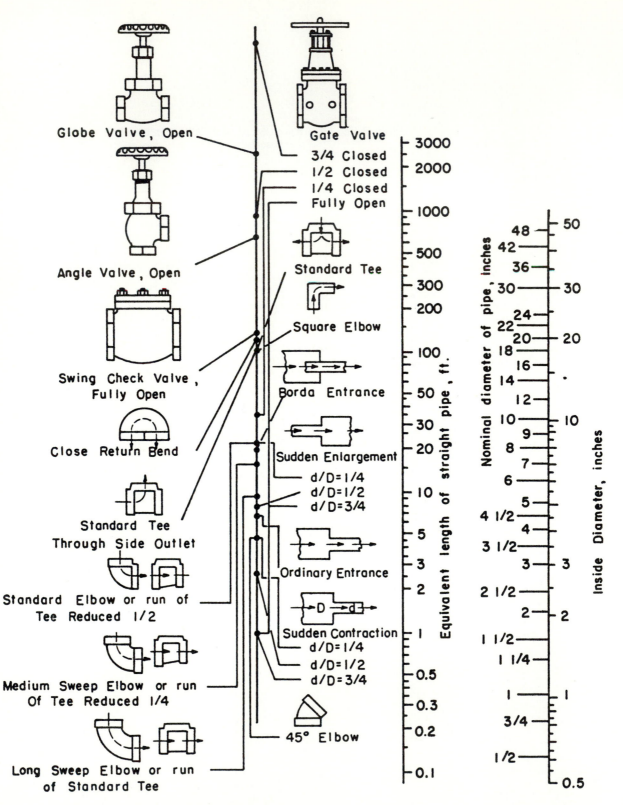

Figure B–1 Resistance of valves and fittings to flow of fluids

REFERENCES

American Society of Agricultural Engineers. "Design, Installation and Performance of Underground Thermoplastic Irrigation Pipelines" (ASAE Standard S376.1). Revised April, 1982. St. Joseph, MI: American Society of Agricultural Engineering, 1983–84.

Chow, V. T. *Hydrologic Determination of Watering Areas for the Design of Drainage Structures in Small Drainage Basins,* University of Illinois Engineering Experiment Station Bulletin No. 462. Urbana, IL, 1962.

Davis, S. N. and R. DeWiest. *Hydrogeology.* New York, NY: John Wiley and Sons, Inc., 1966.

Freeze, R. A. and J. A. Cherry. *Groundwater.* Englewood Cliffs, NJ: Prentice-Hall, Inc., 1979.

Hamilton, C. L. and G. H. Jepson. *Stock-water Developments: Wells, Springs and Ponds,* USDA Farmer's Bulletin No. 1859. Washington, D.C: 1940.

Hancor, Inc. *Drainage and Water Management Products.* Findlay, OH: Hancor, Inc., 1977.

Hanson, A. A. and F. V. Juska. *Turfgrass Science*

(Monograph No. 14). Madison, WI: American Society of Agronomy, 1969.

ITT Marlow. Engineering Section, ITT Marlow Catalog. Midland Park, NJ: 1980.

Jensen, M. E. (editor). *Design and Operation of Farm Irrigation Systems* (ASAE Monograph No. 3). St. Joseph, MI: American Society of Agricultural Engineering, 1980.

Kirpich, P. F. *Time of Concentration of Small Agricultural Watersheds, Civil Engineering* 10:362, 1940.

Pira, E. S. *Golf Course Irrigation System Design.* Amherst, MA: University of Massachusetts, 1982.

Rain Bird. *Turf Irrigation Equipment.* Glendora, CA: Rain Bird, 1982.

Rain Bird. *Rain Bird Specialty Valves.* Glendora, CA: Rain Bird, 1977.

Rain Bird. *Technical Data.* Glendora, CA: Rain Bird, 1976.

Rain Bird. *Irrigation Systems Design Handbook.* Glendora, CA: Rain Bird, 1974.

Rain Bird. *Design Guide for Turf and Ornamental Irrigation Systems.* Glendora, CA: Rain Bird, 1967.

Royal Coach-Buckner. *Irrigation Equipment.* Fresno, CA: Royal Coach Sprinklers, Inc., 1983.

Schwab, G. O., Frevert, R. K., Barnes, K. K., Edminster, T. W. *Elementary Soil and Water Engineering.* New York, NY: John Wiley & Sons, Inc., 1971.

Toro. *Irrigation Equipment.* Riverside, CA: Toro Irrigation Division, 1983.

Toro. *Turf Design Manual for Large Turf Areas.* Riverside, CA: The Toro Company, 1972.

Toro. *Rainfall-Evapotranspiration Data.* Minneapolis, MN: The Toro Company, 1966.

Turgeon, A. J. *Turfgrass Management.* Reston, VA: Reston Publishing Co., 1980.

U.S. Weather Bureau. *Rainfall Intensity-Duration-Frequency Curves.* Technical Paper No. 25. Washington, D.C.: U.S. Government Printing Office, 1955.

Waddington, D. V., Zimmerman, T. L., Shoop, G. J., Kardos, L. T., Duich, J. M. *Soil Modification for Turfgrass Areas—Physical Properties of Physically Amended Sites,* Progress Report 337. University Park, PA: The Pennsylvania Agricultural Experiment Station, 1974.

Weather-Tec. *Weather-Tec Sprinkler Catalog.* Fresno, CA: Weather-Tec, 1983.

Wolfe, J. W. *A Pumping Manual for Irrigation and Drainage,* Agricultural Experiment Station Bulletin No. 481. Corvallis, OR: Oregon State College, 1950.

Worthington. *Pump Catalog.* Mountainside, NJ: Worthington Division, McGraw-Edison, 1983.

Index

Application
  depth 10
  rate 27, 42, 48
Approaches 21, 23
Athletic areas 3

Backflow preventer 60
  air gap 60
  atmospheric vacuum 61
  double-check 61
  pressure vacuum 61
  reduced pressure 61

Control systems 72
  automatic 25, 26
  manual 26
Controllers 69
  automatic 69, 85
    electric 73, 82
    hydraulic 73

Controllers (Contd.)
  central 72
  computer 70
  master 72
  micro-processor 70
  multiple program 72
  satellite 72
  stations 26
Coverage area 9

Design depth 43, 49
Drainage of
  athletic fields 194
    baseball 196
    field hockey 194
    football 194
    prescription athletic turf (PAT) 196
    soccer 194
  greens 193
  homes 196

Drainge, subsurface 145, 146, 148, 173
  gravitational water 147
  gridiron 174
  herringbone 175
  inlets 177
  interceptor 175
  outlets 179
  pipe see *pipe, drainage*
    sizing 181
      area 185
      design charts 187, 188
      drainage coefficient 185
      rate of drainage 185
  random 174
Drainage, surface 145, 146, 148, 159
  diversions 171
  outlet channels 168
  rainfall-runoff 160
    rainfall intensity 161
    rational formula 165
    runoff coefficients 163
    time of concentration 161
  random drains 166
  soil erosion 148
  soil modification 169
  terraces 170
    bench 170
    tile outlet 171
Drains, irrigation 135

Elevations 153, 154
Environment
  atmospheric 4
  biotic 6
  soil 5
Evapotranspiration 8, 10, 45, 46
  transpiration 4

Fairway 34, 85
  dog-leg 30
  wide 30

Grades 153, 154, 182
Greens 19, 20, 193
  circular 23
  large 23
  oblong 23

Head
  discharge 121
  friction 101, 106, 122
  operating 122
  pressure 98

Head *(Contd.)*
  suction 121, 125
  system 122
  total 106, 123
  loss 102
  valve-in 22, 26
  valve-under 22
Hydraulics, irrigation 97
  Bernoulli's equation 104
  elevation 101
  friction head 98, 101
  head loss 102, 219–237
    pipe, in 106, 219–237
    valves, fittings 102. 238
  pressure 98
  surge pressure 107, 109
  water hammer 107, 108
Hydraulics, well 118
  cone of depression 118
  drawdown 118, 121

Infiltration rate 8, 28
Irrigation interval 45, 49

Lawn turf 3
Leveling 155
  carpenter 155
  hard 155
  line 155
  tripod 156

Management 16, 22, 24, 33, 41, 47, 51

Natural soils 44

Pipe, drainage 176
  clay 177
  concrete 176
  corrugated plastic 177
  depth 181
  field layout 183
  grades 182
  sizing see *subsurface drainage*
  spacing 181
  time of installation 190
Pipe, irrigation 97
  circuits 22
  flow rate 82
  layout 79, 85
    dead-end 80
    loops 81
    mains 80
  performance data 219–237

Pipe, irrigation *(Contd.)*
    friction   19–237
    velocity   219–237
  sizing   27, 79, 81, 82, 91
  swing joint   22
Precipitation (rainfall)   4, 47
  rate   9, 13, 162
Pressure tanks   127
Pumps   115, 119
  booster   126
  centrifugal   119
  characteristic curves   123
  circuit   72
  discharge   48
  discharge head   121
  efficiency   123
  friction head   122
  injection   119
  in-parallel   126
  in-series   120, 125
  jockey   127
  net positive suction head   124
  operating head   122
  positive displacement   119
  power input   124
  priming   120
  selection   128
  sprayer   119
  suction head   121, 125
  system head   122
  total head   106, 123
  vertical turbine   119, 120
    bowl,   120
    multistage   120, 125

Root zone   5, 43
  depth   8

Sand traps   34
Scheduling, irrigation   136
Seed germination   5
Sewage effluent   6, 119
Slopes   153
Soil mixes   43
Soil moisture   5, 10, 146
  available moisture   43, 44
  field capacity   5, 43, 146
  gravitational water   5, 147
  water content   5
  water holding capacity   8
  wilting point,   5, 43
Soil salinity   6
Specific heat

Specific heat *(Contd.)*
  of soil   5
  of water   5
Sport turf   3
Sprinkler
  approach   21, 23
  collar   23
  diameter   12
  effective coverage   10, 12, 16, 26, 42
  fairway   11, 13, 20, 21, 22, 25, 28, 29, 30, 34
  full circle   20, 24
  green   14, 20, 30, 34
  nozzles   6
  part circle   20
  performance data   16, 210–218
  pop-up   26
  radius   10, 12
  selection   11, 38
  single permanent   21
  single portable   21
  spacing   13, 20
    single-row   15, 22, 25, 26, 27
     two-speed   16, 28
    triple-row   22
    two-row   25, 26, 27, 30, 89
     square   14, 30
     triangular   15, 20, 23, 28, 30, 31, 37, 38
     wall-to-wall   25
  % spacing   14, 15, 16
Subsurface drainage   see *drainage, subsurface*
Superintendent   4, 19, 41, 48
Supplemental irrigation   4, 5
Surface drainage   see *drainage, surface*
Swing joint   22
Syringing   5, 73

Tees   30
Tensiometers   137
Thrust blocks   133
Timeliness   148
Topographic map   8
Trafficability   148
Turf manager   4, 73

Uniformity of distribution   6, 9, 10, 11, 12, 13, 14, 15, 27, 28
  water   20
Utility turf   3

Valves   21
  automatic   22, 62, 69
  ball   59
  check   58

Valves *(Contd.)*
  gate 57
  globe 57, 62
  in-head 22, 26
  in-line 21, 25, 26
  manual 57
  pressure-regulating 16, 58
  pressure relief 58
  quick-coupling 20, 25, 88
  remote control 22, 62, 69
    electric 62, 63, 73, 82
    hydraulic 62, 73, 74
    normally closed 64
    normally open 64
  shut-off 20, 22
  speciality 59
  under-head 22
Vents 186

Water application efficiency 43
Water supplies 8, 34
  groundwater 115, 117
  municipal 115, 116
  surface 115, 116
    pond 116
      seepage 116
      evaporation 116
      stream 116
Well 117
  deep well 117
  groundwater 117
  hydraulics 118
    cone of depression 118
    drawdown 118, 121
  shadow well 117
  specific capacity 118
Wind 13, 22